Shakespeare & His Biographical Afterlives

Shakespeare &

Series Editors:
Graham Holderness, *University of Hertfordshire*
Bryan Loughrey

Volume 7
Shakespeare & Money
Edited by Graham Holderness

Volume 6
Shakespeare & His Biographical Afterlives
Edited by Paul Franssen and Paul Edmondson

Volume 5
Shakespeare & the Ethics of War
Edited by Patrick Gray

Volume 4
Shakespeare & Creative Criticism
Edited by Rob Conkie and Scott Maisano

Volume 3
Shakespeare & the Arab World
Edited by Katherine Hennessey and Margaret Litvin

Volume 2
Shakespeare & Commemoration
Edited by Clara Calvo and Ton Hoenselaars

Volume 1
Shakespeare & Stratford
Edited by Katherine Scheil

Shakespeare &
His Biographical Afterlives

Edited by
Paul Franssen
&
Paul Edmondson

berghahn
NEW YORK · OXFORD
www.berghahnbooks.com

Published in 2020 by
Berghahn Books
www.berghahnbooks.com

© 2020 Berghahn Books

Originally published in three special issues of *Critical Survey*:
volume 21, number 3; volume 24, number 3; and volume 25, number 1.

All rights reserved. Except for the quotation of short passages
for the purposes of criticism and review, no part of this book
may be reproduced in any form or by any means, electronic or
mechanical, including photocopying, recording, or any information
storage and retrieval system now known or to be invented,
without written permission of the publisher.

Library of Congress Cataloging-in-Publication Data

[TO COME]

British Library Cataloguing in Publication Data

A catalogue record for this book is available from the British Library

ISBN 978-1-78920-687-6 hardback
ISBN 978-1-78920-688-3 paperback
ISBN 978-1-78920-689-0 ebook

*This volume is dedicated to the memory of
Wolfgang Weiss (1932–2019),
who passed away while it was being put together.*

Contents

List of Illustrations	ix
Acknowledgements	x

Setting the Stage

Introduction Paul Edmondson and Paul Franssen	3
Chapter 1 **Shakespeare's Afterlives** *Raising and Laying the Ghost of Authority* Paul Franssen	9

Biography

Chapter 2 **The Debate about Shakespeare's Character, Morals and Religion in Nineteenth-Century Germany** Wolfgang Weiss	31
Chapter 3 **'Talk to Him'** *Wilde, His Friends and Shakespeare's Sonnets* Reiko Oya	48
Chapter 4 **Fighting over Shakespeare** *Commemorating the 1916 Tercentenary in Wartime* Clara Calvo	68

Chapter 5
The Shakespeare Courtship in the Millennium
Katherine Scheil
94

Chapter 6
Biographical Aftershocks
Shakespeare and Marlowe in the Wake of 9/11
Robert Sawyer
107

Fiction

Chapter 7
Performance and Life Analogies in Shakespeare Novels for Young Readers
Marga Munkelt
123

Chapter 8
Shakespeare as Character in Two Works by José Carlos Somoza
Ángel-Luis Pujante and Noemí Vera
139

Chapter 9
The Bard-Baiting Model in *Upstart Crow* and *Something Rotten*
Richard O'Brien
150

Select Bibliography 173

Index 185

List of Illustrations

4.1.	Hamlet and Don Quixote. Cartoon on the cover of the weekly *España* (1916).	69
4.2.	*Shakespeare Tercentenary Observance for Schools.* Notes on Shakespeare the Patriot.	78
4.3.	*Shakespeare Tercentenary Observance for Schools.* Female characters.	80
4.4.	*Shakespeare Tercentenary Observance for Schools.* Male characters.	81
9.1 & 9.2.	Laurie Davidson and David Mitchell, playing Shakespeares of roughly equivalent ages in *Will* and *Upstart Crow*.	156

Acknowledgements

We are grateful to Prof. Sonja Fielitz (University of Marburg) for writing an updated biographical note on Wolfgang Weiss, and for her assistance in matters relating to his critical legacy.

Earlier versions of most of the chapters in this book appeared in *Critical Survey* 21.3 (2009), *Critical Survey* 24.3 (2012), and *Critical Survey* 25.1 (2013). We are grateful to the editors of *Critical Survey* for enabling us to bring out this material in a revised, updated and enlarged form.

Introduction

Paul Edmondson and Paul Franssen

This volume is dedicated to the life of Shakespeare, from a variety of angles ranging from biofiction to what we would recognize as more traditional biography. To begin with the latter: from one perspective, Shakespearean biography may be said to be booming, with a major new account of the life, or even two, coming out just about every year. Paradoxically, from another perspective, Shakespearean biography might be said to be in crisis: not a crisis of dearth, but one of plenty. How can standards of quality be maintained as the quantity burgeons? Such questions are raised by the inconsistent, often even contradictory views on Shakespeare's life aired by biographers. One reason for this plurality is undoubtedly gaps in the record of Shakespeare's life, particularly where his private affairs are concerned. This is not to say that we know hardly anything about him, but rather that each new biographer will have a different way of joining the dots together.

It is almost inevitable that some speculation will be mixed in with the biography proper. Perhaps, as Graham Holderness has it, 'there

Notes for this section begin on page 8.

is no such thing as a speculation-free biography of Shakespeare' to begin with.[1] Taking the example of Shakespeare's death as narrated in half a dozen biographies, Holderness shows how this topos has lent itself to as many different readings, which to a greater or lesser extent reflect the biographer's own background or agenda. Some female biographers, for instance, focus on the role of Anne, one (Katherine Duncan-Jones) seeing her as the victim of her irascible husband, who becomes more and more intractable as the end (from syphilis) comes nearer; another (Germaine Greer) casts Anne as the loving provider of care (Holderness, 11). Similar analyses could be made of many other episodes in Shakespeare's life, for whereas we have a reasonable insight into his finances and his writing, his heart has remained locked to posterity. The role of his parents, his attitude to his children, the emotions to be read into his last will and testament, with its notorious bequest of the second-best bed, have all been subject to endless speculation, with vastly different outcomes. The same is true for his religious and political affiliations.

In this volume, Katherine Scheil investigates how the circumstances of Shakespeare's marriage have been rendered in almost antithetical ways in half a dozen recent scholarly biographies, and Robert Sawyer looks at representations of the relations between Shakespeare and his nearest rival, Christopher Marlowe, in the light of the reactions to the acts of terrorism carried out on the World Trade Center on 11 September 2001. Both confirm that not only is Shakespeare biography (like, to some extent, all biography) a matter of speculation, but also that the biographer's own historical or personal background is likely to determine what the resulting portrait will be like. Nor is this plurality of scholarly views a recent phenomenon. As Wolfgang Weiss shows in his contribution to this volume, Shakespeare's religious affiliation was a topic of often heated discussion in Germany in the nineteenth century, fuelled less by the emergence of new documents than by internal German political tensions over the place of religion in the new nation state. Clara Calvo, similarly, shows how the 1916 Tercentenary, in the middle of the Great War, was an occasion for the various belligerent nations to claim Shakespeare, his person and his works, for their own side. This applied not merely to international politics, but also to rivalry between Stratford and London over the right to commemorate Shakespeare, and to the British class divide; and to the careful reader, it also reveals the incipient tensions between Britain and its colonies. Much as Shakespeare was used to wallpaper over faultlines at the time, by now the incompatibility between Shakespeare the English patriot and the German construction of *unser Shakespeare*, just to mention one example, has become glaringly obvious.

Perhaps the most challenging of all possible questions to ask a biographer is 'How do you decide which are the most important moments in Shakespeare's life?' – challenging because it exposes a major faultline which runs through all Shakespearean biography: fiction. The way in which biographers decide which story they want to tell and how to give it shape will always include, to some extent, the same process as the writing of fiction.

Acknowledged fictions about Shakespeare's life are the subject of three chapters in this volume. All of these attempt to lay bare the discourses underlying the fantasies. Marga Munkelt asks herself what messages young readers may learn from juvenile novels featuring Shakespeare, focusing on the analogies between life and performance. Ángel-Luis Pujante and Noemí Vera have chosen two works by the contemporary Spanish author José Carlos Somoza in which Shakespeare features as a character. These turn him into a gifted craftsman, but otherwise a pretty ordinary, fallible man. In his chapter on what he calls 'Bard-baiting', Richard O'Brien discusses some recent developments in fictions about Shakespeare, which are less obviously bardolatrous. On the surface, these contemporary biofictions appear to cut Shakespeare down to size; yet, O'Brien argues, in the end they do subscribe to the canonization of his works, whatever their take on his person.

As we no longer find fault with Shakespeare's history plays for anachronisms or inaccuracies, we also accept a large degree of poetic licence in fiction about Shakespeare. But does that also apply to serious scholarly biographies? Should we welcome the multiplicity of possible readings of his life as more testimony to Shakespeare's myriad-mindedness, not merely in his works but even in his life? Perhaps we should just accept, as Holderness suggests, that we are incapable of transcending our historical moment, so that we can never know, only speculate; and we may accept, with Holderness, that an intelligent critic like Stephen Greenblatt, in *Will in the World*, can make sense of Hamlet's dilemma by comparing it to his own, and, what is more, that he is then justified in speculating that Shakespeare himself might have experienced a similar emotional state at the time he wrote *Hamlet*. Holderness argues that it is possible to arrive at what he calls 'empathic speculation' that has the 'critical and satirical detachment necessary to distinguish between genuine critical revelation and narcissism in the biographical form' (17). Without that detachment, we may well end up with an infinite number of autobiographical readings. Oscar Wilde has said that 'the highest, as the lowest, form of criticism is a mode of autobiography', and suggested that biography, too, is often a mode of autobiography, in his 'Portrait of Mr W. H.'.[2] Wilde's own thinking about Shakespeare as a person, and his gradual recognition that, indeed, he himself was also projecting his own personality and experience onto his hero in 'The Portrait of Mr W. H.', is the subject of Reiko Oya's chapter. Oya focusses on Wilde, but juxtaposes his views with those of others in Wilde's circle, such as Lord Alfred Douglas and Frank Harris, who also came to define themselves with reference to Shakespeare's *Sonnets*.

Is such total detachment demanded by Holderness even possible, however? Those who argue the impossibility of transcending one's own period and culture often hold that a similar limitation obtains when it comes to emotions: as every culture dictates or at least limits the emotions that are available to the subject in any given circumstance, this also casts doubt on whether, say, Greenblatt's emotions in the present really have any bearing on Hamlet's emotions described four hundred years earlier – let alone Shakespeare's emotions. If Greenblatt's emotional response is actually vastly different from that of someone in the early-modern period, how reliable does that make his interpretations of Shakespeare's emotional world? More practically, if biography is really no more than a species of fiction, albeit one that seems to follow a different set of rules, does it then have any claim to public funding, at a time when the academy is increasingly expected to prove its legitimacy – precisely by acting as a healthy counterbalance to the fact-free politics and fake news that have been with us for many years now? Many biographies are, after all, written by academics working for universities. In 2011, a leading Dutch social psychologist, Diederik Stapel, was disgraced for making up the data underpinning his research; how far is a biography based on a mix of real data and fantasy fundamentally different from such fraudulent practices? On the one hand, we may believe that the positivist attitude to biography expounded, for example, in the work of S. Schoenbaum is too restrictive; on the other, we must also heed the warning implied by a book such as Rodney Bolt's

History Play. In what seems at first sight like a scholarly biography of Marlowe, Bolt constructs a theory of how Marlowe faked his own death in Deptford, and then went on writing from the Continent, having his works produced and printed under the name of his junior colleague, William Shakespeare.[3] Rather than propounding a serious anti-Shakespearean argument, however, Bolt's book plays with history to make a serious point: that so-called scholarly biographies, too, are often based on a little fact and a great deal of speculation. As Bolt himself expresses it, borrowing Mark Twain's metaphor, Shakespeare biographies resemble those huge brontosaurus skeletons, reconstructed from 'nine bones and six hundred barrels of plaster of Paris'.[4] Bolt himself, in fact, goes beyond using plaster of Paris, and even hides one of the genuine bones, as he ignores the fact that Marlowe's death is one of the most thoroughly well documented: the coroner's report survives and is signed by sixteen independent jurors. Nevertheless, there may be some truth in Bolt's metaphor; and the least we might do is to follow Graham Holderness's example in his *Nine Lives*, in distinguishing as clearly as we can between what is more or less factual and what is wholly fictional: as if we built up a brontosaurus skeleton where the plaster of Paris has a distinctly different colour from the bones.

There may be an additional reason for being careful about using Shakespeare's name in vain. As Paul Franssen shows in his opening chapter on fictional appearances of Shakespeare's ghost, Shakespeare's authority has often been borrowed to shore up a variety of causes. At first this was more or less seriously intended, but as the special pleading in his name came to be more and more obvious, the very phenomenon of the Shakespearean ghost lost all its credibility, so that he dwindled from a regal spectre into a comic, even ridiculous figure. By analogy, too many biographies of Shakespeare as a man of flesh and blood, all claiming him for different views, may be detrimental to the reputation, not just of the biographical genre, but even of Shakespeare himself.

Paul Edmondson is Head of Research for the Shakespeare Birthplace Trust. He is the author, co-author, and co-editor of many books and articles about Shakespeare, including biographical and performance studies, as well as work on the plays and poems. He is also a priest in the Church of England.

Paul Franssen has been a lecturer in the English Department of Utrecht University since 1979. He obtained his PhD there in 1987. He specializes in early-modern English literature and in South African literature. His main research interest is in Shakespeare. In addition to authoring a wide range of articles on early-modern writers and J. M. Coetzee, as well as reviews of productions of Shakespeare, he has co-edited books on *Shakespeare and War* (Palgrave, 2008, with Ros King), *Shakespeare and European Politics* (AUP, 2008, with Dirk Delabastita and Jozef de Vos) and *The Author as Character* (AUP, 1999, with Ton Hoenselaars). He is the author of *Shakespeare's Literary Lives: The Author as Character in Fiction and Film* (CUP, 2016).

Notes

1. Graham Holderness, *Nine Lives of William Shakespeare* (London: Continuum, 2011), 12.
2. Oscar Wilde, 'The Portrait of Mr. W. H.' (1889), in *Oscar Wilde: Complete Short Fiction*, ed. Ian Small (Harmondsworth: Penguin Classics, 1994), 47–79. The epigram comes from Wilde's preface to *The Picture of Dorian Gray* (Harmondsworth: Penguin, 1985), 21.
3. Rodney Bolt, *History Play: The Lives and Afterlives of Christopher Marlowe* (New York: Bloomsbury, 2005).
4. Bolt, *History Play*, 313, quoting from Twain's 1909 pamphlet, *Is Shakespeare Dead?*

Chapter 1
Shakespeare's Afterlives
Raising and Laying the Ghost of Authority

Paul Franssen

One of the most impressive contributions to Shakespeare scholarship of recent years famously opens as follows: 'I began with the desire to speak with the dead'. The author, Stephen Greenblatt, explains that the modern critic is in some ways like a shaman who calls up the spirits of the deceased.[1] Greenblatt goes on to argue that such unmediated access to the past is, alas, impossible, as we are always bound by the preconceptions of our own era. Yet the longing for such ultimate authority remains. A similar desire to speak with the dead, translated into a fantasy, lies behind many texts that do allow us unmediated contact with dead writers, including Shakespeare. Such fantasies often take the form of Shakespeare's ghost appearing on earth, or of mortals being granted an interview with his shade in Elysium. Before 1800, it is almost exclusively in the form of a ghost that Shakespeare is deployed as a literary character, in prologues, epilogues, plays, novels and narrative poems.[2] Nor are such

Notes for this section begin on page 26.

apparitions confined to Britain alone: in broadly similar ways, from the late eighteenth century onwards, Shakespearean ghosts also appear on the European Continent. I will study this phenomenon from the perspective of authority: the authority invested in Shakespeare's ghost itself; and hence, in the later author who ventriloquizes through that ghost, making Shakespeare the mouthpiece for her or his ideas and values; and the eventual loss of that authority in Britain, though not so much in Continental Europe.

How Shakespeare (and therefore his ghost) acquired that authority has been analysed by Michael Dobson. According to Dobson, Shakespeare is primarily constructed as a figure of authority by being proclaimed the poet of Nature (29–32), which makes him a national figure, too, as the antithesis of everything classicist and French (198 ff.). The kinds of discourses to which Shakespeare's ghost lent his authority differed widely. As Dobson puts it, 'Summoned from the dead with ever more frequency to appear as a prologue, the Bard's spectre returns to the London stage in order to endorse, in particular, a series of prescriptive and corrective rewritings of his comedies' (101). In addition, the ghost often served political purposes, which according to Dobson ranged from Royalist sympathies to embodying the national spirit in international conflicts. Whatever his role, for Dobson the ghost is always a figure of authority, appropriated by all and sundry. It is all the more surprising, then, that in many twentieth-century instances, so little of that authority remains; as we shall see, modern Shakespearean ghosts are often comic figures. However, as I will argue, the seeds of that undermining of his authority were already present in the earliest examples.

In the earliest texts, as befits a national symbol, Shakespeare's ghost is not usually a remorseful one worrying over his sinful past, but rather a vengeful, regal spirit, returned from the afterlife to castigate posterity. Not surprisingly, he is often identified with Old Hamlet. Historically, the emergence of this type seems to coincide with the earliest records of Shakespeare himself having acted that part. This tradition goes back to Rowe's 1709 edition of the works. Discussing Shakespeare as an actor in his prefatory 'Life', Rowe states that he 'could never meet with any further Account of him this way, than that the top of his Performance was the ghost in his own *Hamlet*'. Rowe gives the actor and theatre manager Thomas Betterton, who had travelled to Stratford to find out all he could about Shakespeare, as his general source.[3] It was the same Betterton who, at the turn of the century, made more use of Shakespearean ghosts in his theatre productions than anyone else. Fittingly, at a 1709 benefit performance for him, Rowe's epilogue to Congreve's *Love for Love* told the audience that if it 'had ... with-held [its] Favours on this Night, Old *Shakespeare*'s Ghost had Ris'n to do [Betterton] Right'.[4] Apart from Old Hamlet, Shakespeare's ghost is sometimes identified with Caesar's ghost, or with that of Duke Prospero.[5]

These monarchical figures clearly have a political dimension, as Dobson points out. In the prologue to Dryden's 1679 adaptation of *Troilus and Cressida*, probably the earliest instance of a Shakespearean ghost, Shakespeare, played by Betterton himself, appears as Hamlet Sr 'to smuggle a guarded royalist polemic onto the stage' (73); that is, Dryden's topical adaptation of the play is rendered seemingly neutral and inoffensive by the appeal to the king of poets rather than the real king. Besides, Dobson points out, this Shakespeare is very much the untutored poet of Nature, which suggests an impartiality the adaptation does not possess: 'Untaught, unpractis'd, in a barbarous Age, / I found not, but created first the Stage'.[6] But what a falling off there was: the ghost cannot rest because of those who currently rule the stage, whose dramatic power is nothing compared to his:

> Now, where are the Successours to my name?
> What bring they to fill out a Poets fame?
> Weak, short-liv'd issues of a feeble Age;
> Scarce living to be Christen'd on the Stage![7]

Apart from the political and poetical aspects, however, there were the more immediate concerns of legitimizing the ghost's true literary heir (i.e., Dryden) and criticizing usurpers of his laurels. In this respect, Shakespeare's ghost remains a figure of authority, but ironically that authority is used to undermine the authority of Shakespeare's original text. Casting Shakespeare as the poet of Nature enables Dryden to appropriate and adapt his text: after all, the ghost himself calls his own work a 'rough-drawn Play', written in a 'barbarous Age'. In this self-deprecating stance, the ghost implicitly authorizes Dryden to rewrite the text: Dryden is the proverbial dwarf standing on a giant's shoulders, who can see further because he lives in more sophisticated times. The ghost claims that Dryden respected his text: '... he, who meant to alter, found 'em [the original's 'Masterstrokes'] such / He shook; and thought it Sacrilege to touch'.[8] Yet, as Dobson has observed, in practice Dryden rewrote the play to suit his own neoclassical principles (75). Dryden's ostensible reverence signals that he is Shakespeare's true heir; all the same, he has in fact 'touched' the work and, to his own mind, improved it. As in many Bloomian-cum-Oedipal situations, the seemingly obedient son is, in fact, appropriating his father's authority under the guise of respect. Shakespeare's ghost is a marionette in Dryden's hands.

A more transparent example of such an appropriation can be found in George Granville's *The Jew of Venice* (1701), which is introduced by the ghosts of Shakespeare and recently deceased Dryden.[9] Shakespeare somewhat naively admires the splendour of the modern stage, but is informed by Dryden of its depravity, including its love of 'French Grimace' and its endorsement of homosexuality. Shakespeare's ghost, though shocked by the revelation of 'These Crimes unknown, in our less polisht Age', proceeds to admire Granville's technical improvements, and calls his own work no more than 'rude Sketches'. This Shakespeare, too, is clearly the child of Nature, whose moral superiority to the corrupt present is counterbalanced by his lack of technical perfection; in that respect, Granville has now 'improv'd' his play.

Granville's adverse comments on the stage also bring into focus the more mundane aspects of the appropriation of Shakespeare's ghost: his usefulness for interventions in theatrical disputes. Precisely because of their trivial nature, in the long run such uses of Shakespeare's ghost undermine his authority altogether, turning him into a comic figure that cannot be taken seriously any longer. Betterton's company at the Lincoln's Inn Fields theatre, where Granville's play was acted, made a habit of raising the Bardic ghost at the turn of the century. A year earlier, Shakespeare's ghost had spoken Oldmixon's epilogue to Gildon's *Measure for Measure* (1700) there, praising this production while inveighing against the rival company 'on yonder stage', Drury Lane, whose Falstaff was unrecognizable to his author. The ghost complains of his fate at the hands of modern adapters and actors, which reminds him of his sufferings during his lifetime:

> Enough your Cruelty Alive I knew;
> And must I Dead be Persecuted too?
> Injur'd so much of late upon the *Stage*,
> My *Ghost* can bear no more; but comes to Rage.[10]

Here the mythical sorrows of Shakespeare, the neglected genius, begin. But the culprits are only to be found on the rival stage; Lincoln's Inn Fields has always done him justice.

This clear-cut appropriation did not go unchallenged: in a sharp retort, Rich's Drury Lane added a new prologue to Farquhar's *The*

Constant Couple in which Oldmixon was ridiculed for trying to 'Fright the *Boxes* with Old *Shakespear's GHOST*: The *Ladies*, of such *Spectres*, should take heed; For, 'twas the *DEVIL* did Raise that *Ghost* indeed'. The Prologue admonishes the rival company:

> Let *Shakespear* then lye still, *Ghosts* do no good;
> The *Fair* are Better Pleas'd with Flesh and Blood:
> What is't to them, to mind the *Antient's* Taste?
> But, the Poor Folks are Mad, and I'm in haste.[11]

Clearly, the authority of Shakespeare's ghost was not universally acknowledged, in particular when the appropriation for some private end was so painfully obvious.

Similar mockery of the Bardic spectre can be found in a fairly even-handed account of the dispute between the theatres in the anonymous dialogue *A Comparison between the Two Stages* (1702). Sullen, one of the speakers, describes how Betterton's company appropriated Shakespeare to recover from a theatrical slump:

> But to prevent this heavy Calamity, *Batterton* [sic], being a cunning old Fox, bethought himself of a Project, whereby he might be rid of this beggarly Trade, and 'twas a sure way to save the third Night to himself; he enters his Closset, and falls down on his Knees, and Prays.
>
> O Shakespear, Shakespear! *What have our Sins brought upon us! We have renounc'd the wayes which thou hast taught us, and are degenerated into Infamy and Corruption: Look down from thy Throne on* Mount Parnassus, *and take commiseration on thy Sons now fallen into Misery: Let down a Beam of thy brightness upon this our forlorn Theatre; let thy Spirit dwell with us, let thy Influence be upon our Poets, let the Streams of thy* Helicon *glide along by* Lincolns-Inn-Fields, *and fructifie our Soil as the Waters of the* Nile *make fruitful the barren Banks of* Egypt.
>
> He rose, and rose much comforted: With that he falls to work about his Design, opens the Volume and picks out two or three of *Shakespears* Plays; and now, says he, I'll feague it away ifaith: Blessed be the Relicks of this Saint; they're more precious than those at *Loretto,* and a Penny that comes in from so pious a Shrine must needs prosper.[12]

John Rich of the rival Drury Lane theatre, Sullen continues, was stung by Betterton's success:

> Well, this lucky hit of *Batterton's* put *D.Lane* to a non-plus: *Shakespear's* Ghost was rais'd at the New-house, and he seem'd to inhabit it for ever: What's to be done then? Oh, says *Rich* I'll pray as well as he – What? Shall a *Heathen Player* have more Religion than a *Lawyer?* No, it shall never be said – (43)

Rich prays to Ben Jonson in similarly idolatrous language. However, the mock-heroic treatment of Shakespeare (as well as Jonson) as an idol does not wholly undercut his authority; Chagrin the Critick, not easily pleased, responds to Sullen's mockery that, where Shakespeare is concerned, 'no Author ever writ with that Felicity, or had such a prodigious compass of Thought' (42). The prime target of the mockery is the hypocrisy of the moderns, the managers of the rival theatres, who dress their greed (trying 'to save the third Night', the income of which was due to the play's author) in seeming reverence for the truly great dramatists from the past.

Thus, in the eighteenth century, a new variant develops alongside the earlier serious-minded appropriation of Shakespeare's ghost of the late seventeenth century: the spectre as a comic device. As one might expect in this age, the ghost occasionally has a function analogous to that of classical and biblical figures in a mock-heroic: as a standard against which the efforts of the contemporaries are judged wanting. In particular, theatrical figures are often confronted with their illustrious forebears whose authority they try to appropriate. Just like Shadwell is ridiculed for posing as Ben Jonson's successor in Dryden's *Macflecknoe*, those who try to arrogate the Shakespearean heritage do so at their peril, too. This in itself does not undermine Shakespeare's authority, but it does cast doubt on representations of the Bard praising or criticizing his successors; deconstructed Shakespearean ghosts *can* be ridiculous.

One theatrical figure in particular is frequently visited by the ghost: Shakespearean actor David Garrick. Mostly, Shakespeare descends from Elysium to praise him, but sometimes to criticize him. In various poems and prologues, the ghost asks Garrick to avenge him by restoring the original texts for the adaptations; or, indeed, to give Garrick carte blanche to '[f]reely correct [his] Page'. He offers him half his laurel wreath, declares him his 'representative' on earth and his 'living monument', which outshines all the statues erected in his honour. After Garrick's death, the ghost is among the mourners who come to pay tribute. But the ghost also warns Garrick against tampering with his sacred text,[13] or, as we shall see, against hiring French actors. In this way, the ghostly apparitions compete for authority, shedding much of their dignity in the process.

Not all ghosts were comical or satirical, however; especially where international politics were concerned, they tended to assume a grim seriousness. As the century wore on, the Bardic ghost was increasingly called upon in the interest of a nationalistic discourse, in particular against the French. In 1707, during the War of the

Spanish Succession, John Dennis wrote a prologue to *Julius Caesar*, in which Shakespeare's ghost boasts that his play about tyrannicide had roused the English to stand up against the Spaniards, and hopes that now it will inspire them to oppose the French drive for a 'fifth Monarchique Reign'.[14] In a poem by Mark Akenside, the spectre rouses the nation against the French as he had agitated against the Spaniards during his lifetime.[15] In 1803, the anonymous 'broadside Shakespeare's Ghost! . . . features Shakespeare "in the character of A TRUE ENGLISHMAN and A STURDY JOHN BULL, indignant that a FRENCH ARMY should WAGE WAR IN OUR ISLE" speaking a mishmash of patriotic speeches drawn in part from *King John*'.[16]

In this strain of anti-Gallicanism, the political is rarely divorced from the cultural, and Shakespeare's ghost joins those of other writers to deplore French cultural influence. As early as 1671, Ben Jonson's ghost had derided the modern taste for 'Farce, the trifling mode of *France*',[17] while Dryden's ghost complained to Shakespeare's of the currency on the English stage of 'French Grimace, Buffoons, and Mimicks' some 30 years later.[18] Shakespeare, having an even better right to be associated with the anti-French cause, appeared as a ghost to take his self-appointed disciple, Garrick, to task for employing French actors. Proudly pointing to his *Henry V*, the ghost makes Garrick promise that, in expiation of his sins, he will soon produce that play.[19]

It is not only in England that Shakespeare's ghost was conjured up to ward off French influence. In 1775, the German author Jakob Michael Reinhold Lenz wrote a satirical sketch on the state of German letters in his era, persistent French cultural influence being a recurrent theme. For a brief moment, the light breaks through when Herder conjures up the Shakespearean spirit: 'Come amongst us, Shakespeare, blessed spirit! Descend from your high heaven'.[20] Shakespeare's ghost duly appears, announcing his presence in flawless German: 'Da bin ich', 'Here I am'. The French dramatists, who are also present, scarcely look up from their drawing work, copying Greek patterns. Shakespeare befriends the German poet Friedrich Klopstock, but the latter suddenly starts and says, 'Where are my Greeks? Do not leave me!'. Shakespeare's ghost disappears into thin air again, angered by Klopstock's refusal to renounce his adherence to classicism. Obviously, Lenz's sketch portrays Shakespeare as the exponent of the Germanic school of Nature, which is opposed to the inferior French classicist tradition.[21] A year later, in 1776, Friedrich

Schröder began a series of Shakespeare productions in Hamburg, the first major such venture in German history (Habicht, 5). In the same year, Lenz wrote a poetic monologue that may well have been a response to this Shakespearean upsurge, which is hardly less hagiographical than his sketch. In 'Shakespeare's Ghost: A Monologue', Shakespeare's ghost visits a London theatre where Garrick is playing *Hamlet*, and is thrilled at the audience that has come to see his play.[22] He realizes that the spell will not last: after the play, they will again spit in his face, crown him with thorns and crucify him. Shakespeare realizes that God, who gave eternal bliss, received no better treatment than he, who only beguiled the audience for two hours in the playhouse. The emphasis on the neglect of Shakespeare by his own countrymen may owe something to the sorrows of many a Shakespearean ghost in the English theatre, complaining about his maltreatment by a rival company, as in Oldmixon's prologue discussed above. Lenz, it seems, loses sight of the polemical context, and generalizes it into a universal complaint of the treatment of prophets and geniuses. In hindsight, it even reads like a prelude to later German attempts to appropriate Shakespeare as a thoroughly German poet, far too good for those ungrateful Englishmen.[23]

In 1780, Johann Friedrich Schink wrote a brief comic play entitled *Shakespeare in der Klemme* [Shakespeare in Trouble], which begins by satirizing Jean-François Ducis, whose neoclassical rewriting of *Hamlet* provokes Shakespeare's ire.[24] First, Shakespeare's ghost, residing in Elysium, is confronted with the newly arrived ghost of his French adapter, still smelling of lavender. Shakespeare has not yet heard of Ducis, but when the latter foolishly presents his *Hamlet* adaptation, Shakespeare glances through it and is very angry at its impertinence. He complains to Garrick, his best friend in Elysium, that Ducis has reduced his 'huge mighty giant, Hamlet to a Duodecimannikin'; has cut a piece out of his dignified tapestry and turned it into a pair of cuffs. The remainder of the plot turns on Shakespeare's anger with the Germans themselves, who are so obsessed with his plays that everyone is acting them, even second-rate actors and children. Clearly, Shakespeare as a (regal) ghost is a figure of authority here, which can be turned against modern appropriations by the French and the Germans alike.

Still in Germany, Friedrich Schiller deployed Shakespeare's ghost to inveigh against modern domestic theatre. In Schiller's late poem

'Shakespears Schatten: Parodie' [Shakespeare's Shade: A Parody, 1804], the narrator has a vision of Shakespeare's ghost in the realm of the dead.[25] In the dialogue that follows, the speaker complains to the astonished shade (whose replies are enclosed between quotation marks) that tragedy is dead, and has been replaced by bourgeois sentimentalism and low farce:

> Only Christian moralism can touch us,
> And whatever is truly popular, homely and bourgeois.

Astonished, Shakespeare's ghost asks:

> 'What? No Caesar is allowed to show himself on your stages,
> No Achilles, no Orestes, no more Andromache?'
> Nothing! With us, you only see parsons, businessmen,
> Ensigns, secretaries, or cavalry officers.

Shakespeare asks how such lowly characters can play a part in great events:

> 'So where do you find the gigantic Destiny,
> Which elevates man, while it destroys him?'
> Those are silly ideas! Only ourselves and our good friends,
> Our complaints and distress do we seek and find here [on the stage].

Shakespeare notes that one might find these at home far more easily, and concludes:

> 'So it is just your own miserable nature that you find on your
> Stages, but not great, unlimited nature?'

which the speaker can only consent to.

Subsequently, in Holland, which long embraced French neoclassical taste, Schiller's poem was loosely translated in such a way that Shakespeare's ghost explicitly supported neoclassical principles in the French tradition. In the (unacknowledged) translation by A. van der Hoop Jr, entitled 'De Schim van Shakespear' [Shakespeare's Shade, 1829], the ghost asks incredulously whether Corneille has been forgotten, while the speaker complains that modern plays are in prose, not verse. The ghost approves of 'nature', but here that seems to imply following the neoclassical rules. Van der Hoop's Shakespeare is a figure of immense authority, but defends values that he usually derides in other countries.[26]

In France, supposedly the antithesis of everything Shakespeare stood for, Shakespeare's ghost made a brief appearance in George Sand's playlet *Le Roi Attend*, written in the revolutionary year 1848.

It is not poetics but politics that the ghost is interested in, when he joins the shades of Sophocles, Aeschylus, Euripides, Voltaire, Rousseau and Beaumarchais, to inspire the living poet, Molière, with revolutionary fervour.[27]

In all these very different appropriations, mostly of a nationalist character, Shakespeare's ghost is clearly regarded as a figure of authority, not as a comic device. Even when, with Sand, he has lost his regal status and turned republican revolutionary (identified with Brutus), the ghost remains larger than life and nearly infallible in the political ideas ascribed to him.

A ghost obviously also has a different potential; as the example of Hamlet Sr reminds us, ghosts were traditionally thought of as restless spirits condemned to roam the earth on account of unexpiated sins. This side of the ghost is usually hidden in the appearances discussed so far; insofar as his return from the afterlife is motivated at all, it is usually because of unease at the doings of his theatrical or political heirs rather than as a result of his own sins. An exception seems to be what Dobson has called 'the first novel to include Shakespeare as a character'. In the anonymous *Memoirs of the Shakespear's-Head in Covent Garden: By the Ghost of Shakespear* (London, 1755), the narrator meets Shakespeare's ghost in a tavern, who tells him that he has to haunt there as punishment for the errors of his youth, beginning with the deer-poaching at Charlecote.[28] Dobson stresses the abstraction from the theatre and the moralism of the story,[29] but perhaps equally remarkable is that here, for the first time, Shakespeare's ghost is not abstracted altogether from his individual background, but instead is seen as a private person with all the attendant frailties. He is not just equated with his characters, such as Hamlet Sr. and Prospero, but anecdotes about his life and career (poaching, holding horses outside the theatre) are worked into the story as well. This points forward to later, more sophisticated fictions about Shakespeare, in which not the ghost but the fallible man is represented.

In embryonic form, then, the early tradition of Shakespearean ghosts, in Britain and on the Continent, contains a number of features that characterize many later Shakespeare stories: he is identified with his own characters; he is undervalued by his contemporaries and posterity alike; he is a figure of authority in moral, cultural, political and national terms, yet in the way he is appropriated for various discourses there is often an element of silent rebellion as well; and occasionally, facts and anecdotes about Shakespeare's life on earth are woven into representations of his ghost.

Whereas there seems to be some continuity between the eighteenth-century Shakespearean ghost and later fictions, it is mainly in the apparition's authority that major changes have occurred since then. Shakespeare may still be a valuable ally to those who appropriate him because of his immense reputation, which not only extends to matters of artistic value, but also to political issues, and in some cases even moral probity. Yet, in the enduring crisis of authority that has engulfed the West over the last century, Shakespeare's authority has also come to be questioned. As a consequence, twentieth-century Shakespearean ghosts tend to be little more than laughing stocks, particularly in Britain. Like the symbols by which he was represented, Shakespeare has undergone a devaluation: as a ghost, he has lost his authority along with the waning belief in the supernatural; as a king, he is subject to the democratic controls that bind modern constitutional monarchies.

In his rare appearances in the twentieth century, Shakespeare's ghost is often a comic figure, as in a play by J. B. Fagan entitled *Shakespear v. Shaw* (1905).[30] In a send-up of various aspects of the Shakespeare industry, which is still remarkably funny today, Shakespeare is conjured up by spiritistic means in a law court to substantiate his libel suit against George Bernard Shaw, who had claimed to be better than Shakespeare. Shakespeare's ghost is a regal presence who, like Hamlet Sr, calls out 'Swear!' at appropriate moments. His pretensions to dignity are ridiculed, however, as when he asks for a pedestal rather than a chair to sit on. His attempts to flirt with a pretty actress in the witness box, by quoting Romeo's praise of Juliet to her, are of no avail: she just sees him as a dirty old man.

The main thrust of the satire is against the financial entanglements resulting from Shakespeare's virtual monopoly on the English stage, which makes a fair and unbiased assessment of his talent impossible: too many vested interests depend on him. Theatre managers queue up in front of the court to pay Shakespeare royalties for productions of his plays, but disappear into thin air when his ghost really does materialize. A vindictive cockney actress asks the judge to hang him, as her locution is not deemed suitable for playing Shakespeare, so that she is jobless. The jury is far from objective as it consists wholly of modern dramatists, who find it hard to compete with this myth from the past who does not even charge royalties.

As in the eighteenth century, Shakespeare's ghost challenges his successors; but in an age that recognizes the importance of money, even in the arts, sympathy is no longer automatically on his side.[31]

In the 1920s, Shakespeare's ghost made another appearance in a comic verse attributed to Guy Boas:

> I dreamt last night that Shakespeare's ghost
> Sat for a Civil Service post;
> The English paper for the year
> Had several questions on *King Lear*
> Which Shakespeare answered very badly
> Because he hadn't read his Bradley![32]

Terence Hawkes discusses this poem in the context of hermeneutical questions in general, and Bradley's notion of transparency in particular;[33] but it is also worth investigating this manifestation of Shakespeare's ghost in relation to those of the eighteenth century. As befits a ghost, he is capable of transcending time and place, so that we find him detached from the flesh and all associations with his life, sitting for a twentieth-century exam. The obvious irony at Bradley's expense, too, is reminiscent of the earlier ghost's wrath at misappropriations of his plays; the acts of adapting and of commenting on the works both imply the making of meaning, and in both cases, it appears, the ghost's authority privileges one meaning – the author's – over any other.

Still, here the hierarchy of meanings is less clearly defined than in the eighteenth-century examples: after all, here the Shakespearean ghost himself is subject to some of the irony. He was expected to read his Bradley, has not done so, and failed the test. Apparently he was incapable of explaining his own meaning to the examiners so as to convince them that this, too, was a possible reading. The ghosts of eighteenth-century prologues frequently disagreed with their descendants' efforts at rewriting their texts, but at least they were aware of these efforts, as befits a nearly omniscient semi-divine being, and rose from the grave to condemn the results. By comparison, this ghost looks less divine or regal; would a king aspire to a civil service post to begin with?

My reading of this simple comic verse may seem like an exercise in attributing my own ingenuity to its anonymous author, who may not have realized the full implications of his representation of Shakespeare; but I do believe that the way he imagines Shakespeare's ghost as a bit of a loser rather than a regal presence is typical of the change in attitude between the bardolatrous eighteenth century and modern scepticism. Intentionally or not, Shakespeare's ghost has lost his crown.[34]

In late 2007, Shakespearean actor Mark Rylance produced a play entitled *I Am Shakespeare*, in which the ghost is conjured into the present. It is not just his authority, but the very authorship of his plays that is at stake: a host of 'rival contenders – Francis Bacon, the Earl of Oxford, the Countess of Pembroke [pursue him] – for the intellectual property right on the Works'.[35] It should come as no surprise that Rylance is known for his anti-Stratfordian views. If earlier Shakespearean ghosts had punished those who had appropriated his plays, here the situation is comically inverted, as Shakespeare himself stands accused of stealing others' works.

Strangely enough, this tendency to raise Shakespeare's spirit only to ridicule him seems to be largely a British phenomenon. The few examples in Continental Europe I know seem far more respectful towards Shakespearean ghosts. In 1935, Danish author Kaj Munk invented a visit by Shakespeare's ghost to explain how he had come to write his modern Danish adaptation of *Hamlet*.[36] While musing about a play to castigate the lack of determination in the Danish spirit, Munk receives a visit from Shakespeare's ghost, who suggests rewriting *Hamlet*. Munk is full of respect for his visitor and hesitant about updating his masterpiece, yet Shakespeare good-naturedly persuades him that it would be wrong to treat his work as a museum piece. Munk's apologia for his politically charged adaptation of Shakespeare's text is remarkably similar to the prologues of the Restoration.

In modern Romanian productions of Shakespeare's plays, the author's ghost is also occasionally raised. In a *Hamlet* directed by Tompa Gabor at the Craiova National Theatre (1997), Old Hamlet's ghost was made up to resemble the Droeshout portrait. Odette Blumenfeld interprets this as a symbol of the relationship between text and performance:

> If the Ghost's command sets the play in motion, i.e., urges Hamlet to turn the heard into the visible, this Ghost (alias Shakespeare, the writer of the script) also seems to urge Hamlet to turn the script into an enacted/visible performance. In other words, if the Ghost wants him to be a dutiful son, the Ghost alias Shakespeare wants him to be his stage manager.[37]

Hamlet himself stands for the director, Tompa Gabor:

> As for Hamlet, dressed in black jeans and a black pullover, wearing spectacles with thin metallic frames, a twentieth-century man according to his looks, with his detached and ironic way of looking at/talking to the others, with his omniscient presence, he seems to stage not only the play-within-the-play, but also his own sacrifice for an idea, for a moral cause, for an artistic creed. Thus he can be regarded as a successful stage manager .... Being given this position, no wonder that Hamlet is the only character in the production to be dressed in modern clothes. In short, he can be viewed as Tompa Gabor's alter ego. (Blumenfeld)

This is a simplified rendering of a far more complex interplay of symbolical elements; yet it suggests strongly that, for contemporary Romanians, Shakespeare, even as a ghost, is still a figure of authority, not of comedy.

Shakespeare's ghost has been raised for a broad range of purposes, most of which have become obsolete by now: rival theatre companies, resisting French expansionism or neoclassical rules, are no longer vital issues. What has remained is the authority to adapt Shakespeare's texts, what Rosenthal has identified as the issue of intellectual property. In various ways, all the twentieth-century examples I have considered are concerned with the right to stage, adapt, or interpret Shakespeare's work. Curiously, the modern examples from Britain tend to treat Shakespeare's ghost as a figure of fun, while those from Continental Europe are more respectful. The only explanation for this I can offer is the tentative theory that a compensatory mechanism is at work. While the British have regained their respect for Shakespeare's original texts since the days of Edmond Malone, they compensate for their bardolatrous practice by poking fun at the ghost. Continental Europeans, by contrast, are forced to translate the texts for productions, which constitutes a kind of tampering with Shakespeare's original; they compensate for this by raising Shakespeare's ghost and propitiating him by acknowledging his ultimate authority. Thus, whereas Shakespeare's ghost still has great cultural prestige abroad, in Britain he seems to have fallen from the heights of bardolatry to the status of a prophet in his own country, even if his texts, in productions and editions, are still widely respected as part of the national heritage.

Coda

Ghosts not only make their appearances; they are also notorious for their sudden exits, disappearing into thin air. Shakespeare's ghost, too, pulls off a disappearing act in S. T. Coleridge's *Biographia Literaria*. In a passage clearly imitated (nowadays we might say plagiarized) from Schiller's poem 'Shakespears Schatten: Parodie' discussed above, Coleridge takes over part of the text of the dialogue, but replaces the interlocutors by a figure called the Plaintiff, who voices Coleridge's own ideas, and an imaginary supporter of the new drama – the Defendant.[38] Schiller's protest against the realism of the sentimental and the bourgeois drama is rendered quite adequately, but embedded in a more general, political, analysis.

The unacknowledged borrowing from Schiller is framed in a letter written from Germany to a Lady, in which Coleridge explains how he went to see a French comedy, and was disappointed by its lack of naturalness. It was 'worse than our modern English plays!' (358). He then generalizes his disapproval into a wholesale attack on 'the pantomimic tragedies and weeping comedies of Kotzebue and his imitators': 'such is the *kind* of drama, which is now substituted every where for Shakespeare and Racine' (358). Modern drama, Coleridge argues, does not do justice to the Aristotelean universal: the older poets regarded all drama as a kind of poetry, as art, not just entertainment, and refused to offer their spectators 'fac-similes of their own mean selves in all their existing meanness, or to work on their sluggish sympathies by a pathos not a whit more respectable than the maudlin tears of drunkenness' (359).

At this point, Coleridge's straightforward argument changes into a dialogue between his alter ego – the Plaintiff – and a supporter of the new drama – the Defendant. In the latter's arguments we recognize the speaker of Schiller's poem, whereas the Plaintiff borrows his arguments from Shakespeare's ghost.

> DEFENDANT. Hold! are not our modern sentimental plays filled with the best Christian morality?
> PLAINTIFF. Yes! just as much of it, and just that part of it which you can exercise without a single Christian virtue – without a single sacrifice that is really painful to you! – ... No Caesar must pace your boards – no Antony, no royal Dane, no Orestes, no Andromache! (360)

If such noble characters are not to be seen on the stage, what heroes has the sentimental muse provided instead? the Plaintiff asks.

> D. O! our good friends and next-door neighbours – honest tradesmen, valiant tars, high-spirited half-pay officers, philanthropic Jews, virtuous courtezans, tender-hearted braziers, and sentimental rat-catchers! ...
> P. But I pray you, friend, in what actions great or interesting, can such men be engaged?
> D. They give away a great deal of money; find rich dowries for young men and maidens who have all other good qualities; they browbeat lords, baronets, and justices of the peace, (for they are as bold as Hector!). (362)

These actions do not impress the Plaintiff, who goes on to ask:

> P. But how can you connect with such men and such actions that dependance of thousands on the fate of one, which gives so lofty an interest to the personages of Shakespeare, and the Greek Tragedians? How can you connect with them that sublimest of all feelings, the power of destiny and the controlling might of heaven, which seems to elevate the characters which sink beneath its irresistible blow?
> D. O mere fancies! We seek and find on the present stage our own wants and passions, our own vexations, losses, and embarrassments.
> P. It is your own poor pettifogging nature then, which you desire to have represented before you? not human nature in its heighth [sic] and vigour? But surely you might find the former with all its joys and sorrows, more conveniently in your own houses and parishes. (362)

So far, it will be clear, Coleridge is following, by and large, the argumentation of Schiller's poem, allowing himself some liberties in the translation. Interestingly enough, he identifies his own voice as the Plaintiff with that of Shakespeare's ghost.

Yet he also places his complaint against ordinary characters, who are deemed untragic, in a wider, more political, context. This becomes evident in a later passage, which does not correspond to anything in Schiller's poem. The Defendant praises modern plays for their happy endings, which make light of conventional morality and social order. The Plaintiff replies indignantly:

> [T]he whole system of your drama is a moral and intellectual *Jacobinism* of the most dangerous kind ... For the whole secret of dramatic popularity consists with you in the confusion and subversion of the

natural order of things, their causes and their effects; in the excitement of surprise, by representing the qualities of liberality, refined feeling, and a nice sense of honour (those things rather which pass among you for such) in persons and in classes of life where experience teaches us least to expect them; and in rewarding with all the sympathies that are the dues of virtue, those criminals whom law, reason, and religion, have excommunicated from our esteem! (363)

Here we see clearly what really bothers Coleridge about sentimental drama: not only does it undermine morality, but it also interferes with the social order. Whereas Schiller's argument limits itself to poetics, Coleridge adds a political dimension, speaking out against the egalitarian potential of sentimental and bourgeois drama. As we have seen, Coleridge's Plaintiff speaks on behalf of Shakespeare's ghost as imagined by Schiller; but in doing so, he attacks the *political* substratum of sentimental drama. Ironically, some of that egalitarian potential was also present in Shakespeare's representation of the lower orders in his tragedies, his mixing of genres being a mixing of social class as well. Coleridge's admiration for Shakespeare here is rather selective, and the authority derived from that shadow of a ghost is as thin as a wisp of fog.

Paul Franssen has been a lecturer in the English Department of Utrecht University since 1979. He obtained his PhD there in 1987. He specializes in early-modern English literature and in South African literature. His main research interest is in Shakespeare. In addition to authoring a wide range of articles on early-modern writers and J. M. Coetzee, as well as reviews of productions of Shakespeare, he has co-edited books on *Shakespeare and War* (Palgrave, 2008, with Ros King), *Shakespeare and European Politics* (AUP, 2008, with Dirk Delabastita and Jozef de Vos) and *The Author as Character* (AUP, 1999, with Ton Hoenselaars). He is the author of *Shakespeare's Literary Lives: The Author as Character in Fiction and Film* (CUP, 2016).

Notes

1. Stephen Greenblatt, *Shakespearean Negotiations* (Oxford: Clarendon Press, 1988), 1.
2. Mary E. Knapp lists some Shakespearean ghosts in her *Prologues and Epilogues of the Eighteenth Century* (New Haven: Yale University Press, 1961), 107. Michael Dobson discusses additional examples from several genres in *The Making of the National Poet* (Oxford: Clarendon, 1992). My debt to Knapp and especially to Dobson will be obvious. Laura J. Rosenthal argues that appearances of Shakespearean ghosts in the eighteenth century served to distinguish between derivative, commercial writing and true, original authorship, between material profit and cultural capital. Being disembodied, the ghost features as the guarantor of the latter, more prestigious kind of authorship. See 'The Author as Ghost in the Eighteenth Century', *1650–1850: Ideas, Aesthetics, and Inquiries in the Early Modern Era* 3 (1997), 29–56.
3. In *Eighteenth Century Essays on Shakespeare*, ed. D. Nichol Smith (1903; 2nd ed. Oxford: Clarendon Press, 1963), 3, 19.
4. Pierre Danchin, ed., *The Prologues and Epilogues of the Restoration, 1660–1700* (Nancy: Publications Université de Nancy II, 1981ff), vol. 2, 430.
5. Theobald invoked the ghost in his prologue to *Hamlet*, curiously also linking him to Caesar's ghost, but apparently it does not materialize (*London Daily Post and General Advertiser* 12 April 1739; Dobson, 140). For Shakespeare as the ghost of Prospero, see Dobson, 212, and *passim*.
6. Danchin, vol. 3, 157.
7. Danchin, vol. 3, 157. Cf. Dobson, 74; Rosenthal, 43–45.
8. Danchin, vol. 3, 157.
9. Pierre Danchin, ed., *The Prologues and Epilogues of the Eighteenth Century: A Complete Edition* (Nancy: Publications Université de Nancy II, 1990ff.), vol. 1, 8–9. Cf. Knapp, 107; Dobson, 121–22; Rosenthal, 45–50.
10. Danchin, *Restoration*, vol. 6, 632–33. See Danchin's *Eighteenth Century*, vol. 2, 739, for a similar invocation of Shakespeare's ghost against Colley Cibber, some twenty years later.
11. Danchin, *Restoration*, vol. 6, 674; cf. vol. 5, xxxv–xxxvi, for the context of theatrical rivalry.
12. *A Comparison between the Two Stages* (London, 1702. Rpt. New York and London: Garland, 1973), 41–42.
13. For these various apparitions to Garrick, see respectively: *London Magazine* (June 1750), 278–79, Dobson, 167, Rosenthal, 52–53; *The Plays of Richard Cumberland*, ed. Roberta F. S. Borkat (New York: Garland, 1982), vol. 2, 82, Dobson, 174–75; *Gentleman's Magazine* (Nov. 1758), 539, Dobson, 169; *London Magazine* (Nov. 1758), 539, Dobson, 182; *A Poetic Epistle from Shakespear in Elysium to Mr. Garrick at Drury-Lane Theatre* (1752), Dobson, 167–68; Samuel Jackson Pratt, *The Shadows of Shakespeare: A Monody, in irregular verse, Occasioned by the Death of Mr. Garrick*, in *Miscellanies* (London, 1785), vol. 2, 25, Dobson, 183 n94; and Arthur Murphy, *Hamlet, with Alterations: A Tragedy in Three Acts*; in Jesse Foot, *The Life of Arthur Murphy, Esq.* (London, 1811), 256–74, Dobson, 172–73.
14. Danchin, *Eighteenth Century*, vol. 1, 359–60. Cf. Dobson, 154; and his 'Accents Yet Unknown: Canonisation and the Claiming of *Julius Caesar*', in *The Appropriation of Shakespeare: Post-Renaissance Reconstructions of the Works and the Myth*, ed.

Jean I. Marsden (New York and London: Harvester Wheatsheaf, 1991), 11–28, esp. 15.
15. *The Remonstrance of Shakespeare* (1749) in *The Poetical Works of Mark Akenside* (Edinburgh, 1781), vol. 1, 73; Dobson, 201–2.
16. See Nicola J. Watson, 'Kemble, Scott, and the Mantle of the Bard', in Marsden (cf. note 14 above), 76. Watson's note refers to *Gentleman's Magazine* 73 (1803), 664.
17. See the second prologue to Edward Howard's *The Womens Conquest*, in Danchin, *Restoration*, vol. 2, 359.
18. In the prologue to Granville's *Jew of Venice*, see above.
19. *The Visitation; or an Interview between the Ghost of Shakespear and D—v—d G—rr—ck, Esq* (1755); rpt. in Maurice J. O'Sullivan, ed., *Shakespeare's Other Lives. An Anthology of Fictional Depictions of the Bard* (Jefferson NC and London: McFarland, 1997), 205–9. For commentary, see Dobson 202–3 and Rosenthal, 53–54.
20. *Pandämonium Germanicum,* in Jakob Michael Reinhold Lenz, *Werke und Schriften,* ed. Britta Titel and Hellmut Haug (Stuttgart: Goverts, 1966–67), vol. 2, 250–77; 274.
21. For the topical context, see Werner Habicht, *Shakespeare and the German Imagination,* International Shakespeare Association Occasional Paper No. 5 (Hertford: Austin, 1994), 4.
22. Lenz, 'Shakespears Geist: Ein Monologe', *Werke*, vol. 1, 166.
23. On this argument, which was especially current in the First World War, see Habicht 14. Habicht traces it to Friederich Kreyssig's *Vorlesungen über Shakespeare* (1877) (28, n50).
24. *Shakespeare im Narrenhaus: Deutschsprachige Shakespeare-Parodien aus zwei Jahrhunderten,* ed. Gerhard Müller-Schwefe (Tübingen: Francke Verlag, 1990), 126–34.
25. *Schillers Werke: Nationalausgabe,* ed. Norbert Oellers (Weimar: Hermann Böhlaus Nachfolger, 1983), II.1.306–7. Translations are mine.
26. A.v.d.H[oop]. Jr, 'De Schim van Shakespear', *De Nederlandsche Mercurius* 26 (4 March 1829), 409–10.
27. George Sand, *Le Roi Attend: Prologue* (Théâtre de la République – 9 avril 1848), in *Théâtre Complet,* I (Paris: Lévy, 1876), 125–42, in particular 137–38. For the reference to Sand, I am indebted to Gretchen E. Smith, 'Aurore Dupin Dudevant and Jean-Baptiste Poquelin: George Sand Reconstructs Molière', in *The Author as Character: Representing Historical Writers in Western Literature,* ed. Paul Franssen and Ton Hoenselaars (Madison: Fairleigh Dickinson, 1999), 141–56.
28. *Memoirs of the Shakespear's-Head in Covent Garden: By the Ghost of Shakespear* (London, 1755), 5–6.
29. Dobson, 212.
30. Produced 1905; typescript in Spielmann Coll., University of Birmingham.
31. Cf. Laura Rosenthal's argument, summarized in note 2 above.
32. Quoted from Katharine Cooke, *A. C. Bradley and his Influence in Twentieth-Century Shakespeare Criticism* (Oxford: Clarendon Press, 1972), 191–92. In a footnote, Cooke traces the poem further to an undated issue of *Punch*, and to Boas's 1926 *Lays of Learning.*
33. Terence Hawkes, *That Shakespeherian Rag* (London: Methuen, 1986), 31.

34. A similar tendency to take Shakespeare down a peg is common in science fiction stories involving time travel. See, for instance, Isaac Asimov's story 'The Immortal Bard', in his *Earth is Room Enough* (1953, rpt. St. Albans: Panther, 1960), 149–51, which also has Shakespeare puzzled by his modern critics. The topic of Shakespeare and time-travel is discussed in my *Shakespeare's Literary Lives* (Cambridge: Cambridge University Press, 2016), 228–46.
35. Mark Rylance, 'The Big Secret Live! "I am Shakespeare" Webcam Daytime Chatroom Show!!!', 2007, unpublished typescript. I am indebted to Mr Rylance for making this material available to me. The summary is quoted from Paul Taylor, 'The Bard's Big Year: A Nation still in Love with Shakespeare', *Independent*, Monday 24 December 2007, 8–9; 9.
36. 'Kaj Munk taler med Shakespeare', *Forum, Tidsskrift for Musik og Teater*, vol. 3 (March 1935), 8–10. I am indebted to Niels Bugge Hansen for this material, which also features in his 'Something is rotten ...', *Shakespeare and War*, ed. Ros King and Paul Franssen (Houndmills, Basingstoke: Palgrave, 2008), 153–65.
37. Odette Blumenfeld, private communication. I am deeply indebted to Professor Blumenfeld for this information, which would have been wholly inaccessible to me otherwise.
38. Samuel Taylor Coleridge, Letter II from 'Satyrane's Letters', in his *Biographia Literaria*, ed. Adam Roberts (Edinburgh: Edinburgh University Press, 2014), 349–63. According to the editor, the passage in question was added in 1808 or 1809 (363n), so considerably after Schiller's poem.

Biography

Chapter 2
The Debate about Shakespeare's Character, Morals and Religion in Nineteenth-Century Germany

Wolfgang Weiss

This chapter traces the process of the naturalization of Shakespeare on the Continent and especially in nineteenth-century Germany, with special attention to the constant oscillation between the Protestant and Catholic poles in biographical studies by Shakespeare scholars up to the twentieth century. In the second half of the eighteenth century, when German poets and critics discovered Shakespeare and chose his dramas as their literary models, they were not chiefly interested in his biography, character and religious beliefs. Instead, his German admirers, especially of the school of *Sturm und Drang* (Storm and Stress) and the early Romantics, concentrated on coming to terms with his dramatic art and defining his poetological position.

This critical and poetological debate about the Bard began to change when, in the first decades of the nineteenth century, Shakespeare not only became widely known but was also naturalized in

Germany and enthroned as the third classic German poet besides Goethe and Schiller. In the course of the nineteenth century and the first decades of the twentieth century, this cultural naturalization became more and more a cultural appropriation of the Bard, with jingoistic overtones mixed with disdainful remarks on the British nation for its supposed neglect of its great countryman and its incompetence to understand him properly.

For Georg Gottfried Gervinus, Shakespeare's naturalization was part of a cultural exchange between England and Germany. In his *Shakespeare* (1849–1850), Gervinus compares the dramatist's naturalization in Germany with Georg Friedrich Handel's naturalization in England: 'As England has conquered Handel we have conquered Shakespeare'.[1] And he continues as follows: 'We like to pride ourselves that we did more justice to the Englishman Shakespeare; it is true that we have conquered him with diligence and love, though England did not allow itself to be deprived of him to the same extent as we did of our Handel'.[2]

Rudolph Genée, Shakespeare scholar and theatre historian, was one of the rare critics of this increasing nationalism in German bardolatry. In his book on Shakespeare (1872) he writes:

> Misled by the justified approval with which the ingenious studies of our A.W. Schlegel were received in England, the German Shakespeare critics have prided themselves for some time on having overtaken the English in the proper appreciation of their poet, and this notion has also found willing consent in the general public.[3]

Friedrich Theodor Vischer's *Shakespeare-Vorträge* in 6 volumes (1899–1905) were some of the most popular books on Shakespeare at the beginning of the twentieth century. In the Introduction he wrote:

> We Germans are now used to consider Shakespeare as one of us. Most of his plays have been rendered palatable for mouth and ear in translation, which is Wilhelm Schlegel's merit. The German research on Shakespeare is rich and fruitful. Without being ungrateful to England, which gave us this greatest of all poets, we can proudly say, that it was the German mind that first perceived Shakespeare's nature more deeply. It has also liberated the English mind from the old prejudice that Shakespeare is a wildrunning genius.
>
> It was in German literary criticism that an approach to Shakespeare was made from the viewpoint of aesthetic philosophy, and from here it spread to England, as if Shakespeare were not a Briton but a German. We have thus returned the present with interest.[4]

This cultural jingoism culminated in the middle of World War I. The famous German dramatist and Nobel Prize winner Gerhart Hauptmann said in an address:

> There is no nation, not even the English nation, that can lay a better claim to Shakespeare than the German nation. Shakespeare's characters are part of our world, his soul has merged with ours: and though he was born and buried in England, Germany is the country where he really lives.[5]

The most absurd proposal in this debate was put forward by Ludwig Fulda in 1916:

> And if we succeed in defeating England, then, I think, we should insert a clause into the peace treaty, that William Shakespeare has to be formally transferred to Germany. I even believe that the English would be rather prepared to consent to this transfer, because they do not know how to deal with him properly anyway.[6]

As late as 1934 the minor German poet Paul Wolf closed his *Shakespeare-Hymne* with the lines: 'More than to any other country you belong to this nation which has born you a second time'.[7]

As a member of the German literary triumvirate Shakespeare became one of the great authorities and moral leaders of the German nation. In Gervinus' words:

> He displays a wisdom and knowledge of man for all general and special situations of inner and outward life that make him a teacher of undoubted authority; he obtained his moral world view from the comprehensive observation of the outward world, and clarified it in a rich inner life, so that he perhaps more than any other man deserves to be elected as a trustworthy leader through world and life.[8]

Shakespeare's exalted status along with the biographical turn in literary criticism also directed the interest of German Shakespeare scholars and critics to the dramatist's personality, his philosophy and religious beliefs. Since the 1840s, hardly a book about Shakespeare and his dramas was published that did not contain a lengthy chapter in which Shakespeare's biography and personality were extensively discussed and different portraits of the Bard by other critics were refuted. These fictitious portraits did not only reflect the ideological positions of their authors but also played an important part in the philosophical and religious controversies of the nineteenth century. The debate about the man Shakespeare appears to have started with Hermann Ulrici's monumental *Shakespeare's dramatische Kunst* (1839) [Shakespeare's Dramatic Art], which was published in many revised and augmented editions and was translated into English in 1846, 1876 and 1888. Ulrici, first President of the *Deutsche Shakespeare-Gesellschaft* [German Shakespeare Society], founded in 1864, portrays Shakespeare and his life according to romantic notions of an ideal poetical existence: a life in seclusion wholly devoted to the creation and improvement of his art:

> After the first youthful indiscretions and their consequences had been overcome, his external life – according to all that we know of him – passed by very quietly and peacefully, even though not without brilliancy and distinction. His was a true poetical life, wholly devoted to free creation, and to the everlasting development of his art. Shakespeare was no minister of state, no professor, or any kind of official; he was not even a Court-poet nor the associate of any Academy of arts or learned Society. He was simply himself, neither more nor less than a poet.[9]

Ulrici was also convinced of Shakespeare's noble character: 'But the poet could not attain what was greatest and highest, without himself possessing a great and noble nature. "Worthy", "noble" and "beloved" are without exception the epithets with which contemporaries adorned his name' (Ulrici, 238).

Shakespeare's noble character became a commonplace in nineteenth-century Germany, but almost all other attributes of his fictitious personality were subject to controversy. In the 1870s Ulrici's romantic portrait of the German cultural hero as a withdrawn poet was no longer considered as appropriate in a period of booming economy and wild speculation, of growing national self-confidence, especially after the victory over France and the foundation of the Second Reich (1871). In chapter VII, 'Shakespeares Charakter, seine Welt- und Lebensanschauung' [Shakespeare's character and world view], of his *William Shakespeare* (1876), Karl Elze deals at length with the poet's character and mind.[10] He confirms Ulrici's notion of Shakespeare's great and noble nature but portrays him according to the contemporary ideal of an energetic and enterprising middle-class man full of willpower. Elze's Shakespeare was no mean flatterer or toady but a proud and ambitious man, a social climber who wanted to become a gentleman but only on the basis of his fortune and properties and not because of his fame as a dramatist, although he was fully conscious of his poetical talents and proud of his achievements as a playwright. For Elze, he was also a devoted friend and knew the passions of love. Elze's image of the Bard corresponds not only to the masculine ideal of his time but is also a vigorous defence of Shakespeare against Thomas Kenny's portrait in his book *The Life and Genius of Shakespeare* (1864). For Kenny, the scarcity of documents about Shakespeare's life proves that the poet lived a noiseless and unobtrusive life: 'There is one conclusion clearly deducible from this slight notice, or this complete silence. Shakespeare mixed noiselessly and unobtrusively with the world around him. He was animated by no visible and striking energy of purpose; he had no firm, commanding originality of character; he pressed himself on no man's admiration'.[11]

Using the *Sonnets* as his main source, Kenny describes Shakespeare as a weak, almost despicable man without self-respect: 'The greatest imaginative genius the world has ever known prostrates himself before some obscure idol, and, in the frenzy of a tremulous devotion, renounces his self-respect, and abdicates the commonest rights of humanity'. Kenny even discerns feminine traits (in his definition) in Shakespeare's character:

> There is, necessarily, perhaps in creative imagination, as in all creative power, a feminine element. It is through a yearning tenderness, through an unsatisfied want, through a vague and insatiable sensibility, that the genius of the poet is most nearly allied to the mighty forms of the world around him. ... We must maintain that they [*The Sonnets*] bear throughout the marks of a nature strangely impressionable, swayed by vague and subtle impulses, without any proud reserve, without any immovable, all-controlling self-dominion.

For Kenny, therefore, it is evident that Shakespeare neither lived a great life nor had a strong personality:

> Shakespeare, we have the most direct evidence, was the greatest of poets; and upon evidence almost equally direct, and, for every reasonable purpose, equally conclusive, we believe, that Shakespeare lived no great life .... That very imaginative faculty which was the talisman of his art is itself a revelation of character. He who passed so readily and so completely into the personality of others had no strong, tenacious personality of his own to maintain.

According to Kenny, it was the want of individuality that enabled Shakespeare to create the universe of his plays: 'His very want of a firm, distinctly marked individuality enabled him the more readily to restore its own boundless life to the wonderful universe beyond him.'

Shakespeare's status as a major cultural authority and spiritual leader also led to an extensive discussion of his morals and his philosophy, and, since morals and religion were then thought to be closely linked to each other, to an extended controversy about the question of whether Shakespeare was a Protestant or a Catholic, a humanist or an atheist.

For Ulrici there was no doubt that Shakespeare was a faithful Protestant, which he tried to prove by numerous quotations from *Henry VIII*, *Measure for Measure*, *Richard III*, *Macbeth* and other plays. All attempts to prove that Shakespeare was a crypto-Catholic on the evidence of Richard Davies' remark that he 'died a papist' and of the spiritual testament of John Shakespeare were refuted by Ulrici as being nothing but an intrigue based on clumsy forgeries. For Shakespeare's Protestantism Ulrici could also refer to Goethe's authoritative testimonials. Goethe thought that Shakespeare was born and educated as a Protestant, and that his living and working in a short liberal Protestant period were the essential and shaping conditions of his work. In his famous essay 'Shakespeare und kein Ende!' [1813–1816; 'Shakespeare and no end!'], he wrote:

> He certainly had the advantage, that he lived in a flowering period, that he was allowed to work in a vital, Protestant country where the bigoted delusion was silenced for a time, so that a true, naturally religious man like Shakespeare was free to develop his pure inner religious life without relation to any distinct religion.[12]

In his review 'Tochter der Luft' [1821; 'Daughter of the Air'] of Calderón's *La hija del aire* (1653) he wrote:

> It should be regarded as one of the greatest advantages of his life that Shakespeare enjoyed that he was born and educated as a Protestant. Everywhere he appears as a human being, perfectly familiar with human nature. He is above illusion and superstition and only plays with them. He presses supernatural beings to serve his ends; he engages tragic ghosts, farcical goblins for his purpose which clarifies everything so that in the end the poet is never embarrassed to have to idolize the absurd, which would be the most deplorable situation into which a man can get who is conscious of his reason.[13]

Shakespeare's supposed Protestantism furthered his popularity in the Protestant parts of Germany, and many books and articles in Protestant journals were published which argued that his dramas were in accordance with the Bible and Protestant teachings.

But there also started a debate within the Protestant world, whether Shakespeare was a faithful and devout member of the Protestant church or a liberal Protestant. In 1851, Eduard Vehse's book was published under the significant title *Shakespeare als Protestant, Politiker, Psycholog, und Dichter* [Shakespeare as a Protestant, Politician, Psychologist and Poet], in which the author describes his religious and political convictions as Protestant and aristocratic Whig. But Vehse goes on to qualify Shakespeare's Protestant belief. After quoting passages from *Richard III, Henry V, Hamlet* and *Henry VIII*, he writes:

> [F]rom these passages it becomes evident that Shakespeare somehow professed to the main teachings and main stories of the Christian faith, namely the Protestant, the popular-biblical Christian belief. It is inconceivable how this could have been put in doubt, let alone have been denied. ... Shakespeare refused all intentionally instructive and sermonizing admixtures from a special theology or dogmatic system which is the capacity of a hierarchy of priests.

And Vehse concludes:

> This sovereign manly point of view of Shakespeare's Protestantism, which directly opposes the Catholic as well as the Protestant hierarchical childish points of view, is the soul of Shakespeare's soul: this point of view is, if I am not mistaken, that which explains all in him. The self-guidance, the self-government in religious matters is his innermost and basic conviction.[14]

Rudolph Genée, one of the few scholars who warned against the nationalistic appropriation of Shakespeare, also criticized all attempts to claim Shakespeare for any religious denomination or any political or philosophical ideology. In his *Shakespeare. Sein Leben und seine Werke* [Shakespeare. His Life and his Works] (1872) he wrote:

> Shakespeare's creations have been misused in the most disgraceful way. They have tried hard to distil everything out of them! The mania to construct Shakespeare's personality out of the poet's dramatic characters has led to the result, that he has been made a Catholic on the one hand, and a zealous and incarnate Protestant on the other; that he has been described as an atheist here, and there as a pietist; that they alleged to discern him as a dyed-in-the-wool aristocrat and a people's friend, a cosmopolite and a true-blue Englishman at the same time![15]

It was Georg Gottfried Gervinus who presented a different Shakespeare to German readers. In his monumental *Shakespeare*, published in four volumes between 1849 and 1852 and translated into English as *Shakespeare Commentaries* by F. E. Bunnett in 1863, he did not only provide exhaustive interpretations of each play but also dealt extensively with Shakespeare's moral system and world view.

For Gervinus, Shakespeare was neither a Protestant nor a Catholic, nor a dramatist who propagated the teachings of the Bible, but an enlightened intellectual whose moral system was strictly secular and could be called Christian only insofar as he professed the love of men as the highest value. He did not believe in biblical revelations but in the revelation God places in every human heart. According to Gervinus, Shakespeare's message means that man is supposed to lead a self-determined and self-controlled life and does not need spiritual guidance or church-laws: 'In the same way as Bacon expelled religion from science, so Shakespeare [expelled it] from art; and as the former complained of teachers of religion taking side against science, so they did against the stage. ... But morals were just as much his aim as poetry itself'.[16] 'Shakespeare's morals are based on the simple principle that man is born with faculties of activity which he should use and with faculties of self-government and self-control which should guide this use in the right direction.'[17] Therefore, Gervinus concludes, Shakespeare the humanist can only be fully understood by the educated classes but never by the multitude, who are in need of strong religious guidance. Gervinus' portrait tried to defend the Bard against two sides: on the one hand against critics of Shakespeare such as W. J. Birch or W. Gifford. For Birch, Shakespeare was an atheist, a blasphemer and a despiser of all religions. In order to prove this he did not hesitate to misquote Shakespeare on purpose. In *A Midsummer Night's Dream* he makes Shakespeare say: 'the religious, the lunatic, and the poet are of imagination all compact', instead of: 'the lover, the lunatic and the poet'. Birch was also convinced that Shakespeare's Sonnet 74 contained a denial of the Redemption.[18]

Another author who suspected Shakespeare of being a scoffer at religion was the admirer and editor of Ben Jonson, W. Gifford. He wrote: 'Shakespeare is in truth the coryphaeus of profanation'.[19] On the other hand, Gervinus defended him against Protestants and Catholics who tried to claim the famous dramatist as a faithful member of their respective churches. Gervinus' portrait met with strict opposition, especially from Protestant Shakespeareans. Heinrich von Friesen, an admirer of Gervinus' brilliant analyses of Shakespeare's works, wrote an essay in order to refute Gervinus' portrait of Shakespeare as a liberal humanist. For von Friesen, Shakespeare was a pious Protestant, whose plays were in full accordance with the Bible and Protestant teachings.[20]

Karl Elze, another scholar who followed Gervinus in the defence of Shakespeare's liberal humanism against all attempts to turn the Bard into a devoted member of one of the denominations, quoted with approval the angry words of the famous eighteenth-century actor James Quin, who exclaimed on hearing that Bishop Warburton was about to publish an edition of Shakespeare: 'I wish he would stick to his own Bible and leave us ours!' (Elze, 443).

Not only Protestants but also Roman Catholics tried to claim Shakespeare for the Old Faith. They tried to assert their claim by referring to Richard Davies' dictum in clergyman Fuller's manuscript and to John Shakespeare's spiritual testament (see above) but also to passages from Shakespeare's plays. The Romantics in particular, with their nostalgic longing for the Middle Ages and the Catholic Church with its rituals appealing to emotions rather than to reason, saw Shakespeare as a crypto-Catholic poet whose mind was not framed by the atheism and scepticism of the Renaissance but by medieval Catholicism, and thus compared him to Dante and Calderón.

François-René de Chateaubriand (1768–1848) appears to have been among the first who supposed that Shakespeare may have been a Catholic. In his *Essai sur la littérature anglaise* (1836) he wrote: 'Shakespeare ... if he was anything, was a Catholic.'[21] In Germany, the Romantic poet Joseph von Eichendorff in his *Zur Geschichte des Dramas* [1854; On the History of Drama] presented Shakespeare as a Christian dramatist, whose mental attitude he defined as closer to Catholicism than Protestantism. Roman Catholics also used to quote Thomas Carlyle's remark on Shakespeare:

> In some sense it may be said that this glorious Elizabethan Era with its Shakespeare, as the outcome and flowerage of all, which had preceded it, is itself attributable to the Catholicism of the Middle Ages. The Christian Faith, which was the theme of Dante's Song, had produced this Practical Life, which Shakespeare was to sing. For Religion then, as it now and always is, was the soul of Practice, the primary vital fact in men's life. And remark here, as rather curious, that Middle-Age Catholicism was abolished, so far as Acts of Parliament could abolish it, before Shakespeare, the noblest product of it, made his appearance. ... We called Dante, the melodious Priest of Middle-Age Catholicism. May we not call Shakespeare the still more melodious Priest of a true Catholicism, the 'Universal Church' of the Future and all times?[22]

In 1854 and 1858 Richard Simpson's articles about Shakespeare's supposed Catholicism were published in the *Rambler*, a Catholic journal, followed by another article in the *Edinburgh Review* 251 (1866), which were also read on the Continent. After Simpson's articles, what had hitherto been an assumption cherished by many Catholics, for some Roman Catholic authors became an undoubted fact. For the French author A. F. Rio it was evident that Shakespeare was not only a faithful Roman Catholic but also that he led a most virtuous life according to the teachings of the Roman church. Rio's line of reasoning is highly speculative throughout the book. For instance, the fact that Shakespeare's first daughter was born five months after his marriage with Anne Hathaway and named Susanna was interpreted by Rio as proof that there must have been a secret Catholic marriage ceremony before the Protestant wedding. Otherwise, Shakespeare would never have dared to name his daughter Susanna after the heroine of chastity in the Old Testament.[23] By fanciful speculations like these, Rio did rather a disservice to the Catholic cause, and his book was harshly censured in M. Bernays' review in the first volume of the *Shakespeare Jahrbuch* in 1865.[24]

The tone of the debate about Shakespeare's religion between Protestants and liberal humanists on the one side and Catholics on the other became sharper after the founding of the *Second Reich* in 1871, which in contrast to the *Old Reich* (dissolved in 1806), came under the hegemony of Protestant Prussia. Chancellor Bismarck's policy to unite the German kingdoms and principalities into a nation dominated by Protestantism, liberalism and nationalism was observed with growing concern by the Vatican authorities, who saw in it a weakening of the influence of Catholicism. As early as 1864, Pope Pius IX had published the *Syllabus Errorum* [List of Errors] in which he condemned political ideologies such as nationalism, liberalism, or socialism as incompatible with the teachings of the Roman Catholic Church. In 1870 at the First Vatican Council, the Pope declared the dogma of the Pope's infallibility in all matters of religion and morals when speaking *ex cathedra*. Bismarck interpreted these efforts of the Vatican to strengthen its influence among Roman Catholics living in secular societies as attacks on the unity of the Reich. He accused the Catholics as ultramontanists of disloyalty to the Reich because of their obedience to the 'ultramontane' Pope (residing beyond the Alps), and declared them enemies of the nation. In the *Kulturkampf* [War of Cultures] that followed – the word was coined in 1872 by the famous physician Rudolf Virchow, an ardent supporter of Bismarck's policy who was a liberal member of the Reichstag – Chancellor Bismarck took a number of harsh measures against the Catholic Church, strongly opposed in the Reichstag by the *Zentrum*, the political party of the Catholics, who insinuated that Bismarck planned the final accomplishment of the reformation in Germany that had been initiated by Martin Luther. Among Bismarck's measures were the expulsion of Jesuits and other orders, putting Catholic schools under the control of the government, prohibiting priests from using the pulpit for political comments, introducing compulsory civil marriage and breaking off the diplomatic relations with the Vatican. The *Kulturkampf* – its climax being between 1872 and 1879 – did not end in a defeat of political Catholicism but rather strengthened it. Bismarck's measures turned out to be counterproductive and increased rather than diminished the political influence of the *Zentrum*, especially in traditionally Catholic countries. When Pope Pius IX died in 1878 and the more diplomatic Leo XIII ascended the papal throne, Bismarck slowly began to change his policy against the Catholics. *The Kulturkampf* ended in 1878.

As Thomas Richter has shown,[25] in this political-religious controversy Shakespeare was the only one of the three classic 'German' poets whose religious conviction was not known for certain and whose work could thus be used as an argument for the cultural superiority of one of the religious denominations. A typical example of the polemical tone in which Shakespeare's religion was discussed appears in a passage in Karl Elze's *Shakespeare* published in 1876 when the *Kulturkampf* was in full swing:

> A Catholic by name, it is quite possible, Shakespeare may have been; but a Catholic in deed or in character, never! ... Catholicism in its logical consequences is an institution that exhibits the greatest possible one-sidedness, not to say narrowness, of the human mind, and Shakespeare's was not only a many-sided mind, but one that embraced every point of view. His, the freest and most independent of minds, could not possibly have tolerated the mental restraint or limitation such as the Catholic Church casts upon its followers, and which in fact it must cast upon them for the sake of its own preservation. Nay, the Catholic Church in its narrow-mindedness, its police-like supervision, intolerance and love of persecution must have been positively repulsive to Shakespeare, and, indeed, the very same reasons kept him aloof from Protestant Churchism.[26]

On the Catholic side, critics and literary historians continued to plead in favour of Shakespeare's Catholicism on the basis of arguments presented by Carlyle, Simpson and others. They also pointed to features of his works, such as the fair presentation of Catholic characters or Shakespeare's exact knowledge of Catholic rituals, features that were explained away by Protestant authors with Shakespeare's *'hohe Objektivität'* ['high objectivity'], which Goethe had praised in the dramatist. Catholic Shakespeareans like August Reichensperger, one of the founding members of the *Zentrum*, in his book of 1871 repeated Carlyle's thesis that Shakespeare's mind was entirely formed by the spirituality of the Middle Ages, although he lived in Protestant Elizabethan England.[27]

In order to support Shakespeare's Catholicism, Catholic literary historians rejected the prevailing tendency in the national, liberal and Protestant-oriented literary historiography of the nineteenth century to portray Shakespeare as the Protestant Renaissance champion in the struggle for progress towards Protestantism, humanism and enlightenment in which the Germanic nations of northern Europe had taken the lead, a progress that culminated in the literary achievements of the Weimar classic era. In contrast to this nationalistic model, the literary historian Peter Norrenberg in his three volumes of *Allgemeine Geschichte der Literatur* (1882–1884)[28] [General History of Literature] developed his concept of a truly catholic (that is, including the poetry of all nations) history of world literature with different standards of evaluation and rankings. In his literary history, the literatures of the Middle Ages, of the Counter-Reformation and of Catholic Romantics were revaluated, and Dante, the Catholic Shakespeare and Calderón were established as the true triumvirate against the three classic 'German' poets.

In 1884, the Catholic theologian J. M. Raich published his monograph *Shakespeares Stellung zur katholischen Religion*[29] [Shakespeare's Attitude toward the Catholic Religion], which was the most exhaustive study of the subject in Germany up to then. On its basis, the exiled Jesuit Alexander Baumgartner, one of the most esteemed Catholic literary historians of his time, and notorious among Goethe-admirers for his attack on the 'Goethe-Cult', wrote three articles on Shakespeare's Catholicism published in 1885, 1897 and 1899.[30] Especially in his article of 1897, in the post-*Kulturkampf* era, Baumgartner refrained from any polemics and carefully and objectively weighed the pros and cons of the issue. He even admitted:

No contemporary author called Shakespeare a Catholic or even hinted at it. There is no contemporary file in which he is mentioned as such. His name is missing completely in the lists of Stratford recusants, which contain unusually many names at that time. The growing wealth and the reputation which he enjoyed in Stratford, are in favour of the assumption that he was generally thought a Protestant and, therefore, escaped all prosecutions which Catholics were exposed to.[31]

On the other hand, Baumgartner is convinced that Shakespeare the poet was no Protestant: 'As a poet Shakespeare was no Protestant. He belongs to us. The Romantics were right to put him together with Dante and Calderón on their banner'.[32] But Baumgartner also admitted 'that the existing evidence is not sufficient to decide the question of Shakespeare's religion simply and with full certainty'.[33] This statement may well serve both as an epilogue to the long and passionate debate in nineteenth-century Germany and also as a prologue to the more moderate discussion of Shakespeare's religion in our days.

Wolfgang Weiss (1932–2019) was Full Professor of English Literature at the University of Munich. He studied English, French and Celtic philology at the University of Munich, where he also completed his PhD, and from 1960 to 1962 he taught at the German Department of the University of Glasgow in Scotland. Back in Germany, he was appointed Professor of English Literature at the University of Cologne in 1970, from where he returned to Munich in 1974 to take over the prestigious Chair of English Literature with a focus on Shakespeare and the Early Modern Period, as well as the directorship of the Munich Shakespeare Library. In 2000, he became Professor Emeritus, and he passed away in July 2019. His main areas of academic research and teaching included Shakespeare and the early modern period (*Das Drama der Shakespeare Zeit*, 1979; *King Lear*, 2004; *Shakespeare in Bayern und auf Bairisch*, 2008), Elizabethan poetry (*Die elisabethanische Lyrik*, 1974), Jonathan Swift and 18th-century British satire (*Swift und die Satire des 18. Jahrhunderts*, 1992), and campus novels (*Der anglo-amerikanische Universitätsroman*, 1988). From 1997 to 1999, he was editor of *Shakespeare Jahrbuch*. During his academic career, he published 11 books, about 70 articles, and numerous reviews and shorter dictionary entries.

Notes

1. 'So wie England Haendel haben wir Shakespeare erobert'. Georg Gottfried Gervinus, *Shakespeare*, 2 vols (Leipzig: Engelmann, 1862), vii. All translations are my own unless otherwise noted.
2. 'Dem Englaender Shakespeare ruehmen wir uns gern sein groesseres Recht gethan zu haben; gewiß ist, daß wir ihn durch Fleiß und Liebe, so gut wie England unseren Haendel, uns erobert haben, wenn auch England nicht in dem Masse, wie wir jenen ihn sich rauben liess' (Gervinus, viii).
3. Verleitet durch die Anerkennung, welche die geistvollen Arbeiten unsers A.W. Schlegel auch in England fanden, bildet sich die deutsche Shakespeare-Kritik seit laengerer Zeit etwas darauf ein, die Englaender in der richtigen Wuerdigung ihres Dichters ueberfluegelt zu haben, und diese Ansicht hat bei uns auch im grossen Publikum willige Zustimmung erfahren.
   Rudolph Genée, *Shakespeare. Sein Leben und seine Werke* (Hildburghausen: Bibliographisches Institut, 1872), 6.
4. Wir Deutsche sind nun also gewohnt, Shakespeare als einen der Unsern zu betrachten. Seine Dramen sind uns zum groessten Teil mund- und ohrgerecht uebersetzt: das ist Wilhelm Schlegels Verdienst. Die deutsche Forschung ueber Shakespeare ist reichlich und umfassend fruchtbar. Ohne undankbar zu sein gegen England, das uns diesen groessten aller Dichter geschenkt hat, duerfen wir es mit Stolz sagen: dass der deutsche Geist zuerst Shakespeares Wesen tiefer erkannte. Er hat auch den englischen befreit aus dem alten Vorurteil, Shakespeare sei ein wildlaufendes Genie.

   In der deutschen Litteratur [sic] ist der Anfang damit gemacht worden, Shakespeare aesthetisch, kunstphilosophisch zu nehmen, und von ihr aus ist diese Auffassung in England selbst erst geweckt worden, als waere er nicht ein Brite, sondern ein Deutscher. Wir haben also das Geschenk mit Zinsen heimgegeben.
   Friedrich Theodor Vischer, *Shakespeare-Vorträge*, 6 vols (Stuttgart, Berlin: Cotta, 1899–1905), 2.
5. Es gibt kein Volk, auch das englische nicht, das sich ein Anrecht wie das deutsche auf Shakespeare erworben haette. Shakespeares Gestalten sind ein Teil unserer Welt, seine Seele ist eins mit der unsern geworden: und wenn er in England geboren und begraben ist, so ist Deutschland das Land, wo er wahrhaft lebt.
   Gerhart Hauptmann, 'Deutschland und Shakespeare', *Shakespeare Jahrbuch* 51 (1915), xii.
6. Und falls es uns glueckt, England niederzuringen, dann, meine ich, wir sollten in den Friedensvertrag eine Klausel setzen, wonach William Shakespeare auch formell an Deutschland abzutreten ist. Ich glaube sogar, für diese Abtretung werden die Englaender noch am ehesten zu haben sein, weil sie ohnehin nichts Rechtes mit ihm anzufangen wissen.
   Ludwig Fulda, *Deutsche Kultur und Ausländerei* (Leipzig: Hirzel, 1916), 13f.
7. 'Bist du zu eigen nun vor aller Welt / Dem Land, das dich zum zweitenmal geboren'. Paul Wolf, *Rufe vom anderen Ufer* (Weimar: Alexander Duncker, 1934), 139.

8. Er entfaltet fuer alle allgemeinen und besonderen Lagen des inneren und aeußeren Lebens eine Weisheit und Kenntniss des Menschen, die ihn zu einem Lehrer von unbestreitbarer Autoritaet macht; er hat eine moralische Weltsicht aus reicher Beobachtung der aeußeren Welt so geschoepft, und in einem reichen innern Leben so gelaeutert, dass er mehr vielleicht als jeder Andere verdient, zu einem Fuehrer durch Welt und Leben vertrauensvoll gewaehlt zu werden. (Gervinus, 3)
9. Hermann Ulrici, *Shakespeares dramatische Kunst* (Leipzig: T. O. Weigel, 1839). English ed. 1888, 238.
10. Karl Elze, *William Shakespeare* (Halle: Waisenhaus, 1876).
11. Thomas Kenny, *The Life and Genius of Shakespeare* (London: Longman, Green, 1864). The following quotations are from 79 and 101.
12. Freilich hat er den Vorteil, dass er zur rechten Erntezeit kam, dass er in einem lebensreichen protestantischen Lande wirken durfte, wo der bigotte Wahn eine Zeitlang schwieg, so dass einem wahren Naturfrommen, wie Shakespeare, die Freiheit blieb, sein reines Innere, ohne Bezug auf irgend eine bestimmte Religion, religioes zu entwickeln.
Johann Wolfgang von Goethe, 'Shakespeare und kein Ende!', *Jubilaeumsausgabe*, vol. 6 (Frankfurt, Leipzig: Insel, 1998), 305.
13. Es sei fuer den groessten Lebensvorteil, welchen Shakespeare genoss, zu achten, dass er als Protestant geboren und erzogen worden. Ueberall erscheint er als Mensch, mit Menschlichem vollkommen vertraut, Wahn und Aberglauben sieht er unter sich und spielt nur damit, ausserirdische Wesen noetigt er, seinen Unternehmen zu dienen; tragische Gespenster, possenhafte Kobolde beruft er zu seinem Zwecke, in welchem sich zuletzt alles vereinigt, ohne dass der Dichter jemals die Verlegenheit fuehlte, das Absurde vergoettern zu muessen, der allertraurigste Fall, in welchem der seiner Vernunft sich bewusste Mensch geraten kann. (Goethe, 338)
14. [A]us diesen Stellen ist wohl mit Evidenz zu ersehen, dass Shakespeare sich schlecht und recht zu den Hauptlehren und zu den Hauptgeschichten des Christenthums und zwar des protestantischen, des populair-biblischen Christenthums bekannt hat. Es ist unbegreiflich, wie das nur hat in Zweifel, geschweige in Ablaeugnen gestellt werden koennen. ... Durchaus hielt sich Shakespeare fern von aller absichtlich lehrenden und predigenden Beimischung aus einer speziellen Theologie und Dogmatik, dem doktrinairen und disziplinairen Ruestzeug einer Hierarchie der Priester.
Dieser souveraine maennliche Standpunkt des Protestantismus Shakespeares, der direct dem katholisch sowohl als protestantisch hierarchischen Kinderstandpunkt entgegensteht, ist die Seele der Seele Shakespeares: dieser Standpunkt ist, wenn mich nicht alles taeuscht, der, der bei ihm Alles erklaert. Die Selbstfuehrung, das Selfgovernment in der religioesen Sphaere ist seine innerste Grunduebperzeugung.
Eduard Vehse, *Shakespeare als Protestant, Politiker, Psycholog, und Dichter* (Hamburg: Hoffmann, 1851), 83f.
15. Man trieb mit seinen inhaltsreichen Schoepfungen den schnoedesten Missbrauch. Was hat man nicht alles daraus zu destillieren versucht! Die Sucht, aus den dramatischen Charakteren des Dichters Shakespeares Persoenlichkeit zu konstruieren, hat dahin gefuehrt, dass man ihn auf der

einen Seite zum Katholiken auf der anderen zum eifrigsten und inkarnierten Protestanten gemacht hat; dass man ihn hier als Atheisten, dort als Pietisten schilderte; dass man ihn gleichzeitig einen eingefleischten Aristokraten und einen Volksfreund, einen Weltbuerger und prononcirten Englaender zu erkennen vorgab! (Genée, 7)

16. 'Ganz wie Bacon die Religion aus der Wissenschaft wies, so Shakespeare aus der Kunst; und wie sich jener beklagte, dass die Lehrer der Religion gegen die Naturwissenschaft Partei waren, so waren sie es gegen die Buehne ... Die Sittlichkeit aber war ihm so sehr Zweck wie die Dichtung selber' (Gervinus, 522).

17. 'Shakespeares sittliche Anschauung geht von dem einfachen Gesichtspunkte aus, dass der Mensch mit Kraeften der Thaetigkeit geboren wird, die er brauchen soll, und mit Kraeften der Selbstbestimmung und Selbstlenkung, die diesen Gebrauch der handelnden Kraefte richtig steuern sollen' (Gervinus, 553).

18. W. J. Birch, *An Inquiry into the Philosophy and Religion of Shakespeare* (London, 1848), quoted from Elze, op. cit., English ed. 1901, 440f.

19. William Gifford, ed., *The Works of Ben Jonson* (London: Moxon, 1853), lv.

20. See Heinrich von Friesen, *Das Buch: Shakespeare von Gervinus. Ein Wort über dasselbe* (Leipzig: Baensch, 1869).

21. 'Shakespeare ... s'il était quelque chose, était catholique.' François-René de Chateaubriand, *Essai sur la littérature anglaise* (Paris: Furne et Gosselin, 1836), vol. 1, 203.

22. Thomas Carlyle, *On Heroes, Hero-Worship, and the Heroic in History; The Hero as Poet. Dante; Shakespeare*, Lecture III, 12 May 1840. Quot. from *Oxford Anthology of English Literature*, vol. II, 824f.

23. Alexis François Rio, *Shakespeare Catholique* (Paris: Charles Douniol, 1864), 46 ff.

24. Michael Bernays, 'Shakespeare ein katholischer Dichter', *Shakespeare Jahrbuch* 1 (1865), 220–99.

25. Thomas Richter, '"Shakespeare's Katholicität" – Die Kontroverse um Shakespeares Konfession in Deutschland zur Zeit des Kulturkampfes', *Shakespeare Jahrbuch* 136 (2000), 108–30. The following passages are indebted to Richter's article.

26. Ein Katholik dem Namen nach haette Shakespeare moeglicherweise sein koennen, ein Katholik der That und dem Wesen nach nimmermehr! ... Der Katholizismus in seiner strengen Consequenz ist die groesste Einseitigkeit, um nicht zu sagen Beschraenktheit des menschlichen Geistes, Shakespeare aber besaß nicht nur einen vielseitigen, sondern einen allseitigen Geist. Er, der freieste und unabhaengigste Denker, konnte sich unmoeglich einer geistigen Gebundenheit und Fesselung unterwerfen, wie sie die katholische Kirche ueber ihre Bekenner verhaengt und um ihrer Existenz willen verhaengen muß. Ja, die katholische Kirche mit ihrer Engherzigkeit, ihrer polizeilichen Ueberwachung, ihrer Unduldsamkeit und Verfolgungssucht musste Shakespeare geradezu abstossen, wie ihn ja dieselben Gruende auch vom protestantischen Kirchenthum, insbesondere vom Protestantismus fernhielten. (Elze, 528f.)

27. August Reichensperger, *William Shakespeare, insbesondere sein Verhältnis zum Mittelalter und zur Gegenwart*. Franz Hülskamp, ed., *Zeitgemäße Broschüren*, vol. 7, nos. 9 and 10 (Münster: Russell, 1871).

28. Peter Norrenberg, *Allgemeine Geschichte der Literatur: Ein Handbuch der Geschichte der Poesie aller Völker*, 3 vols (Münster: Russell, 1882–84).
29. J. M. Raich, *Shakespeare's Stellung zur katholischen Religion* (Mainz, 1884).
30. See Richter, 'Shakespeare's Katholicität', 126, n 71.
31. Von keinem zeitgenoessischen Schriftsteller wird Shakespeare als Katholik bezeichnet oder auch nur angedeutet. Kein zeitgenoessisches Aktenstueck erwaehnt ihn als solchen. Sein Name fehlt vollstaendig auf den Rekusantenlisten von Stratford, die zu dieser Zeit sonst ungewoehnlich viele Namen enthalten. Die steigende Wohlhabenheit und das Ansehen, dessen er in Stratford genoss, beguenstigen die Annahme, dass er allgemein daselbst als Protestant galt und deshalb allen Verfolgungen entging, welche die Katholiken trafen.

    Alexander Baumgartner, 'Shakespeares Religion', *Stimmen aus Maria Laach* 53 (1897), 487–505. Quoted from Richter, loc. cit., 128.
32. 'Als Dichter ist Shakespeare kein Protestant. Er gehoert zu uns. Die Romantiker haben ihn ganz richtig mit Dante und Calderón zugleich auf ihr Banner erhoben' (Baumgartner, quoted from Richter, 129).
33. 'Wir geben zu, dass die vorhandenen Zeugnisse nicht ausreichen, um die Frage nach Shakespeares Religion einfach und mit voelliger Sicherheit zu entscheiden' (Baumgartner, quoted from Richter, 128).

Chapter 3
'Talk to Him'
Wilde, his Friends and Shakespeare's *Sonnets*

Reiko Oya

'It is curious how the problem of the Sonnets haunted Oscar Wilde for years!'[1]

A Brief Encounter

George Bernard Shaw vividly recalls the only time he saw Oscar Wilde and his aristocratic boyfriend Alfred Douglas together. It was on the eve of Wilde's libel trial over the offending inscription ('For Oscar Wilde posing Somdomite [*sic*]') that Douglas's father, the Marquess of Queensberry, had sent him. Wilde came to see Shaw's editor Frank Harris at London's Café Royal, to ask him 'to testify at the trial that *Dorian Gray* was a masterpiece of literature and morality'. Harris pleaded with Wilde to flee the country immediately:

> It was no use. Wilde was in a curious double temper. He made no pretence either of innocence or of questioning the folly of his proceedings against Queensberry. But he had an infatuate haughtiness

Notes for this section begin on page 65.

as to the impossibility of his retreating, and as to his right to dictate your [i.e., Harris's] course. Douglas sat in silence, a haughty indignant silence, copying Wilde's attitude as all Wilde's admirers did, but quite probably influencing Wilde as you suggest, by the copy. Oscar finally rose with a mixture of impatience and his grand air, and walked out with the remark that he had now found out who were his real friends; and Douglas followed him, absurdly smaller, and imitating his walk, like a curate following an archbishop.[2]

Personal contact among the four friends would become sporadic thereafter. Wilde would soon be imprisoned (1895–97) and, after a brief reunion with Douglas, would die in exile in Paris (1900), while the other three would be based in different parts of England, Europe and America the rest of their lives. Nonetheless, they maintained their dialogue not only through writing letters to each other,[3] but also by writing about each other. During his two-year prison term, Wilde wrote a dramatic monologue and autobiography, posthumously entitled *De Profundis*, addressed to Douglas, while Douglas himself reflected on his relations with his one-time lover in a series of publications: *Oscar Wilde and Myself* (1914; largely ghost-written by T. W. H. Crosland), *Autobiography* (1929; retitled in America as *My Friendship with Oscar Wilde*, 1932) and *Oscar Wilde: A Summing-Up* (1940). Harris wrote biographies of both Wilde (*Oscar Wilde: His Life and Confessions*, 1916) and Shaw (*Bernard Shaw: An Unauthorised Biography*, 1931), and Shaw contributed chapters to both. Harris's ambition to author 'The Life and Confessions of Lord Alfred Douglas' did not materialize,[4] but he did publish 'The Full and Final Confession by Lord Alfred Douglas' in the 1930 edition of his Wilde biography by citing a private letter with explicit content from Douglas without the sender's consent.

The relationship of Wilde and the three men was anything but straightforward, to which the complicated publication history of their respective biographies attests. The most explosive portions of *De Profundis* were only released more than a decade after Wilde's death and, to the everlasting dismay of Douglas, loudly decried the younger friend's avarice and cruelty. In order to promote the sales of his Wilde biography, Harris printed the name of Shaw 'in golden letters' on its cover 'as if it were a book about Oscar Wilde by Bernard Shaw'.[5] In the book, Harris not only exaggerated his role in events – Hesketh Pearson's criticism that the book 'is not the story of Oscar Wilde but the story of Frank Harris' was apt[6] – but also portrayed Douglas's responsibility for the downfall of Wilde in a vilifying manner. The biography remained unpublishable in Britain until 1938, when Shaw pacified Douglas by rewriting the most libelous passages and attaching an explanatory preface in the form of a reply to yet another biography, Robert Harborough Sherard's *Bernard Shaw, Frank Harris and Oscar Wilde* (1936).

Their convoluted conversation also continued on a literary plane in their interpretations of Shakespeare's *Sonnets* and, in the years after the death of Wilde in particular, this book of brilliant and enigmatic love poems would be a medium through which his friends kept thinking about and talking to the fallen angel. But, first of all, a quick review of the use that Wilde himself made of Shakespeare in his literary work and in the courtroom is due.

Wilde, the *Portrait* and the Trials

Ever since the 'discovery' of the *Sonnets* by the Romantics as a source of information on Shakespeare's life, scholars and literati have searched for the sentiments and actual circumstances of the poet's life in the 1609 publication. While the mysteries associated with the identities of the Fair Youth, the Dark Lady and the Rival Poet, as well as with 'Mr W. H.' of the dedication, elicited heated discussion about the patronage and literary climate of Shakespeare's day, readers traced the homosexual and adulterous experiences that the sonnet sequence purportedly recorded, and hazarded some wild speculations about the emotional and sexual life of the Bard.[7] The interpretations thus obtained, however, tended to unlock the heart, not of the poet (as Wordsworth put forward in 'Scorn not the Sonnet'), but of the interpreter of the poems.

Such self-projection in literary criticism should hardly surprise us, when Wilde had already pointed out in the preface to *The Picture of Dorian Gray* (1890; revised 1891) that '[t]he highest, as the lowest, form of criticism is a mode of autobiography'.[8] One of the interlocutors of his Platonic dialogue, *The Critic as Artist*, also insists that 'by curious inversion, it is only by intensifying his own personality that the critic can interpret the personality and work of others, and the more strongly this personality enters into the interpretation, the more real the interpretation becomes, the more satisfying, the more convincing, and the more true' (1131). In *The Portrait of Mr W. H.* (1889; revised 1889–93?), the 'wonderfully handsome' and 'effeminate' Cyril Graham, who used to play Shakespeare's female parts while at Cambridge, certainly envisioned Shakespeare's Fair Youth in his own image when he commissioned a portrait of a boy actor 'of quite extraordinary personal beauty, though evidently somewhat effeminate' to vindicate his interpretation of the *Sonnets* (302, 304). As he 'read and re-read' the poems, the (unnamed) narrator of this short story also felt as if 'I was deciphering the story of a life that had once been mine, unrolling the record of a romance that, without my knowing it, had coloured the very texture of my nature, had dyed it with strange and subtle dyes' (343).

Wilde's *Portrait* delineates an attempt by three dilettante readers (Graham, the narrator and their mutual friend Erskine) to identify the mysterious dedicatee of Shakespeare's *Sonnets* through analysis of internal evidence, such as the supposed double pun on 'Will' (in Sonnets 134, 135, 136 and 143) and *'Hews'*, or Hughes, in the erotically charged Sonnet 20:

> A woman's face with nature's own hand painted
> Hast thou, the master mistress of my passion;
> A woman's gentle heart, but not acquainted
> With shifting change, as is false women's fashion;
> An eye more bright than theirs, less false in rolling,
> Gilding the object whereupon it gazeth;
> A man in hue, all hues [*Hews*, in the 1609 Quarto] in his controlling,
> Which steals men's eyes and women's souls amazeth;
> And for a woman wert thou first created,
> Till nature as she wrought thee fell a-doting,
> And by addition me of thee defeated,
> By adding one thing to my purpose nothing:
>> But since she pricked thee out for women's pleasure,
>> Mine be thy love, and thy love's use their treasure.[9]

Graham believes that Mr W. H. was an enchanting boy actor, Willie Hughes, and, lacking external evidence, goes on to fake a portrait of the imaginary youth to 'prove' the theory. When his forgery comes to light, Graham kills himself as an act of confirmation of his faith. The cause of Willie Hughes is then taken up successively by the narrator and Erskine, the latter of whom also dies to vindicate it. To finish off the story's paradox of faith and deception, this second literary suicide itself turns out to be a fake in the end, Erskine's death having been actually caused by consumption.

The three men's quest after the elusive Mr W. H. in the *Portrait* is a parable of biographical literary criticism aglow with male same-sex desire and fervent aestheticism. According to Harris, it was this story that 'set everyone talking and arguing' about its author Wilde's sexual inclinations and did him 'even more damage [than his *Intentions*] by appearing to justify the peculiar rumours about his private life'. Wilde's portrayal of Shakespeare and Willie Hughes was seen as an allegory of the writer's own love life, and 'did Oscar incalculable injury', the Bard's homosexuality being the 'universal belief' of the day. Wilde's *Portrait*, Harris continues, 'gave his enemies for the first time the very weapon they wanted and they used it unscrupulously and untiringly with the fierce delight of hatred'. As a matter of fact, at the time of the story's first publication, most reviewers focused on the interpretation of the *Sonnets* as developed in it and did not scrutinize its author's sexual orientation.[10] In the ill-starred lawsuits of 1895, however, the *Portrait* would certainly be conjured up to prove Wilde's homosexuality, and the flamboyant author and his examiners would carry on Cyril Graham and company's discussion over the validity of such biographical reading of a piece of literature.

In the first libel trial concerning his 'pose' as a sodomite, Wilde was cross-examined not only about his past relationships but also about such literary outputs as his flirtatious letters to Douglas, *Dorian Gray*, and the 1894 issue of the *Chameleon*, which contained two poems by Douglas ('Two Loves' and its sequel, 'In Praise of Shame') alongside his own 'Philosophies for Use of the Young'.

Wilde maintained the literary pretence of these somewhat racy pieces of writing with recourse to Shakespeare and his *Sonnets*. Defending his reference to Douglas's 'red rose-leaf lips' and 'slim gilt soul' in one of his compromising letters,[11] Wilde argued for priority of beauty to propriety and demanded the same artistic privilege as had been accorded to Shakespeare, thereby establishing his standing as a man of letters, as opposed to a perverted lover:

> I think it was a beautiful letter. If you ask me whether it is proper, you might as well ask me whether *King Lear* is proper, or a sonnet of Shakespeare is proper. It was a beautiful letter. It was not concerned with – the letter was not written – with the object of writing propriety; it was written with the object of making a beautiful thing.[12]

The phrase 'I quite admit that I adored you madly' from *Dorian Gray* triggered a heated exchange between Edward Carson, Queensberry's lawyer, and Wilde:

Carson:	Have you ever felt that feeling of adoring madly a beautiful male person many years younger than yourself?
Wilde:	I have never given adoration to anybody except myself. (*Loud laughter.*)

....

Carson:	Then, you never had that feeling that you depict there?
Wilde:	No, it was borrowed from Shakespeare I regret to say. (*Laughter.*)
Carson:	From Shakespeare?
Wilde:	Yes, from Shakespeare's sonnets.[13]

Wilde disengaged himself from the homoerotic emotion that the novel conveyed by consigning it to Shakespeare's literary heritage.

As Lawrence Danson has shown, the first libel trial was indeed 'a contest of hermeneutic principles' in which Carson's literal-minded construction perpetually undermined the subversive indeterminacy of Wilde's amorous writings. According to Carson's 'forensic' reading, 'Wilde posed as a sodomite; only a pervert would pose as a sodomite; the pose told the truth; and the truth was available for all to read'.[14] In this clash between Carson's literalism and Wilde's literariness, it was actually the former that embraced Cyril Graham's biographical approach to literature: the lawyer tried to 'unlock' Wilde's heart by the internal evidence which his writing afforded.[15] Carson went on to ask about Wilde's interpretation of the *Sonnets* in the *Portrait*:

Carson:	I believe you have written an article pointing out that Shakespeare's sonnets were practically sodomitical [*sic*]?
Wilde:	On the contrary, Mr Carson, I wrote an article to prove that they were not so.

....

> I was explaining that the love of Shakespeare to the young man to whom he dedicated them, was the love of an artist for a personality which I imagine to be a part of his art.[16]

According to Wilde's explanation, the *Portrait* vindicated the artistic integrity of the *Sonnets* by rationalizing Shakespeare's liaison with the Fair Youth as aesthetic, as opposed to carnal, experience. In the course of the second trial over Wilde's violation of the 1895 Criminal Law Amendment Act, it was Shakespeare, along with some other classical authorities, who helped justify contemporary homosexual literature. Wilde was asked to interpret the final line ('Love that dare not speak its name') of Douglas's 'Two Loves', which was a variation on Shakespeare's Sonnet 144 ('Two loves I have, of comfort and despair...'):

> C. F. Gill: What is the 'Love that dare not speak its name'?
> Wilde: 'The Love that dare not speak its name' in this century is such a great affection of an elder for a younger man as there was between David and Jonathan, such as Plato made the very basis of his philosophy, and such as you find in the sonnets of Michelangelo and Shakespeare. It is that deep, spiritual affection that is as pure as it is perfect. It dictates and pervades great works of art like those of Shakespeare and Michelangelo, and those two letters of mine, such as they are. It is in this century misunderstood, so much misunderstood that it may be described as the 'Love that dare not speak its name', and on account of it I am placed where I am now. It is beautiful, it is fine, it is the noblest form of affection. There is nothing unnatural about it. It is intellectual, and it repeatedly exists between an elder and a younger man, when the elder man has intellect, and the younger man has all the joy, hope, and glamour of life before him. That it should be so the world does not understand. The world mocks at it and sometimes puts one in the pillory for it.[17]

While Wilde's repartees might rightly be described as inspired (his eulogy on the Shakespearean 'affection of an elder for a younger man' certainly provoked 'loud applause', if 'mingled with some hisses', from the public in the gallery), they were totally inconsequential in legal terms. Unlike the characters of the *Portrait*, Carson was ready to produce not only the internal but also external evidence of Wilde's guilt in the shape of the numerous juvenile delinquents with whom the playwright had enjoyed criminal intimacy. Nevertheless, Wilde's Shakespearean discourse as developed in the *Portrait* and in the courtroom would help his literary-minded friends not simply to draw analogies between Shakespeare and themselves, but think about and redefine their relationship to the disgraced genius with reference to the Poet, the Fair Youth and the Dark Lady of the *Sonnets*.

Apologia pro Vita Sua: Douglas, the Fair Youth and 'Two Loves'

Alfred Douglas was obsessed with Shakespeare's fair friend. He liked Wilde's construction of Mr W. H. as Willie Hughes and found it 'a thousand pities that he did not write it and put it forth as a theory', rather than as a fanciful story of a forged portrait and precarious literary faith.[18] Like Cyril Graham, Douglas even went about hunting for external evidence to demonstrate the Willie Hughes theory and incredibly, in 1938, actually succeeded in unearthing a reference to one Will Hewes, apprentice to shoemaker John Marlowe – Christopher Marlowe's father – in the archives of Canterbury Cathedral.[19] When he reflected on Wilde's trials in his 1929 *Autobiography*, however, it was misguided use of internal evidence that preoccupied him most. According to Douglas, Wilde's incriminating love letters only 'proved, what neither Wilde nor I ever denied, that Wilde had an exaggerated devotion to me and an unbounded admiration for my personal appearance' and should not have contributed to his prison sentence:

> He compared me to Hylas and Hyacinthus, and the language he used was of course extravagant and unusual. But there is nothing whatever in his letters which could not be matched in Shakespeare's *Sonnets* (also written to a boy), and though I believe it is the fashion nowadays to accuse Shakespeare of having had the same vices as Wilde, this merely shows the ignorance and baseness and stupidity of those who make such accusations on such grounds.[20]

Here Douglas's contention is twofold: he justifies Wilde's letters on the strength of the *Sonnets*, before exonerating Shakespeare himself from the charge of homosexuality. Douglas goes on to elucidate Sonnet 20, in 'the last six lines' of which Shakespeare 'refuted his detractors, by anticipation':

> 'Nature', says he, 'who intended thee for a woman, "fell a-doting" and, "by addition, thee of me defeated"'. Could anything be clearer? 'If you had been a woman ... but unfortunately you were a boy, so that I was defeated.' To rub it in still more strongly he goes on to say:
>
> > But since she pricked thee out for woman's pleasure,
> > Mine be thy love, and thy love's use their treasure.
>
> The effect of the lines referred to is even stronger because they are so obviously not deliberately made in answer to, or in anticipation of, any adverse suggestion. Shakespeare exculpates himself, in the eyes of any reasonable being, quite definitely and quite unconsciously. Obviously it never occurred to him that anyone would put a bad interpretation on his love and adoration for 'Master W. H.'[21]

The *Portrait* should not have done any 'incalculable injury' to Wilde, when the very sonnet where Willie Hughes originated quashes the charge of Shakespeare's inversion. Moreover, similar reinterpretation would have exempted Wilde's love letters from criminal charge very easily. Douglas continues: 'In the same way, I repeat, I will challenge anyone who is not prejudiced to find anything in any letter of Wilde's to me that exists, or ever has existed, that is not consistent with a perfectly pure devotion.'

The curious thing is that Douglas frankly admits that Wilde 'was guilty of what my father had accused him of' in the same autobiography.[22] He has also confided to Harris elsewhere that Wilde did treat him 'as an older boy treats a younger one at school, and he added what was new to me and was not (as far as I know) known or practiced among my contemporaries' though '[s]odomy never took place'.[23] The central point of Douglas's argument is not that Wilde was innocent of homosexual practices but that there was no evidence to prove his guilt in his 'Shakespearian' letters to him, when '[t]he gentle Harris and others ... are so ready, for reasons best known to themselves, to fling at me the accusation of having "ruined" Wilde and "sacrificed" him to gratify my "hatred of my father"'.[24] Reference to Shakespeare mitigates Douglas's responsibility for Wilde's misfortune: if Wilde had made better use of the *Sonnets* and guarded himself more carefully, his downfall could have been avoided.

Douglas then went on to publish a study of the *Sonnets* (*The True History of Shakespeare's Sonnets*, 1933), and set about defending Shakespeare and himself all over again. Douglas was aware of the analogy to be drawn between the story that Shakespeare's love lyrics convey and his own biography and knew that it would be considered 'awkward' for him to write about them. However, 'having a perfectly clear conscience, and being, moreover, prepared to defend Shakespeare at all costs and risks', he 'has long ceased to be influenced by such considerations'.[25] Douglas's publication was inspired by Samuel Butler's *Shakespeare's Sonnets Reconsidered* (1899) and he followed Butler's early dating of the *Sonnets* (to 1585–88, when Shakespeare was between the ages of twenty-one and twenty-four) as well as the identification of Mr W. H. as Will Hughes by both Butler and Wilde. Douglas, however, sharply repudiates Butler's 'charge of homosexual[i]ty against Shakespeare on the evidence of the Sonnets', and 'utterly rejects the notion that Shakespeare was a homosexualist'.[26] He sets out proving Shakespeare's 'innocence' through analysis of

Sonnet 20 (as in his *Autobiography*) and Sonnet 144, on which his now notorious 'Two Loves' was based:

> Two loves I have, of comfort and despair,
> Which, like two spirits, do suggest me still:
> The better angel is a man right fair,
> The worser spirit a woman coloured ill.
> To win me soon to hell my female evil
> Tempteth my better angel from my side,
> And would corrupt my saint to be a devil,
> Wooing his purity with her foul pride;
> And whether that my angel be turned fiend
> Suspect I may, yet not directly tell;
> But being both from me both to each friend,
> I guess one angel in another's hell.
>   Yet this shall I ne'er know, but live in doubt,
>   Till my bad angel fire my good one out.

Reversing the polarities of the wholesome heterosexual love and the 'Love that dare not speak its name' of his own *Chameleon* poem, Douglas contrasts Shakespeare's 'love' for the Fair Youth with his 'affair' with the Dark Lady, and defines the former character as an 'innocent young friend' and Shakespeare's 'saint'.[27]

As a matter of fact, Douglas accepts the possibility that Shakespeare might also have been homosexual in real life. When asked by one of his friends why he should be 'so anxious to acquit Shakespeare of homosexuality', Douglas replies (italics mine):

> if it could be proved that Shakespeare was a homosexualist, it certainly would not invalidate my admiration of his poetry, nor would I consider myself qualified to condemn him or to cast stones at him; but if the accusation (or the inference) is not true, and if there really is no *evidence* at all that he was a homosexualist, and if all the available *evidence*, such as it is, points utterly against it, why should he be libelled and defamed merely to gratify those who really are tarred with that brush on the one hand, and fools and prudes like Hallam on the other?[28]

As in the case of Wilde's amorous writings, there is no hard evidence in the *Sonnets* to either prove or disprove the poet's homosexuality. Echoing the description of his physical intimacy with Wilde, Douglas illustrates the nature of 'evidence' in a sexual relationship once again by referring to boys-only schools: 'Any honest man who has been at a public school or a university must know perfectly well that young men and boys are liable to fall in love with other young men and boys, and they must also know equally well that some of these relationships are innocent and some are not', and only 'evidence' can decide 'into which of the two categories such a state of affairs falls'.[29] As Shakespeare is not known to have attended either a public school or a university, Douglas is concerned in this passage with his own sexuality as much as that of the Bard.

By an odd twist of fate, Butler's study of the *Sonnets* was foreshadowed by his own love affair with a handsome young man, Charles Paine Pauli, who 'sponged off him, at the same time making no effort to conceal his boredom with his benefactor'.[30] Charged likewise with exploitation and cruelty in Wilde's *De Profundis* and Harris's biography, Douglas felt the need to distinguish between Pauli and himself. He criticizes Butler and Harris for confusing Shakespeare's biography with their own life story ('It seems to me that Butler, at this particular point in his investigation, fell into very much the same kind of blunder as the unspeakable Frank Harris ... That blunder consists in trying to read into Shakespeare's life one's own experiences'). Shakespeare as represented in Harris's publications (*The Man Shakespeare and his Tragic Life Story*, 1909; *Shakespeare and his Love*, 1910; *The Women of Shakespeare*, 1911) 'shared his [Harris's] revolting, almost maniacal, sex-obsession about women', while Butler's Mr W. H. was his pitiless former lover under the thinnest of disguises:

> Butler had the misfortune, at one time of his life, to be afflicted with a young friend called Pauli, to whom he was passionately devoted and who treated him in a shocking way; and when he is writing about Shakespeare and Mr W. H., he is terribly inclined to forget that he is not writing about Butler and Pauli.[31]

Defying Butler's denunciation of Shakespeare's, and his own, Fair Youth, Douglas firmly defends the character of Mr W. H.:

> I see nothing whatever in the text of the sonnets to support Butler's furious attack on the character of Mr W. H. Being unafflicted with a Pauli complex, and being, moreover, very sure in my own mind that Shakespeare would not have loved Will Hughes so much unless he had had something more than his good looks to commend him, I see no reason at all to accept Butler's estimate of his character or of his influence on Shakespeare.[32]

By reinterpreting the love letters and the two sonnets that had directly contributed to Wilde's disgrace, and by maintaining the 'innocence' of not only Shakespeare but also the Fair Youth, Douglas persuasively made his case against his own detractors.

Gaiety of Genius: Harris, Shaw and Shakespeare

Although his reminiscences must always be handled with caution, Frank Harris maintains that he talked over the *Portrait* while Wilde was writing it, and told him that he 'thought the whole theory completely mistaken' as it put disproportionate emphasis on the Fair Youth sonnets. According to Harris, 'Shakespeare was as sensual as one could well be; but there was no evidence of abnormal vice; indeed, all the evidence seemed to me to be against this universal belief ... My conviction that Shakespeare was not abnormally vicious, and that the first series of Sonnets [i.e., 1–125/6] proved snobbishness and toadying and not corrupt passion, seemed to Oscar the very madness of partisanship'.[33] In Harris's drama, *Shakespeare and his Love* (published 1910, but composed several years previously) featuring Mary Fitton as the Dark Lady, Shakespeare was certainly just as heterosexual and 'over-sexed' as the author himself, whose claim to fame (or notoriety, to be more precise) rested largely on his seedy autobiography with pornographic content: *My Life and Loves* (1922–27).

Wilde's and Harris's projection of their homo- or heterosexual self-image on Shakespeare was hardly an isolated exception, given that the members of their coterie kept encountering reflections of themselves and of each other in Shakespeare and his *Sonnets*. To Bernard Shaw, Douglas's *True History* was 'by far the best of all those known to me', as:

> Nobody else has understood the case of Mr W. H. in the least; and nobody else has understood the case of Shakespeare so naturally and unstudiously. The first success is the more important; and the explanation is that you yourself have had the experience of Mr W. H.: men fell in love with your personal beauty; and you learnt thereby what neither Wilde nor Butler had discovered, that the attraction of beauty is entirely distinct from the homosexual attraction, and that the one is no evidence of the other.[34]

Being a sonneteer himself, Douglas was equally flattered when Harris remarked that 'as a writer of sonnets', Douglas can 'stand with Shakespeare'.[35]

In the preface to his playlet *The Dark Lady of the Sonnets* (1910), Shaw insisted that Shakespeare 'was very like myself' and that if Shaw 'had been born in 1556 instead of 1856', he 'should have taken to blank verse and given Shakespear a harder run for his money than all the other Elizabethans put together'.[36] In the same preface, however, Shaw also developed an analogy between the Bard and a deceased friend of his. *The Dark Lady* was a light-hearted '*pièce d'occasion*', written for a fund-raising event to promote the cause of a National Theatre commemorating Shakespeare. The play, however, provoked the ire of Harris, who believed that Shaw's identification of Mary Fitton as Shakespeare's Dark Lady was copied from his sentimental play, in which the cruel courtly lady breaks the heart of the dramatist and ruins his life.[37]

In the preface to *The Dark Lady*, Shaw good-humouredly rebuts the charge of plagiarism from as inconsequential a playwright as Harris, and points to an artistic quality that is crucially lacking in his old acquaintance.[38] According to Shaw, 'Frank Harris is everything except a humorist, not, apparently, from stupidity, but because scorn overcomes humor in him'. Nevertheless, Harris 'knows the taste and the value of humor', and he was 'one of the few men of letters who really appreciated Oscar Wilde, though he did not rally fiercely to Wilde's side until the world deserted Oscar in his ruin'. Shaw recalls the crucial meeting at the Café Royal 'when Harris ... prophesied to Wilde with miraculous precision exactly what immediately afterwards happened to him, and warned him to leave the country'. When Wilde decried Harris as a 'fainthearted friend who was failing him in his hour of need' and angrily left the room with Douglas, 'Harris's idiosyncratic power of pity saved him from feeling or shewing the smallest resentment' in the dismal scene. It was this sense of pity and appreciation of humour in his friends that made Harris a good editor of such celebrated magazines as *The Fortnightly Review* and *The Saturday Review*. But the predominance of sentimentality over gaiety ultimately disqualified him for any Shakespearian endeavour ('The same capacity for pity governs Harris's study of Shakespear, whom, as I have said, he pities too much').[39]

In *Shakespeare and his Love*, Harris's Shakespeare is utterly heart-broken by Mary Fitton and dies in black despair. Shaw believes that there is 'an irrepressible gaiety of genius which enables it to bear the whole weight of the world's misery without blenching'. He explains this essential optimism in Shakespeare on the analogy of the letter that Wilde wrote in the darkest moments of his life at Reading Goal:

> Let me again remind Mr Harris of Oscar Wilde. We all dreaded to read De Profundis: our instinct was to stop our ears, or run away from the wail of a broken, though by no means contrite, heart. But we

were throwing away our pity. De Profundis was de profundis indeed: Wilde was too good a dramatist to throw away so powerful an effect; but none the less it was de profundis in excelsis. There was more laughter between the lines of that book than in a thousand farces by men of no genius.[40]

Needless to say, Shaw's 'comedic view' of *De Profundis* was profoundly heretical. Readers certainly sensed not simply the 'anguish of the poor soul' but also Wilde's literary affectation and his 'artist's joy' in his own tragedy as soon as the abridged version of *De Profundis* was published in 1905.[41] Nobody, however, went as far as Shaw in regarding Wilde's letter from his prison cell as 'quite exhilarating and amusing', or finding in it 'no real tragedy, all comedy'.[42]

According to Shaw, Wilde, like Shakespeare, 'found in himself no pity for himself', and this gaiety of heart constitutes the prime requisite of a good playwright: 'There is nothing that marks the born dramatist more unmistakeably [*sic*] than this discovery of comedy in his own misfortunes almost in proportion to the pathos with which the ordinary man announces their tragedy. I cannot for the life of me see the broken heart in Shakespear's latest works.' Shaw thus extols Shakespeare's 'incorrigible divine levity' and his 'inexhaustible joy that derided sorrow', two qualities that are utterly lacking in Harris.[43]

One could argue that the ultimate dramatist thus defined is redolent not so much of Shakespeare and Wilde as of Bernard Shaw himself, who was fiercely proud of his 'comedic love of anti-climax' and his 'sense of humor' that enabled him to 'enjoy big mischief'.[44] By projecting his own love of comedy onto the ideal playwright, Shaw in effect claimed dramatic preeminence not only for Shakespeare and Wilde but also for himself.

In the preface to the British edition of Harris's Wilde biography, Shaw's theory of the gaiety of genius was woven further into the intricate tapestry of Shakespeare, Wilde, and their respective fair friends. Shaw once again compared Wilde and Douglas to Shakespeare and Mr W. H., but then went on to distinguish between the Irish playwright and his aristocratic boyfriend in terms of genial levity:

> The part played by Wilde in Lord Alfred's life was fateful. There had been nothing like it in literary history since the famous case of Mr W. H., the 'onlie begetter' of Shakespear's sonnets. Without the tragedy of Lord Alfred the story would be impossible. For please let us hear no more of the tragedy of Oscar Wilde. Oscar was no tragedian. He was the superb comedian of his century, one to whom

> misfortune, disgrace, imprisonment were external and traumatic. His gaiety of soul was invulnerable: it shines through the blackest pages of his De Profundis as clearly as in his funniest epigrams. Even on his deathbed he found in himself no pity for himself, playing for the laugh with his last breath, and getting it with as sure a stroke as in his palmiest prime.[45]

Wilde acted the part of a comedian with panache in the drama of his own fall from grace, when his less talented companion only managed a stale tragic gesture.

Douglas resented Shaw's comical reading of *De Profundis* and protested against his 'cruelty of finding comedy or farce in the frightful tragedy of Oscar Wilde's terrible pilgrimage'. He believed that Shaw 'dislike[d]', and therefore was 'unfair to', his fellow playwright.[46] Shaw's love of mischief certainly approximated suspiciously to a malicious sneer when he described Wilde's derogation of Douglas in *De Profundis* as of 'the most amazingly undignified kind, venting all sorts of petty grudges about the sharing of their expenses and omissions to visit Wilde when he had influenza and what not',[47] or when he stated that 'no other Irishman [Shaw himself included, presumably] had yet produced as masterful a comedy as *De Profundis*'.[48]

Shaw's outlook on Wilde's calamity was not free from bias either and even his recollection of the fateful lunch at the Café Royal was somewhat distorted by his predilection for comedy. When Harris nearly persuaded Wilde to flee the country, it was actually Douglas who got up and left the room first, saying, 'Your telling him to run away shows you are no friend of Oscar's'. Wilde merely followed suit by echoing Douglas ('I do not think this is friendly of you, Frank') and walking out. Shaw's account of the slightly built Douglas (the curate) following the gigantic Wilde (the archbishop) presented 'an inimitable picture' but was ultimately false. According to Harris, it was Shaw's 'fine sense of comedy' that played a trick on his memories.[49]

Shaw had never been particularly intimate with Wilde and had met him only around six times in person inclusive of the Café Royal encounter.[50] He was 'in no way predisposed to like' Wilde, whose 'Irish charm, potent with Englishmen, did not exist' for this fellow townsman.[51] Shaw even caused a furore among Wilde's devoted followers by stating that he had 'ended as an unproductive drunkard and swindler'.[52] His admiration for Wilde's irrepressible levity was genuine nonetheless. By comparing Wilde to Shakespeare and distinguishing his gaiety from both Harris's sentimentality and Douglas's tragedy, Shaw paid the highest compliments a dramatist could pay his ill-fated fellow dramatist and his enduring sense of humour.

Haunting Memories

> I dreamed of him last night, I saw his face
> All radiant and unshadowed of distress,
> And as of old, in music measureless,
> I heard his golden voice and marked him trace
> Under the common thing the hidden grace,
> And conjure wonder out of emptiness,
> Till mean things put on beauty like a dress
> And all the world was an enchanted place.
>
> And then methought outside a fast locked gate
> I mourned the loss of unrecorded words,
> Forgotten tales and mysteries half said,
> Wonders that might have been articulate,
> And voiceless thoughts like murdered singing birds.
> And so I woke and knew that he was dead.
>
> *Alfred Douglas, 'The Dead Poet'*

Wilde's demise in Paris on 30 November 1900 did not stop people from dreaming and daydreaming of him, and his ghost was witnessed in such varied locales as Oxford, Paris and New York.[53] While Wilde paid posthumous visitations even to total strangers from time to time, his memories haunted his close friends with obstinate persistence. They would think and write about Wilde the rest of their lives, cross-referring to and hitting back at other people's retellings of the man's life story.

Shaw once remarked that 'Wilde's friends were so contemptuous or jealous of one another that it is impossible to do anything but guess at the truth of their stories about him' and that they were unanimous only in that 'each one of them vouches for the shameless mendacity of all the others'.[54] Their relations with Wilde himself were not of unremitting amity either, and the paradoxical title of Douglas's book of self-justification, *Without Apology* (1938), epitomizes the complexity of their sense of sympathy, antipathy and guilt over their friend's calamitous end.

Recent explorations of sexual orientation and gender have shown the crucial centrality of Wilde's life and writing in the formation of modern homosexual identity.⁵⁵ The word 'homosexual', which I used rather unguardedly in the preceding discussion, had yet to attain general currency at the time of the 1895 trials, and if Wilde strikes us as exemplarily 'homosexual', it is merely because his work and behaviour formed our concept of homosexuality to begin with. Shakespeare, in his turn, helped Wilde to articulate the 'Love that dare not speak its name': as Chris White cogently put it, the Elizabethan playwright, along with some other literary sources, provided 'a language and a frame of reference ... to speak about desires and experiences that have no dictionary anywhere else'.⁵⁶ Moreover, adding to the homoerotic vocabulary, Wilde may also have appropriated the intense joy and pain of love itself from Shakespeare through mystical identification with his sonnet sequence, for '[o]ut of Shakespeare's sonnets they [i.e., people of artistic temperament] draw, to their own hurt it may be, the secret of his love and make it their own' (*De Profundis*, 1031).

In the case of Douglas, Harris and Shaw, however, Shakespeare's *Sonnets* served as a medium to explore not simply their own selfhood, homosexual or otherwise, but more importantly their *relations* with Wilde and with each other. Reusing and adapting the metaphor and rhetoric that Wilde had employed in the *Portrait* and variously identifying each other with Shakespeare and his fair friend, these three writers probed the depth of their mixed feelings towards the disgraced genius. Through their deliberations on the *Sonnets*, these men kept up communication with their deceased friend and would come to terms with, and expiate their guilt over, his misfortune.

Reiko Oya is Professor of English at Keio University, Tokyo. She is the author of *Representing Shakespearean Tragedy: Garrick, the Kembles, and Kean* (2007), and publishes extensively on Shakespeare's reception from the 18th to the 20th centuries. Her recent work includes contributions to *Shakespeare Survey* such as 'Filming "the weight of this sad time": Yasujiro Ozu's Rereading of *King Lear* in *Tokyo Story* (1953)' (2013); 'Authenticating the Inauthentic: Edmond Malone as Editor of the Apocryphal Shakespeare' (2016); and 'The Comedy of Hamlet in Nazi-Occupied Warsaw: An Exploration of Lubitsch's *To Be or Not To Be* (1942)' (2019).

Notes

1. Charles Ricketts, in his and Jean Paul Raymond's *Oscar Wilde: Recollections* (1932). Ricketts painted a 'forged' portrait of Willie Hughes on an old panel as a frontispiece for 'The Portrait of Mr W. H.'
2. Bernard Shaw, 'My Memories of Oscar Wilde', in Frank Harris, *Oscar Wilde: His Life and Confessions* (New York: Blue Ribbon, 1930), 399.
3. For their correspondence, see especially Mary Hyde, ed., *Bernard Shaw and Alfred Douglas: A Correspondence* (Oxford; New York: Oxford University Press, 1989), and Stanley Weintraub, ed., *The Playwright and the Pirate: Bernard Shaw and Frank Harris, a Correspondence* (University Park: Colin Smythe, 1982). The correspondence between Shaw and Douglas was turned into the drama *Bernard and Bosie: A Most Unlikely Friendship* (2002), by Anthony Wynn.
4. 'Introduction' to Oscar Wilde, *De Profundis*, ed. Robert Ross (New York: Modern Library, 1926), [xv].
5. Shaw, 'Preface', in Frank Harris, *Oscar Wilde: His Life and Confessions*, 2nd ed. (London: Constable & Co., 1938), xxii.
6. Hyde, *Shaw and Douglas*, 67 (note).
7. See S. Schoenbaum's overview of the biographical readings of the *Sonnets* in the Victorian era, in *Shakespeare's Lives*, 2nd ed. (Oxford; New York: Oxford University Press, 1993), 314–30. Cary DiPietro observes a Freudian preoccupation with Shakespeare's psychology in the *Sonnets* as explored by Wilde and his contemporaries, in *Shakespeare and Modernism* (Cambridge; New York: Cambridge University Press, 2006), 43–82.
8. *Collins Complete Works of Oscar Wilde*, 5th ed. (Glasgow: HarperCollins, 2003), 17. References to Wilde's literary works are to this edition and are given parenthetically in the text.
9. *Shakespeare's Sonnets*, ed. Katherine Duncan-Jones, Arden 3 (Walton-on-Thames: Thomas Nelson & Sons, 1997). Subsequent references are to this edition.
10. Harris, *Wilde*, 80–81. The reception of the *Portrait* at the time of its first appearance in *Blackwood's Edinburgh Magazine* (July 1889) is studied extensively in Horst Schroeder, *Oscar Wilde, The Portrait of Mr W. H.: Its Composition, Publication and Reception* (Braunschweig: Seminar für Anglistik und Amerikanistik, TU Braunschweig, 1984), 14–21.
11. The letter in question (in *The Complete Letters of Oscar Wilde*, ed. Merlin Holland and Rupert Hart-Davis [London: Fourth Estate, 2000], 544) reads:

    [? January 1893]   [Babbacombe Cliff]
    My Own Boy, Your sonnet is quite lovely, and it is a marvel that those red rose-leaf lips of yours should have been made no less for music of song than for madness of kisses. Your slim gilt soul walks between passion and poetry. I know Hyacinthus, whom Apollo loved so madly, was you in Greek days.

    Why are you alone in London, and when do you go to Salisbury? Do go there to cool your hands in the grey twilight of Gothic things, and come here whenever you like. It is a lovely place – it only lacks you; but go to Salisbury first. Always, with undying love, yours, OSCAR

12. Merlin Holland, ed., *The Real Trial of Oscar Wilde: The First Uncensored Transcript of the Trial of Oscar Wilde vs. John Douglas (Marquess of Queensberry), 1895* (New York: Fourth Estate, 2003), 105.
13. Holland, *The Real Trial*, 91–92.
14. Lawrence Danson, 'Oscar Wilde, W. H., and the Unspoken Name of Love', *ELH* 58 (1991), 979–1000; 982–83. See also his *Wilde's Intentions: The Artist in his Criticism* (Oxford: Clarendon Press, 1997), 102–26, and Rebecca Laroche, 'The Sonnets on Trial: Reconsidering "The Portrait of Mr W. H."', in *Shakespeare's Sonnets: Critical Essays*, ed. James Schiffer (New York: Garland, 1999), 391–410.
15. The elaborate deployment of the Wordsworthian metaphor of the key and the lock in the *Portrait* and in the trials is explored by Kate Chedgzoy, 'Strange Worship: Oscar Wilde and the Key to Shakespeare's *Sonnets*', in *Shakespeare's Queer Children: Sexual Politics and Contemporary Culture* (Manchester; New York: Manchester University Press, 1995), 135–76, and Danson, 'Wilde'.
16. Holland, *The Real Trial*, 93.
17. H. Montgomery Hyde, ed., *The Three Trials of Oscar Wilde* (New York: University Books, 1956), 236.
18. Alfred Douglas, *The True History of Shakespeare's Sonnets* (London: M. Secker, 1933), 34.
19. Hyde, *Shaw and Douglas*, 52–53 ('To Bernard Shaw', 20 May 1938).
20. Alfred Douglas, *Autobiography* (London: M. Secker, 1929), 61.
21. Ibid., 61–62.
22. Ibid., 96.
23. See his 'Full and Final Confession', in Harris, *Wilde*, xlii. Douglas himself was educated at Winchester College (1884–88) and at Magdalen College, Oxford (1889–93).
24. Douglas, *Autobiography*, 62.
25. Douglas, *True History*, 18.
26. Ibid., 19.
27. Ibid., 28.
28. Ibid., 23–24. 'Hallam' refers to Henry Hallam, Alfred's father, who regretted Shakespeare's 'weakness and folly in all excessive and mis-placed affection' as seen in the *Sonnets* and said that 'it is impossible not to wish that Shakespeare had never wrote them' (*Introduction to the Literature of Europe*, 1839; cited in Hyder Edward Rollins, ed., *A New Variorum Edition of Shakespeare: The Sonnets*, 2 vols (Philadelphia; London: J. B. Lippincott, 1944), 2: 359.
29. Douglas, *True History*, 24.
30. Schoenbaum, *Shakespeare's Lives*, 326.
31. Douglas, *True History*, 71–72.
32. Ibid., 211.
33. Harris, *Wilde*, 80–81.
34. Hyde, *Shaw and Douglas*, 15 ('To Alfred Douglas', [June 1933]). See also Shaw's description of Douglas as 'Mr W. H. *redivivus*' in his 'Preface' to Harris, *Wilde*, 2nd ed., xxxvii. It is also worth noting in this context that Wilde had written the *Portrait* (1889) and a substantial portion of its enlarged edition (*The Incomparable and Ingenious History of Mr W. H.*) before he met Douglas in 1891. See Schroeder, *Oscar Wilde*, 22–26. See also Ian Small's 'Introduction' to Wilde, *The Short*

Fiction, in Russell Jackson and Ian Small, gen. ed., *The Complete Works of Oscar Wilde*, 8 vols (to date) (Oxford: Oxford University Press, 2000–), 8: liv–lxxxiii.
35. Douglas, *Autobiography*, 140.
36. Shaw, 'Preface' to *The Dark Lady of the Sonnets*, in *The Works of Bernard Shaw*, 37 vols (Tokyo: Hon-no-tomosha, 1991), 13: 207.
37. The Mary Fitton theory derived from Thomas Tyler and it was Shaw's review of Tyler's edition of the *Sonnets* (*Pall Mall Gazette*, 7 January 1886) that 'had first put Mary into [Harris's] head'. See Shaw's 'Preface' to *The Dark Lady*, 206; and Hyde, *Shaw and Douglas*, 19 ('To Bernard Shaw', 1 July 1933).
38. See also Shaw's detailed review of Harris's play ('Mr Frank Harris's Shakespear', *Nation*, 24 December 1910), in *Bernard Shaw's Book Reviews*, ed. Brian Tyson, 2 vols (University Park: Pennsylvania State University Press, 1991–96), 2: 240–54.
39. Shaw, 'Preface' to *The Dark Lady*, 208–9. See also Harris's *The Man Shakespeare* and *The Women of Shakespeare* for his sentimental interpretation of Shakespeare's plays and poems.
40. Shaw, 'Preface' to *The Dark Lady*, 216.
41. See Karl Beckson, ed., *Oscar Wilde: The Critical Heritage* (London: Routledge & K. Paul, [1970]), 244, 256, 251.
42. Ibid., 244 ('To Robert Ross', 13 March 1905).
43. Shaw, 'Preface' to *The Dark Lady*, 216–17.
44. Shaw, *Sixteen Self Sketches* (London: Constable, 1949), 106.
45. Shaw, 'Preface' to Harris, *Wilde*, 2nd ed., xxxvi–xxxvii.
46. Douglas, *Oscar Wilde: A Summing-Up*, intro. Derek Hudson (London, 1961), 5–6.
47. Shaw, 'Preface' to Harris, *Wilde*, 2nd ed., xlviii.
48. Beckson, *Critical Heritage*, 243 (Letter to *Neue Freie Presse*, 23 April 1905).
49. Shaw, 'My Memories', 399–400 (note).
50. Ibid., 389–92.
51. Ibid., 393.
52. Ibid., 403. See also Robert H. Sherard's *Bernard Shaw, Frank Harris and Oscar Wilde* (London: T. W. Laurie, 1936) for a typical reaction from Wilde's coterie members to Shaw's remark.
53. John Stokes collects many interesting examples of Wilde's visitations, in *Oscar Wilde: Myths, Miracles, and Imitations* (Cambridge: Cambridge University Press, 1996), 1–22.
54. Shaw, 'Preface', in Harris, *Wilde*, 2nd ed., xlii–xliii.
55. For Wilde's contribution to the formation of homosexual identity, see, among many others, Eve Kosofsky Sedgwick, *Epistemology of the Closet* (Berkeley: University of California Press, 1990), Jonathan Dollimore, *Sexual Dissidence: Augustine to Wilde, Freud to Foucault* (Oxford: Clarendon Press; New York: Oxford University Press, 1991) and Alan Sinfield, *The Wilde Century: Effeminacy, Oscar Wilde, and the Queer Moment* (London; New York: Cassell, 1994).
56. Chris White, ed., *Nineteenth-Century Writings on Homosexuality: A Source Book* (London: Routledge, 1999), 117. Chedgzoy (in 'Strange Worship') and Danson (in 'Oscar Wilde') make the same point.

Chapter 4

Fighting over Shakespeare
Commemorating the 1916 Tercentenary in Wartime

Clara Calvo

In a cartoon published in the weekly *España* in 1916, Don Quixote, the man for whom mills were castles and sheep soldiers, sits next to Hamlet and responds to the noise coming from an artillery attack on the Western Front, proclaiming: 'Amigo Hamlet, hear how the cannons salute us' (Illustration 4.1). Don Quixote's delusion suggests that, at the time, it was established opinion that the war was a hindrance to proper Tercentenary celebrations. In 1916, the First World War made it impossible for England and Spain to commemorate the deaths of their national poets, Shakespeare and Cervantes, with a truly pan-European cultural festival. Spain hastily cancelled all official celebrations, whereas England simply toned them down and enlisted Shakespeare for the war effort. In England, the synchronicity of the Great War and the 1916 Tercentenary turned Shakespeare into both a site of conflict and a site of collaboration. This paper explores how Shakespeare was worth fighting for in both local and European

Notes for this section begin on page 89.

terms – how Stratford feared London's claims to Shakespeare as much as England feared German appropriation. It also shows how in France, instead, quoting Shakespeare's words in 1916 was not a belligerent act of appropriation but a gesture meant to erase the memory of Anglo-French enmity at Agincourt and construe a bond between current allies fighting against the same foe in the trenches of the Western Front. Unlike other studies on the 1916 Tercentenary, this paper favours a European approach that integrates England with other European countries.[1] It also departs from previous studies in its approach to the 1914–1919 war, which is not regarded here as a mere background influencing Shakespearean reception but as a dynamic presence, directly triggering appropriations of the playwright as cultural icon and of the plays as revered texts. Don Quixote's

Illustration 4.1. Hamlet and Don Quixote. Cartoon on the cover of the weekly *España* (1916).

words in the *España* cartoon, therefore, contain a measure of truth. The war, which may have impaired the celebrations to some extent, also fostered the commemoration cult of Shakespeare.

Shakespearean Sermons and the Great War

The sermon preached by Anthony C. Deane, Vicar of Hampstead and Hon. Canon of Worcester Cathedral, in the church Shakespeare was baptized and buried in, the Church of the Holy Trinity, Stratford-on-Avon, on 30 April, was fittingly entitled 'His Own Place'. Its opening gambit was a quotation from Gen. xxx., 25: 'That I may go unto mine own place' and a portrayal of Shakespeare as a new incarnation of Jacob, the biblical figure who speaks these words after serving in a foreign, alien land for twenty years.[2] The choice of title and quotation suggests that Shakespeare's life in London was, like Jacob's, a sort of exile, a necessary spell of forced labour in a country *not his own*. Rev. Deane could not retrieve the cultural body of Shakespeare – his professional life in the theatre as actor, author, and theatre impresario would always belong to London – but he could at least stress that the body of Shakespeare the man, and the cultural icon, returned to Stratford at the end of his life, that Stratford was the place he chose for his family, his properties, his investments, his retirement, and his grave. The sermon delivered to the congregation of Holy Trinity Church discloses some of the cracks and *faultlines* the celebrations of Shakespeare's death in 1916 were wrapped in.[3] The tension between Stratford and London over who had a right to celebrate acquires the shape of a fight over the body of Shakespeare. Where does he belong? Who owns him?

The desire to claim Shakespeare back for Stratford in 1916 was possibly triggered by the lavish celebrations the Shakespeare Tercentenary Committee had arranged to take place in London during the 'Shakespeare Week'. With the impulse given by David Garrick's Stratford Jubilee in 1769, the small town on the Avon had transformed itself into a shrine for the canonized Shakespeare and a destination for international tourism during the nineteenth century.[4] The semi-sacred nature of Stratford as a site of pilgrimage went hand in hand with the religious underpinning of the literary cult of Shakespeare. The celebrations of the 1864 Tercentenary of the birth of Shakespeare gave Stratford pride of place over London, and the festivities increased Stratford's national and international visibility as Shakespeare's birthplace.⁵ In the late 1880s, during a visit to Shakespeare's birthplace, the Spanish novelist Benito Pérez Galdós had a chance to assess how much was at stake if one could claim possession of Shakespeare. In 'La casa de Shakespeare' ('Shakespeare's Birthplace'), he recorded his emotional and intellectual responses to the commercial appropriation of the English national poet, concluding that in Stratford the visitor could easily witness the canonization of Shakespeare.⁶ Galdós drew a picture of Stratford which anticipated twentieth-century scholarly opinion. He noticed how the Romantics and the early Victorians had added to Shakespeare's 'eterno expediente de canonización' [eternal canonization process], turning Stratford into the Mecca of a cultural pilgrimage with its own rites and rituals that made bardolatry look like a religious cult.⁷ The stages of this cult were already in the 1880s almost what they are today: the Birthplace, New Place and its garden, Holy Trinity Church, the King Edward VI School, Guildhall (because Shakespeare may have seen his first play there). For Galdós, Stratford is like a theme park in which hotels have rooms named after the plays, Shakespearean characters are ubiquitous in the décor of corridors, bedrooms, and dining rooms, and they look at guests from etchings and prints.⁸ Each character is portrayed in the midst of the scene that even those not familiar with the plays will immediately recognize: 'Here, Lady Macbeth washes her hand; over there Catherine of Aragon claims her rights as queen and mother; or King Lear, with his long beard, shouts and rails against heaven and earth.'⁹ In Shakespeare's Birthplace in Henley Street, he notes, the number of tourists who have signed the visitors' book is recorded as 17,000 for the previous year. And he reflects: 'The number of pilgrims increases every day.'¹⁰ This tourist industry described by Galdós was no doubt responsible at the end of the nineteenth century for the town's prosperity.¹¹ Galdós compares Stratford to London: 'In Stratford one can find shops as good as those in London and the neighbours that stroll on the streets resemble the London upper class.'¹² In 1916 the prosperity of Stratford that Galdós had witnessed in 1887 had been curtailed by the Great War, which brought on a reduction in the number of visitors. It also came under threat from the interest the British Empire's metropolis was taking in Shakespeare's cultural capital.

Around the time of the Tercentenary, the growth of English as a discipline at the new London University and the energy of a Shakespearean Professor, Israel Gollancz, posed a challenge to Stratford's claim to being the sole proprietor of Shakespeare. If London had

Gollancz, Honorary Secretary of the Shakespeare Tercentenary Committee, Stratford found its own champion in Sir Sidney Lee, Shakespeare's renowned biographer and Chairman of the Executive Committee of the Birthplace Trustees. To commemorate the 1916 Tercentenary, Shakespeare's Birthplace held an exhibition of sixteenth- and seventeenth-century documents preserved in Stratford whose main purpose was to foreground Shakespeare's connection to his native town. Before declaring the exhibition open on 22 April, Lee gave an address aptly entitled 'Shakespeare and Stratford'. In his address, after underlining the need to celebrate Shakespeare's achievement in spite of the war and referring to the Tercentenary commemorations as 'a national duty', Lee stressed that 'in spite of his London triumphs, [Shakespeare] was proud to be known as a gentleman of Stratford-upon-Avon.'[13] He also pointed out that Shakespeare entrusted the publication of *Venus and Adonis* – his first venture in the press – to a native of Stratford, Richard Field, and added that 'Practically at every step of Shakespeare's career the links between him and Stratford are very strongly knit.'[14] In the preface to the exhibition catalogue, Lee betrays a certain anxiety about the rival claims of Stratford and London to Shakespeare's life and trade and suggests the capital and the birthplace should share him:

> The ties which bound Shakespeare to the borough of his birth steadily strengthened as his years increased, yet the mighty work which makes him memorable was chiefly done in London. To reach a full conception of his career it is needful to co-ordinate all extant evidence of his experiences, alike in his native place and in the capital city of the country.[15]

Lee had to accept that although the body – his birth and death – belonged to Stratford, his trade – the mighty work – belonged to London, hence this cry for collaboration. In 1916, Stratford could not claim the possession of all the documents of Shakespeare's mortal life; his will was kept at Somerset House in London and the Birthplace could only boast a 'carefully executed' facsimile. In fact, many of the documents proudly exhibited in Stratford in 1916 were related to Shakespeare's father and Shakespeare's own offspring, rather than to the playwright himself. Amongst those documents concerning Shakespeare directly, the visitor would find evidence showing the genius mostly as litigant in local courts, i.e. not exactly in a very heroic, or artistic, light. The exhibition had, however, an added interest. For the first time, the visitor to Stratford could see reunited material proof of Shakespeare's existence that was usually kept apart in the Birthplace and the municipal archives. The Tercentenary had rekindled the question of the authorship of the plays and poems. By 1916 there were plenty of candidates, titled or not, to whom the Complete Works had been attributed, as some found it hard to believe that such great dramas had been composed by a man from Stratford with only a grammar school education. The need to keep Baconians and Oxfordians at bay is also an anxiety that emerges from Lee's address:

> It may be beyond our [the trustees'] power to dissipate all the misgivings which have been harboured of late years in brains prone to scepticism regarding Shakespeare's history, but I am sanguine enough to believe that very few – a negligible minority – of those who inspect our documents will leave the birthplace in any doubt as to Shakespeare's sure relations with this place.[16]

With this exhibition, the Birthplace Trustees and the Corporation of Stratford had taken a step to defend their material possession of William Shakespeare's symbolic power.

London, capital of a world empire, had resources that a small provincial town could not aspire to. It is to Gollancz's credit that, as Secretary of the Tercentenary Committee, he managed to get a substantial array of different people involved in the celebrations, including the king and queen, the Lord Mayor and nobles, politicians, and diplomats, and even players and playwrights, besides schools and ordinary people. He also managed to collect in London, at the time when the Great War divided the world, a considerable group of delegates from Commonwealth countries, America, and Europe. The fear that Rev. Deane's sermon at Stratford's Holy Trinity Church betrays, from its very title, was well grounded. Stratford's Shakespeare industry was at risk, and its practice of turning Shakespeare's cultural capital into material capital suffered from the competition of London.

The rivalry of Stratford and London for possession of the national poet runs concurrently with another fight over the cultural iconicity and symbolic power of Shakespeare. The Great War turned German and British academics, who had previously joined forces to study Shakespeare and his works, into enemies. Before the war, on 1 July 1913, Professor Alois Brandl of Berlin University, then President of the German Shakespeare Society, delivered the British Academy Annual Shakespeare Lecture, on the topic of 'Shakespeare and Germany'. Professor Brandl ended his lecture in 1913 with the wish that during the Tercentenary celebrations England and Germany would 'stand up like one man, and hail him with one voice, as the greatest creator in literature ... *Au revoir* till Shakespeare Day, in 1916!'.[17] By 1916, it could be said, as Manfred Pfister claims, that Shakespeare had been 'appropriated, indeed "nostrified", as the "third German classic", flanked by Goethe and Schiller in the nascent German national canon'.[18] Werner Habicht and Peter Dávidházi have questioned the mythical proportions of the German *nostrification* of Shakespeare and suggest that *unser Shakespeare* was a convenient national myth forged by Lessing, Herder, and the *Sturm und Drang* that ignored the influence of French culture in the reception of Shakespeare in Germany during the nineteenth century.[19] This may be so, but it is also true that, as stage practice shows, during the decade before the Tercentenary celebrations, the Germans claimed that they were doing more for Shakespeare and his works than the country he was born in. In the 1910s, England did not have a National Theatre or a national company dedicated to the performance of the plays of Shakespeare; in Germany, by contrast,

> There are 180 companies, and they maintain in their repertory about twenty-five plays of Shakespeare. ... On an average, throughout the Fatherland, three or four plays of Shakespeare are performed every evening. In Berlin, the theatrical capital, it sometimes happens that on five or six successive evenings as many different plays of his are to be seen.[20]

Brandl also pointed out that the Germans had several advantages over the English that enabled them to understand Shakespeare better than the playwright's countrymen. German audiences enjoyed Shakespeare in modern German and had to struggle with no linguistic difficulties, so 'a German reader and spectator feels himself in a way closer to Shakespeare than a Londoner.'[21] German national customs, Brandl claims, are more similar to sixteenth-century manners than modern English ones, so German Shakespeare can be said to be 'more faithful to the historical Shakespeare'.[22] German critics, Brandl adds, are attuned to Romantic gothic horrors and can appreciate early plays such as *Titus Andronicus* or *Henry VI*, plays often dismissed as failures by English critics.[23]

Brandl was probably echoing other voices when he assumed that to 'many an Englishman the German Shakespeare is sure to appear nationalized to such an extent as to wear the garb of a foreign poet.'[24] Brandl is here noting that when removed from its original national habitus and transferred abroad, the literary cult of a national poet is transformed, adapted, reshaped to fit the new habitus. In 1916, this German nostrification of Shakespeare was widespread and led some Englishmen, during the war and after, to lay a claim to Shakespeare as 'English' and to fight to 'retrieve' him from the Germans. Playwright Henry Arthur Jones in *Shakespeare and Germany ... Written during the Battle of Verdun* voices a fear concerning the German 'annexation' of Shakespeare:

> With this constant evidence before us of German temper and methods, it will be well for England to be prepared for the characteristic official announcement which will doubtless be made in Berlin on 23rd April on the final and complete annexation by Germany of William Shakespeare, with all his literary, poetical, philosophical, and stage appurtenances, effects, traditions, and associations, and all the demesnes that there adjacent lie. Meantime, we may ask by what insolence of egotism, what lust of plunder, or what madness of pride Germany dares add to the hideous roll of her thieveries and rapes this topping impudence and crime of vaunting to herself the allegiance of Shakespeare?[25]

This desire to repossess Shakespeare for England, and deprive the Germans of a foreign bard they had supposedly appropriated, clashes with the also widespread desire to see in Shakespeare a universal genius for humankind. He belonged to humanity, but not to Germany.[26] During the 1916 Tercentenary then, the residual rhetoric, fostered by the anti-German feeling, exposed a faultline between Shakespeare the national poet and the universal genius.

If before August 1914, a German scholar could be invited to give the British Academy Annual Shakespeare Lecture, no German Shakespearean could be asked to contribute to the Tercentenary's literary homage in Gollancz's monumental *A Book of Homage to Shakespeare*. To make up for this absence, Gollancz invited C. H. Herford, an English scholar, to address the issue of 'The German Contribution to Shakespearean Criticism' and English fair play acknowledged how important it had been, in spite of the war:

> The war has made impracticable the co-operation of any German Shakespeare scholar in this collective tribute to his memory. But no estrangement, however bitter and profound – still less that occasional extravagance of German claims – can affect the history of the services rendered by Germany to the study and interpretation of Shakespeare, or their claim to recognition at our hands.[27]

One of the paradoxes of the Great War was that both German and British propaganda made use of Shakespeare and his work to instigate either anti-German or anti-British feelings accordingly.[28] Commenting on Habicht's work on the impact the war had on the Tercentenary in both England and Germany, Michael Neill notes that 'Each side proposed allegorical rereadings of key texts, in which Britain was cast as the vindictive and mercenary Shylock, the dishonourable Falstaff, or the treacherous Iago, while Germany figured as the bloodstained Macbeth.'[29] Jonathan Bate finds in the German Romantics' appropriation of Shakespeare the explanation for this paradox: 'Ironically, Shakespeare had been so fully naturalised by Goethe, Schlegel, and their successors that he was used in German propaganda against England during the First World War, as well as vice-versa.'[30] Between 1914 and 1918 then, battles were not only being fought on the fields of Belgium and France – combat spread to cultural battlegrounds. Shakespearean texts and Shakespeare the national poet were soon turned into sites of conflict.

In his Holy Trinity Church sermon, Rev. Deane could put the Stratford–London rivalry aside, when it was a matter of national pride in the celebrations for the national poet and he could use his works to teach wartime Christian patience:

> 'Mine own place' – there, surely, we have the note giving our festival here to-day its unique character. In London, in scores of other towns, this Tercentenary of William Shakespeare is to be observed. We, who revere his genius, rejoice at this. We are glad that not even the grim preoccupations of war have eclipsed an event so notable. We believe, indeed, its celebration at this time to be peculiarly apposite, since the message breathed from the pages of Shakespeare is one which heartens our England to strive and to endure.[31]

To strive and endure is the message Rev. Deane finds in the plays of Shakespeare the good Christian. The only plays that Rev. Deane could have had in mind are the histories, since most of the tragedies and comedies do not even take place in England and, at face value, provide tales, happy or unhappy, about foreigners. Shakespeare's plays are deployed here as material providing a moral lesson. Around the time of the Tercentenary, Shakespeare was conveniently turned into a moral pattern of excelling nature as well as a national hero.

Shakespeare, the Patriot

Shakespeare's history plays could be easily appropriated to present him as a man who loved his country. Shakespeare was England's first patriot. This was the subject of the lecture English schoolchildren were exposed to on 3 May 1916, the day Shakespeare's Tercentenary was celebrated in schools. Written by Gollancz and entitled 'Notes on Shakespeare the Patriot', it was included in *Shakespeare Tercentenary Observance in the Schools and Other Institutions*, a beautifully printed booklet containing recommendations for the celebrations in educational establishments.[32] The style of this booklet is redolent of the arts and crafts woodcutting technique used at the Kelmscott Press – once again, the Tercentenary looks back to its Victorian roots rather than ahead to the emergent, contemporary art (Illustration 4.2). After its title page, the names of male Shakespearean characters are profusely displayed in banners twined with coiling twigs of leaves and acorns. Female characters are excluded from this right-hand side page announcing 'Shakespeare Day 1916'. Their names are relegated to the left-hand side page, bearing the quotation: 'For never anything can be amiss when simpleness and duty tender it'. Boys and girls keep separate stations in the Shakespeare Tercentenary Observance as they did in schools (Illustrations 4.3 and 4.4). Besides, the proximity of Shakespearean female characters to the moral-enforcing quotation suggests that femaleness is next to simpleness and duty.

Interestingly, Ariel finds a niche amongst the girls, whereas Caliban takes exactly the same position in the opposite page amongst the boys. If the choice of male and female Shakespearean characters reproduced on these pages represents more than simply Gollancz's taste, then the Shakespearean characters schoolchildren were expected to be familiar with in 1916 included the following female characters: Juliet, Portia, Ophelia, Celia, Helen, Cleopatra, Olivia, Cordelia, Constance, Katharine, Jessica, Rosalind, Imogen, Margaret and Titania; and the following male ones: Macbeth, Hamlet, Henry V, Julius Caesar, Caliban, Falstaff, Andronicus, Pericles, Cymbeline, Othello, King Lear, Wolsey, Coriolanus, Romeo, Brutus and Shylock. The selection leaves no doubt about what girls and boys should read. Many of the female characters are drawn from the comedies, whereas the male characters mostly belong to the tragedies and histories and late plays, with the only exception being Shylock.[33]

NOTES ON SHAKESPEARE THE PATRIOT.
BY PROFESSOR I. GOLLANCZ, LITT. D.

IT were well if every year a Shakespeare Day were observed, when those who speak the speech of Shakespeare might reverently pay homage to his memory, and be reminded of all that he stands for on the roll of British fame and of the universal recognition of his exalted genius.

❡ While all the world acclaims him, those who are privileged to be his fellow-countrymen owe to themselves the high duty of gratefully recalling, on this occasion of the Tercentenary of his death, some of the lessons he has left us, and, especially at the present time, how it behoves us as patriots to strive to play our part in war as in peace, and how best to maintain our faith in the ultimate triumph of a noble humanity.

❡ The story of his life, so far as the facts are known, gives us the impression of a man who, while conscious of his genius, did his work with gentle grace and modesty. Happily, he was destined so to use his gifts as to reach all classes of his countrymen—lords, gallants, scholars, and unlettered groundlings.

Illustration 4.2. Shakespeare Tercentenary Observance for Schools. Notes on Shakespeare the Patriot.

Girls should read the comedies and learn to be simple and dutiful daughters. Boys should read the tragedies and histories and learn to be warriors and heroes.

The Shakespeare Tercentenary Observance's division of male and female characters' names follows a quotation by S. T. Dobell that captures some of the discourses of patriotism and imperialism that also pervade Gollancz's 'Notes on Shakespeare the Patriot' and other texts produced for the Tercentenary: 'Children brave and free / of the great mother-tongue – and ye shall be / Lords of an empire wide as Shakespeare's soul, / Sublime as Milton's immemorial theme, / And rich as Chaucer's speech, and fair as Spenser's dream.' Speakers of English are 'lords of an empire' and this empire is as wide as Shakespeare's soul and Milton's religious theme. Language (Chaucer's speech) is a reason to feel proud of one's country; those who have English as their mother-tongue must be brave.³⁴

Together with Gollancz's lecture on Shakespeare the patriot, the programme to be observed at schools on the 1916 Shakespeare Day, with the approval of the Shakespeare Tercentenary Committee, included the reading of scenes or passages and the singing of several songs taken out of Shakespeare's plays. The whole observance began with a reading from the Bible and ended with 'God save the King'. The Bible reading, 'Let us now praise famous men' (Ecclesiasticus xliv) could not have been more appropriate. The text invites us to praise men 'Such as did bear rule in their kingdom, men renowned for their power' and men 'Such as found out musical tunes, and recited verses in writing'. These men will have 'Their bodies buried in peace; but their name liveth for evermore' and 'The people will tell of their wisdom, and the congregation will shew forth their praise'. Brave soldiers and famous writers will enjoy immortal glory – a very fitting preamble to Gollancz's lecture, which presents Shakespeare as playwright and patriot.³⁵

Shakespeare the Christian in sermons is, not surprisingly, similar to Shakespeare the Patriot as he appears in Gollancz's 'Notes' for the Tercentenary schools' observance. Rev. Shawcross, in a 'Popular Address' written for the Tercentenary, begins by presenting Shakespeare's biography in hagiographical terms, reviews his literary production, and presents him as 'the author of nearly all our quotations and homely sayings; we quote him without knowing it'.³⁶ Shawcross then invites his listeners/readers to leave the writer aside and pay attention to Shakespeare the man: 'From Shakespeare the philosopher and poet, let us turn to Shakespeare, the patriot'.³⁷ Shakespeare is a patriot because 'We see in him the typical Englishman who loved his country, and was concerned about its safety and welfare.'³⁸ To illustrate this, Shawcross resorts, like so many others during the Tercentenary, to John of Gaunt's speech on England in *Richard II* (2.1), and suggests that Shakespeare wrote it under the influence of his country's reaction towards the threat of invasion posed by the Spanish Armada, 'sent to bring England under the dominion of Rome'.³⁹ The picture of Elizabethan England summoned by Rev. Shawcross is one of a country united against a common enemy: 'In face of this common peril, all parties and all classes, irrespective of creed or politics, closed their ranks and presented to the enemy

Illustration 4.3. Shakespeare Tercentenary Observance for Schools. Female characters.

a firm, united front'.[40] The relevance of this image of Elizabethan England to the England of 1916 was self-evident. Shakespeare's patriotism is not only found in *Richard II*; *Henry V* follows in his train. After quoting the lines in *Richard II* (2.1) about the 'dear, dear land' that has 'such dear souls' that make their country 'dear for her reputation throughout the world', Shawcross adds: 'Not only here, but elsewhere we find patriotism and self-sacrifice urged as worthy of true Englishmen'.[41] Predictably, the next Shakespearean character to be invoked is Henry V, the 'hero – manly, brave, daring and fearless', the English king that could ask his men not to fear to fall because 'if thou fallest, thou fallest a blessed martyr' for your country and your God.[42]

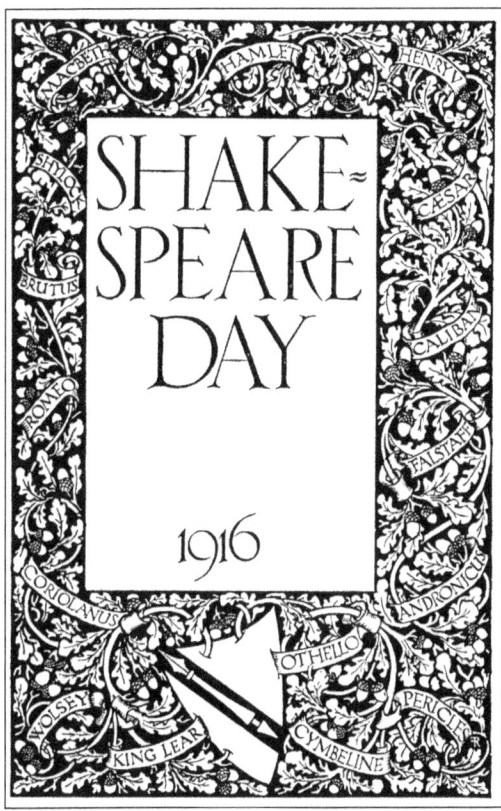

Illustration 4.4. Shakespeare Tercentenary Observance for Schools. Male characters.

Shakespeare the Patriot is also presented as Shakespeare the good Christian. Shawcross confidently answers his own rhetorical question: 'But was Shakespeare (ask some) a religious, God-fearing man? Undoubtedly'.[43] To justify his claim, Shawcross explains that Shakespeare 'nowhere discredits the principles of Christianity or sneers at religious customs and morals'.[44] He also refers to Christ with tenderness, believes in Providence, confidently asserts the triumph of good over evil, condemns suicide, praises mercy, makes sin odious – all of which are generously illustrated by Rev. Shawcross with quotes or allusions to the plays. Shakespeare also 'illustrates the fruitfulness of endurance and of self-sacrifice in deeds of chivalry and of noble heroism' because he is 'the practical, sensible teacher'.[45] Once again, in Rev. Shawcross's popular address, as in Rev. Deane's Stratford Tercentenary sermon, Shakespeare the patriot and Shakespeare the Christian teach Englishmen to strive and endure.

For another churchman, Rev. Fred Askew, Shakespearean texts could do much more than simply teach to strive and endure. Rev. Askew saw no difficulty in extracting the texts of the plays out of their contexts and applying them to contemporary Britain. In his *Shakespeare Tercentenary Souvenir: England's Thoughts in Shakespeare's Words*, he carefully matched an appropriate Shakespearean quotation with a newspaper headline or piece of news relative to the Great War.[46] The subtitle is in itself revealing: England thinks in unison, as a whole body; no possibility of diversity of opinion is contemplated here, and the thoughts of this English soul have already been expressed by Shakespeare. A headline about Germany having abandoned its submarine policy would prompt, for any true Englishman, a line from *Twelfth Night*: 'What think you of this fool ... doth he not mend?' (1.5.65–66). This seems to have been an extended practice, as Francis Colmer's *Shakespeare in Time of War: Excerpts from the Plays Arranged with Topical Allusion* (1916) shows.[47]

During the war, Germany was often represented as a 'bloodstained Macbeth'[48] but Rev. Askew also finds a true representation of the German race in Caliban. This must have been a widespread association at the time, as it appears in a sonnet written by the Cuban man of letters, José de Armas y Cárdenas, for Gollancz's *A Book of Homage to Shakespeare*.[49] Terence Hawkes has unveiled the complex implications of the 'Germanizing' of Caliban, who is divested of his American roots and turned into a European 'wild man', a 'bestial, savage, and deformed man' easily accommodated within a long-standing, particular European world view.[50] For Askew, the German soldier has no second thoughts when he is told to occupy Belgium because 'My man-monster hath drowned his tongue in sack' (*The Tempest*, 3.2.11). Count Ferdinand von Zeppelin is given Prospero's words when referring to Caliban, and Askew makes him boast about his rigid airship: 'This thing of darkness, I acknowledge mine' (*The Tempest*, 5.1.278–79). When German soldiers with their Prussian officers start an attack, Askew, full of pride and confidence in the national army, exclaims, borrowing words from Stephano: 'Lead monster, we'll follow!' (*The Tempest*, 3.2.143). The fact that he was giving England the words of a drunken butler whose attack has no success seems not to trouble Rev. Askew. The words of Shakespeare are national heritage – they can be wrenched out of their context and may easily acquire a new, appropriate meaning in a new context.[51]

Churchmen could concern themselves with Shakespeare, and he could be simultaneously construed as a model Christian and England's leading patriot, perhaps because 'In the late nineteenth century religion and recreation had often gone together'.[52] At the time, the religious and the civil often intermingle, as churches were used for theatrical performances, town halls for religious music:

> In much of provincial Britain they still did, with a wide range of social activities based on church and chapel: girls' friendly societies or lads' clubs, choirs or amateur dramatic groups. Choral works had long been the forte of English music; north-country town halls resounded to performances of oratorios like Handel's *Messiah*, another reflection of the religiosity with which popular culture was still impregnated.[53]

The choice of Handel and the *Messiah* for performance in English town halls can be seen as part of the struggle between England and Germany over cultural icons. Handel's music is not all a matter of religion here but rather, another stab in the *nostrification* battle. Just as the English felt that the Germans had appropriated Shakespeare, the Germans strongly felt that the English had nostrified 'Händel'.[54]

Cet idéal pour lequel on combat

In 1916, the Recteur de l'Université de Nancy, Ch. Adam, in a speech given at the 'Commémoration de Shakespeare' and dedicated 'Aux universités d'Angleterre, d'Ecosse et d'Irlande' provided, in a nutshell, the reason why literary cults draw strength from times of war.[55] Adam began his address with a description of what happens to national poets during wartime:

> In wartime, the great geniuses of a nation appear, in the eyes of their countrymen, much greater than at times of peace. Instinctively, people turn to them, as the benefactors of the nation: their major works, don't they express the ideal of all of us, that ideal for which we fight and which we want to retain the legitimate portion of influence in world civilization?[56]

> [Pendant la guerre, les grands génies d'une nation apparaissent, aux yeux de leurs compatriotes, bien plus grands encore qu'en temps de paix. D'instinct le peuple se tourne vers eux, comme vers

les Bienfaiteurs de la Patrie: leurs chefs-d'oeuvre n'expriment-ils pas l'idéal de tous, cet idéal pour lequel on combat et dont on veut maintenir la part légitime d'influence dans la civilisation du monde?]

Cet idéal pour lequel on combat. Canonical authors, for the Recteur of the University of Nancy, stand for the country, the nation, the *Patrie*. They are not only national poets but national heroes, the 'bienfaiteurs' of the nation. Their works contain the ideas and the foundations of the world and the world view the soldiers, in times of war, fight for. Thomas Carlyle's writing on heroes and hero worship and his reading of the poet as hero in particular may be echoed here.[57] For the Recteur, a major conflagration, such as the one taking place then, is likely to rekindle and stir the cult of major literary authors: 'Books by classical authors have never been so much in demand as in these heroic days, and they are read by many officers and soldiers at the front and even in the trenches'.[58] Canonical authors, like Shakespeare and Corneille, do not only provide the ideal to fight for, but also comfort, even in the trenches. Like a secular Bible, the works of a nation's literary classical authors always lie on the soldier's table. One of these works that bring comfort to soldiers is Shakespeare's *Henry V*, a play that the Recteur analyses and re-interprets in the light of the First World War and the battle fought in 1915 on – very roughly – the same ground as Azincourt. The address ends by stating what many, including Rev. Askew, had already noticed in England, that Shakespeare's works can be found to be applicable – and very conveniently so – when describing the greatest European conflagration ever known at the time: 'While we await the great day of peace, we will re-read Shakespeare's lines that are in advance applicable to today's epic times, given that he celebrates the glory of all those that, fighting for the good cause, become "brothers" and who are "ennobled"'.[59]

The echo of Shakespeare's *Henry V* in the speech of the Recteur of the University of Nancy ('we band of brothers', 4.3.60; 'This day shall gentle his condition', 4.3.63) turns the Tercentenary celebrations into an occasion for wartime propaganda. These words, originally written to imagine the hours prior to a battle that was part of England's invasion of France, are appropriated by a Frenchman to stress the unity of the French and the British in a common *'bonne cause'*. In this good cause, *cet idéal pour lequel on combat* is the defence of democracy and the former enemy of France is now 'its faithful ally, England' [*'sa fidèle alliée, l'Angleterre'*].[60] Germans were not the only Europeans appropriating Shakespeare in, or around, 1916. The works of a *'bienfaiteur de la Patrie'* such as Shakespeare, including his most anti-French play, are deployed to strengthen a sense of unity, a kind of supranational bonding.

The appropriation of Henry V's pre-battle speech for the cult of commemoration and wartime propaganda rewrites Agincourt as a *lieu de mémoire*, reshaping it and endowing it with a different significance. Partly as a result of the war, Shakespeare's Agincourt is no longer a reminder of Anglo-French conflagration but an emblem of reconciliation, of the need to forget past enmity and collaborate in the defeat of current common enemies. The cultural life of Shakespeare's *Henry V* as artistic object in Nancy in 1916 echoes the fate of one of the four casts of Rodin's sculptural group *Les Bourgeois de Calais* encountered in London in 1915. When it was originally erected in Calais in 1895, Rodin's monument symbolized French heroism in the face of English imperialistic aggression. The sculpture commemorates the valour and sacrifice of the six prominent men of Calais who in 1347 took up the challenge of the English king Edward III and offered their lives so the city and its inhabitants would be spared. In 1911, when it was offered to the National Arts Collection Fund, Rodin's statue must have had a different meaning for Englishmen, stressing the mercy of an English king and the *savoir faire* of Queen Philippa, his wife, who begged on the burghers' behalf. In 1915, when the statue was placed in Victoria Tower Gardens, next to the Houses of Parliament on the Thames Embankment, the war fostered new meanings for a work of art that transcended its essence as artistic object and became 'a symbol of fraternity'.[61] In contemporary descriptions, the monument was also seen as 'a bond of courage and sympathy' between England and France against Germany, 'the enemy of Europe'.[62] Like Shakespeare's *Henry V* in the speech of the Recteur of the University of Nancy, Rodin's *Citizens of Calais* becomes part of Anglo-French *commemorabilia* (i.e. objects through which the past is remembered) and as a result of the First World War, the cultural life of these objects reshapes the siege of Calais and the battle of Agincourt as European *lieux de mémoire* that transcend national boundaries.[63] Calais and Agincourt become, partly through Rodin and Shakespeare, sites of remembrance and commemoration that invite two countries to share the same collective memory.

This desire to stress unity and to enhance the value of supranational bonding in wartime through Shakespeare, led some to turn the man not of an age but for all time, into the man for all political persuasions. Behind Edward Salmon's *Shakespeare and Democracy* lies an obvious desire to retrieve Shakespeare from the claws of the Tory party, who like the Germans, have, in Salmon's view, appropriated a national bard that belongs to all.[64] Salmon's agenda is to challenge the view that Shakespeare was 'a Tory devoid of sympathy with the common people'.[65] He claims that '[t]he party man has looked at [Shakespeare] through party spectacles falsely focussed'[66] and that, for this reason, his essay 'is an attempt to show that Shakespeare as revealed in his works was as superior to any mere party or class feeling as it is possible for mortal to be'.[67]

Salmon's discussion of Shakespeare and democracy has a clearly stated departure point: 'In this Tercentenary year of Shakespeare's death what is the message of his works for the Empire and for Democracy?',[68] and the reply to this question is stated in equally unambiguous terms: 'Shakespeare had many messages for mankind, but none more valuable or more opportune than that party is a national bane'.[69] Given that he is against taking sides, Salmon considers Shakespeare as both monarchical and republican. Shakespeare did not take sides, politically speaking, concludes Salmon, because he was a patriot: 'To deny Shakespeare's interest in, and sympathy with, the common people is to rob his patriotism, which no one has called in question, of much of its fire and meaning'.[70] Shakespeare's patriotism and sympathy with the common people are stressed at a time in which the need for unity in national issues, given the war, was clearly desirable. This 'sympathy with the common people', though, stands next to Shakespeare's role in the constitution of the British Empire. At the core of Salmon's construction of Shakespeare as a democrat lies his contribution to the building of the imperial administration:

> For the upbuilding of the Empire, for the enlightened despotism by which it is ruled; for the freedom which has been found the surest guarantee of the loyalty of peoples of every shade of political thought and every religion, for the ideals which move us to seek a union of which no empire ancient or modern provides a pattern, may we not give some measure of credit to Shakespeare?[71]

In 1916, Salmon claims, democracy is a recent political development: 'Democracy, as we know it in Great Britain, has been with us thirty years'.[72] Democratic Britain has to be reconciled, though, to the existence of a British Empire that spreads over 'the four quarters of the earth'.[73] The ideological faultline that lies in Salmon's view of

Great Britain as a democracy and Shakespeare as a democrat is the very existence of an empire whose relation to Britain is necessarily non-democratic. This reconciliation between democratic Britain and non-democratic empire is attempted through the political appropriation of Shakespeare's universality as a genius that speaks to all peoples, and whose plays convey a unique message of political unity: 'Shakespeare stood and stands for Democracy, for Empire, for Humanity; his message for all mankind and for all time is Nature's own; it will ring down the ages, a challenge to prejudice, a clarion call to Patriotism'.[74] The ideological faultline is clearly there, at the core of Salmon's attempt to read Shakespeare for both democracy and empire through 'humanity' and 'patriotism'. Shakespeare represents the 'democratic Imperial sentiment', a rhetorically built notion to reconcile the political clash between the notions of democracy and the Imperial administration that co-existed in British politics at the time of the First World War. Shakespeare is the national poet but 'in an imperial sense'.[75] The imperialistic dream of Shakespeare's King Henry V casts its shadow over Salmon's text when he quotes from F. R. Benson: 'a common ideal of Empire, not for conquest, or exploitation, or lust of greed, but an Empire for expansion and association: an Empire, which in terms of patriotism and intensification of national life shall bring the world a step nearer to the Brotherhood of Man. Of such is the kingdom of Poetry, and Shakespeare wears its crown'.[76]

Through the residual rhetoric of this imperialistic discourse, the brotherhood of England with the nations of its colonial Empire emerges as similar to the brotherhood of King Henry V with his soldiers the morning before the battle of Agincourt. Although his kingdom is poetry, Shakespeare is crowned like his own royal character and, just like Henry V, uses language to bring all nations, and particularly those of the British Empire, into a fictitious democratic equality with Britain in wartime.

Both the Recteur of Nancy and Edward Salmon bring to the foreground the relation between national poets and war, showing how literary cults expand and obtain vigour out of both celebrations and armed conflicts. Both Adam and Salmon avail themselves of discourses that are typical of the texts produced around the Shakespeare Tercentenary celebrations. Both, too, need to glide over the faultlines that appear in their discourse – such as the clash between the notions of democracy and empire, or such as the fact that England and

France have been traditionally at odds and that in 1415, Henry V, whose words in Shakespeare are so quotable in 1916, led the English to defeat the French at Agincourt. Both bridge these faultlines by reconciling ideological contraries through the rhetoric of patriotism and national unity.

Conclusion

The 1916 Tercentenary of Shakespeare's death presents a complex commemoration paradigm. The concurrence of the celebrations and the Great War triggered a considerable amount of Shakespearean appropriations which underlined existing conflicts of interests, between Stratford and London, or between England and Germany. Shakespeare's verse was topically read not only in England and Germany, or in North America and Commonwealth countries, as has already been pointed out, but also in France and several other European countries. The fight over the cultural capital of Shakespeare extended to different texts and objects, from sermons and public addresses to exhibition catalogues, from anthologies of quotations to educational texts. Political readings of Shakespeare's plays in wartime Europe rub shoulders with the rhetorical discourse of the cult of Shakespeare as national bard and universal genius. The desire to counteract the German nostrification of Shakespeare resulted in a contradiction in the Tercentenary's commemorative discourse, presenting the English Bard as both a national poet for England and a universal genius for mankind, but not for Germany, whose unlawful 'annexation' of Shakespeare's works was seen as an act of war. In France, instead, quoting from Shakespeare's *Henry V* was a patriotic gesture signalling Anglo-French bonding against Germany. The 1916 Tercentenary saw how Triple Entente nations and Central Powers equally availed themselves of Shakespeare's symbolic power and his works to indicate their positions vis-à-vis each other. During the Tercentenary, the ideological appropriation of Shakespeare for political purposes or propaganda was not an independent affair in a national context – it often involved the pattern of extant enemies and allies. Any future study of the 1916 Shakespeare Tercentenary should therefore aim to be transnational in scope. During the First World War, military action was not responsible for the only battles fought on European fields – the concurrence of the Tercentenary and the war turned Shakespeare into a cultural battleground.

Acknowledgements

Research for this paper was possible thanks to funding from two research projects, 'Great War Shakespeare II: Myth, Social Agents and Global Culture' (05736/PHCS/07), financed by the Fundación Séneca, and Research Project FFI2011-24347, 'Shakespeare and the Cultures of Commemoration II: Remembering Shakespeare', financed by the Spanish Research Agency MEC-ANEP.

Clara Calvo is Professor of English Studies at the University of Murcia. Her research interests include the afterlives of Shakespeare and Jane Austen, literary adaptation and cultural memory. She is the author of *Power Relations and Fool-Master Discourse in Shakespeare* (1991) and has co-authored, with Jean-Jacques Weber, *The Literature Workbook* (Routledge, 1998). With Ton Hoenselaars, she has edited *European Shakespeares* (*The Shakespearean International Yearbook*, 8, 2008) and a special issue of *Critical Survey* on *Shakespeare and the Cultures of Commemoration* (2011). She has also edited *The Spanish Tragedy* for the Arden Early Modern Series with Jesús Tronch (2013) and *Celebrating Shakespeare: Commemoration and Cultural Memory* (CUP, 2015) with Coppélia Kahn.

Notes

1. Previous, well-known studies of the 1916 Tercentenary include Thomas Cartelli, 'Shakespeare, 1916: *Caliban by the Yellow Sands* and the New Dramas of Democracy', in *Repositioning Shakespeare: National Formations, Postcolonial Appropriations* (London: Routledge, 1999), 63–83; Balz Engler, 'Shakespeare in the Trenches', *Shakespeare Survey* 44 (1991), 105–11; Richard Foulkes, 'The Theatre of War: the 1916 Tercentenary', in *Performing Shakespeare in the Age of Empire* (Cambridge: Cambridge University Press, 2002), 180–204; Werner Habicht, 'Shakespeare Celebrations in Times of War', *Shakespeare Quarterly* 52 (2001), 441–55; Coppélia Kahn, 'Remembering Shakespeare Imperially: The 1916 Tercentenary', *Shakespeare Quarterly* 52 (2001), 456–78.
2. Rev. Antony C. Deane, *'His Own Place'. The Tercentenary 'Shakespeare Sermon'. Preached in the Church of the Holy Trinity, Stratford-on-Avon, 30 April 1916* (Hampstead, N. W.: J. Hewetson and Son, 1916).
3. For the notion of 'faultlines' see Alan Sinfield, *Faultlines: Cultural Materialism and the Politics of Dissident Reading* (Oxford: Oxford University Press, 1992) and, in particular, Alan Sinfield, 'Shakespeare and Dissident Reading', *Cultural Politics – Queer Reading* (London: Routledge,1994), 3–4.

4. See Balz Engler, 'Stratford and the Canonization of Shakespeare', *European Journal of English Studies* 1 (1997), 354–66 and Péter Dávidházi, *The Romantic Cult of Shakespeare: Literary Reception in Anthropological Perspective* (London: Macmillan, 1998), 70–87. For Stratford as a tourist destination see also Nicola Watson, *The Literary Tourist* (London: Palgrave, 2006). See also Richard Schoch, 'The Birth of Shakespeare's Birthplace', *Theatre Survey* 53 (2012), 181–201, for a cultural history of how John Shakespeare's house in Henley Street became the Birthplace.
5. For a detailed cultural history of the 1864 Tercentenary see Richard Foulkes, *The Shakespeare Tercentenary of 1864* (London: The Society for Theatre Research, 1984).
6. Benito Pérez Galdós, 'La casa de Shakespeare', in *Memoranda*, reprinted in *Novelas y Miscelánea* (Madrid: Aguilar, 1973), 1196–203; 1203.
7. To see how Galdós anticipated twentieth-century criticism, see Dávidházi, *The Romantic Cult*.
8. 'The traveller who stays there overnight is assaulted by a multitude of eminent ghosts.' ['El viajero que allí pasa la noche, se ve acosado por la turba de ilustres fantasmas.'] (Pérez Galdós, 'La casa de Shakespeare', 1199).
9. 'Aquí, Lady Macbeth lavándose la mano; más allá Catalina de Aragón reclamando sus derechos de Reina y esposa, o el Rey Lear, de luenga barba, lanzando imprecaciones contra el cielo y la tierra.' (Pérez Galdós, 'La casa de Shakespeare', 1199).
10. 'La peregrinación a la casa natal aumenta cada día.' (Pérez Galdós, 'La casa de Shakespeare', 1200).
11. 'The welfare, the comfort, the aurea mediocritas and the absence of pretentious manners, are evident in the streets of Stratford.' ['El bienestar, la comodidad, la medianía placentera y sin pretensiones, se revelan en las calles de Stratford.'] (Pérez Galdós, 'La casa de Shakespeare', 1199).
12. 'En Stratford se encuentran tiendas tan bellas como las de Londres, y el vecindario que discurre por las calles tiene el aspecto de la burguesía londinense.' (Pérez Galdós, 'La casa de Shakespeare', 1199).
13. 'Shakespeare Commemoration at Stratford', *The Scotsman*, 24 April 1916, 3.
14. 'Shakespeare Commemoration at Stratford', 3.
15. Sir Sidney Lee, *Shakespeare Tercentenary Commemoration, 1616–1916: Shakespeare Birthplace. Catalogue of an Exhibition of Original Documents of the XVIth & XVIIth Centuries Preserved in Stratford-upon-Avon, Illustrating Shakespeare's Life in the Town* (Stratford-upon-Avon: Edward Fox and Sons, 1916), 6. Lee justifies the need to share Shakespeare with Shakespeare's own example. Shakespeare had shared his money with both his Stratford and London friends, since in his will he had left money to buy memorial rings to four Stratford men and three men in London. The latter were his friend the playwright Ben Jonson and his fellow actors John Heminges and Henry Condell.
16. 'Shakespeare Commemoration at Stratford', 3.
17. Alois Brandl, *Shakespeare and Germany. British Academy Third Shakespeare Annual Lecture* (London: The British Academy, 1913), 14.
18. Manfred Pfister, '"In States Unborn and Accents Yet Unknown": Shakespeare and the European Canon', in *Shifting the Scene: Shakespeare in European Culture*, ed. Ladina Bezzola Lambert and Balz Engler (Newark, NJ: Delaware University Press, 2004), 41–63; see 50–51. See also Manfred Pfister, 'Hamlet und der deutsche Geist', *Shakespeare Jahrbuch (West)* (1992), 13–38.

19. Werner Habicht, *Shakespeare and the German Imagination* (Hertford: Stephen Austin & Sons, 1994). Péter Dávhidázi, *The Romantic Cult*, 184.
20. Brandl, 'Shakespeare and Germany', 6–7.
21. Brandl, 'Shakespeare and Germany', 11.
22. Brandl, 'Shakespeare and Germany', 12.
23. Brandl, 'Shakespeare and Germany', 13.
24. Brandl, 'Shakespeare and Germany', 13.
25. Henry Arthur Jones, *Shakespeare and Germany (Written during the Battle of Verdun)* (London: Chiswick Press, 1916), 3–4.
26. The desire to deprive Germany of Shakespeare and punish it for its unlawful 'annexation' of the English Bard extended beyond the Armistice. In March 1919, the English actor Arthur Bouchier said in a public speech that 'Shakespeare never wrote his works for Germany, and the Peace Conference could do worse than ban their production there for a term of years' (*The Times*, 5 March 1919, 7).
27. Israel Gollancz, ed., *A Book of Homage to Shakespeare* (London: Oxford University Press, 1916), 231. For an in-depth analysis of Gollancz's *Homage*, see Kahn, 'Remembering Shakespeare Imperially'.
28. Habicht, 'Shakespeare Celebrations'.
29. Michael Neill, 'From the Editor', *Shakespeare Survey* 52 (2001), iii–x; see ix.
30. Jonathan Bate, *The Genius of Shakespeare* (London: Picador, 1997), 196; see also Engler, 'Shakespeare in the Trenches'.
31. Deane, '*His Own Place*', 3–4.
32. *Shakespeare Tercentenary Observance in the Schools and Other Institutions* (London: Geo W. Jones, 1916).
33. Although *The Merchant of Venice* is usually placed amongst the comedies, Shylock's status as a comic character is problematic. Since the Romantic period, and particularly since Edmund Kean's success in this role, Shylock has been performed as a tragic hero. See John Gross, *Shylock: Four Hundred Years in the Life of a Legend* (London: Chatto and Windus, 1992), 89 and ff.
34. For a discussion of the presence of discourses of nationalism and colonialism in the Tercentenary celebrations and the role played by language, see Clara Calvo, 'Shakespeare and Cervantes in 1916: The Politics of Language', in *Shifting the Scene: Shakespeare in European Culture*, ed. L. Bezzola Lambert and B. Engler (Newark, NJ: University of Delaware Press, 2004), 78–94.
35. For a more detailed analysis of Gollancz's use of the histories to construct his image of Shakespeare the patriot, see Calvo, 'Shakespeare and Cervantes in 1916', 82–83.
36. J. P. Shawcross, *The Shakespeare Tercentenary: A Popular Address* (London: Skeffington and Son, 1916), 7.
37. Shawcross, *The Shakespeare Tercentenary*, 8.
38. Shawcross, *The Shakespeare Tercentenary*, 8.
39. Shawcross, *The Shakespeare Tercentenary*, 8.
40. Shawcross, *The Shakespeare Tercentenary*, 8.
41. Shawcross, *The Shakespeare Tercentenary*, 9.
42. Shawcross, *The Shakespeare Tercentenary*, 9. Since Shawcross's 'popular address' bears no indication of the day or month when it was (if it was) delivered, it is possible that he had written it after *Shakespeare Tercentenary Observance* had been made available at English schools. If this is the case, it would show how the circulation and the circularity of discourses affected the Tercentenary.

43. Shawcross, *The Shakespeare Tercentenary*, 9.
44. Shawcross, *The Shakespeare Tercentenary*, 10.
45. Shawcross, *The Shakespeare Tercentenary*, 11.
46. Rev. Frederick Askew, *Shakespeare Tercentenary Souvenir: England's Thoughts in Shakespeare's Words* (Lowestoft: Flood and Son, 1916).
47. Francis Colmer, *Shakespeare in Time of War: Excerpts from the Plays Arranged with Topical Allusion* (London: Smith, Elder & Co, 1916). For Colmer's work and how it shows the mark left by the Great War on the 1916 Tercentenary, see Habicht, 'Shakespeare Celebrations'.
48. See Neill, 'From the Editor,' ix; see also Habicht, 'Shakespeare Celebrations'.
49. For this sonnet see Calvo, 'Shakespeare and Cervantes in 1916', 88–90.
50. Terence Hawkes, 'Swisser-Swatter: Making a Man of English Letters', *Alternative Shakespeares*, ed. John Drakakis (London: Methuen, 1985), 26–46.
51. This was standard practice during the Tercentenary, and another well-known example of this is Percy McKay's community masque *Caliban by the Yellow Sands*.
52. Peter Clarke, *Hope and Glory: Britain 1900–1990* (London: Penguin, 1996), 50.
53. Clarke, *Hope and Glory*, 50.
54. For Shakespeare and Handel, see also Georg Gottfried Gervinus, *Händel und Shakespeare. (Eine Parallele.) Zur Ästhetik der Tonkust* (Leipzig: Verlag von Wilhelm Engelmann, 1868).
55. Ch. Adam, *Commémoration de Shakespeare. Aux Universités d'Angleterre, d'Ecosse et d'Irlande.* (1916) BL Ac. 382.b (1).
56. Adam, *Commémoration*, 1.
57. For Carlyle's views of Shakespeare as model poet and hero, see Thomas Carlyle, *On Heroes, Hero-Worship and the Heroic in History*, ed. Michael K. Goldberg (Oxford: University of California Press, 1993).
58. 'Les livres classiques n'ont été plus demandés qu'en ces jours d'héroisme, et qu'ils sont lus par beaucoup d'officiers et des soldats sur le front et jusque dans les tranchées.' Adam, *Commémoration*, 2.
59. 'En attendant le grand jour de la paix, nous relirons les vers de Shakespeare qui s'appliquent si bien par avance a l'épopée actuelle, lorsqu'il célèbre la gloire de tous ceux qui, combatant pour la bonne cause, deviennent "autant de frères", et en sont tous "anoblis".' Adam, *Commémoration*, 3.
60. Adam, *Commémoration*, 3.
61. Axel Lapp, 'Rodin's *Bourgeois de Calais*: Commemorating a French National Ideal in London', in *Memory and Memorials: The Commemorative Century*, ed. William Kidd and Brian Murdoch (Aldershot: Ashgate, 2004), 13–25; 13.
62. *Country Life* 31 (1915), 151. Quoted in Axel Lapp, 'Rodin's *Bourgeois de Calais*', 13.
63. The concept of *commemorabilia* has been borrowed from Lapp, 'Rodin's *Bourgeois de Calais*,' 16.
64. Edward Salmon, *Shakespeare and Democracy* (London and New York: McBride, Nast & Co., 1916).
65. Salmon, *Shakespeare and Democracy*, 3.
66. Salmon, *Shakespeare and Democracy*, 1.
67. Salmon, *Shakespeare and Democracy*, 2.
68. Salmon, *Shakespeare and Democracy*, 1.
69. Salmon, *Shakespeare and Democracy*, 4.
70. Salmon, *Shakespeare and Democracy*, 55.

71. Salmon, *Shakespeare and Democracy*, 56.
72. Salmon, *Shakespeare and Democracy*, 1.
73. Salmon, *Shakespeare and Democracy*, 57.
74. Salmon, *Shakespeare and Democracy*, 58.
75. Colmer, *Shakespeare in Time of War*, xvii. For a discussion of Colmer's view of Shakespeare as national and imperial poet, and the implications for his being both an English and a universal genius, see Calvo, 'Shakespeare and Cervantes', 91.
76. Salmon, *Shakespeare and Democracy*, 58.

Chapter 5

The Shakespeare Courtship in the Millennium

Katherine Scheil

Every biographer of Shakespeare must sort out a number of issues related to his wife Anne Hathaway. How did William and Anne meet? What were the circumstances of the conception of daughter Susanna? Why are there two different names on the two documents related to the Shakespeare marriage – Anna Whateley of Temple Grafton on the marriage licence in the Bishop's Register, and Anne Hathwey of Stratford on the marriage registry?[1] How did they negotiate William's move to London, leaving behind his wife and three small children? What were the terms of their long-distance relationship? How often did William visit Anne and family in Stratford? What were the circumstances of Shakespeare's return to Stratford? And how might one explain the fact that William and Anne Shakespeare are buried next to each other in Stratford's Holy Trinity Church, yet she receives only the 'second best bed' in his will?

Notes for this section begin on page 104.

Any one of these issues would provide copious material for analysis, but for the sake of space, I will focus on just one topic. An analysis of how the Shakespeare courtship/marriage is interpreted in millennial biographies can serve as a microcosm, both for biographical studies of Shakespeare, and for the way his relationship with his wife impacts interpretation of his life, and (perhaps) his work.[2] In the larger scheme of biographical studies, the various configurations of the Shakespeare courtship help determine how the Stratford parts of Shakespeare's life fit into the larger biographical design.

Within the topic of the Shakespeare courtship and marriage, we might see a further subset of questions for biographers. What impact did the age difference have on the Shakespeares? What was the relationship between their families? Was daughter Susanna's conception a single instance of Shakespeare sowing his wild oats, or was it the physical consummation of a longer relationship? How is the Anne Hathaway/Anna Whateley situation explained? What was Shakespeare's attitude toward his marriage? And what evidence is used to support answers to these questions?

The spate of millennial biographies offers an opportunity to analyse this topic in a succinct critical, cultural, and historical climate.[3] I will focus on six biographies from this cluster: Park Honan's *Shakespeare: A Life* (1998), Katherine Duncan-Jones's *Ungentle Shakespeare: Scenes from his Life* (2001), Stephen Greenblatt's *Will in the World: How Shakespeare Became Shakespeare* (2004), Peter Ackroyd's *Shakespeare: The Biography* (2005), René Weis's *Shakespeare Revealed: A Biography* (2007) and Jonathan Bate's *Soul of the Age: A Biography of the Mind of William Shakespeare* (2009), with a brief detour to Germaine Greer's biography of Anne Hathaway, *Shakespeare's Wife* (2007).[4] A glimpse into the window of 'Shakespeare as lover' may reveal how biographers and readers around the millennium would like him to be as a wooer, lover, and husband.[5]

Park Honan, *Shakespeare: A Life* (1998)

In his 1998 biography *Shakespeare: A Life*, Park Honan vows to avoid '[i]maginative reconstructions and elaborate psychological theories' (ix), focusing instead on illustrating the 'Tudor social milieu' (xi) alongside 'the complex evolution in Shakespeare's mind and being' (xii). The 'evolution' that Honan charts is grounded in

Stratford; as such, this 'milieu' entails a sympathetic reading of the Warwickshire components as part and parcel of the overall life story, combining the Stratford man with the poet.

In Honan's account, the Shakespeare courtship involves a couple who have been friends from their youth; 'at no time, in his school years or later, had [Shakespeare] been a stranger at Anne's door' (74), and the two families knew each other well, since some of Richard Hathaway's debts were paid off by John Shakespeare. Despite this apparent financial inequality, the Shakespeare family respected the Hathaways, and they found Anne's 'age and practicality of benefit to their son', whose youth provided him with 'small practical experience', compared to her 'maturity of outlook' (82, 80). Honan sees the age difference between the Shakespeares as a virtue, rather than evidence of a predatory older woman. The death of her father and marriage of her brother may have inspired Anne 'to take a lover', and Honan's terminology gives both agency and choice to Anne (80). In this account of the courtship, Shakespeare felt a reciprocal love for Anne and was concerned to provide for her. As Honan puts it, Shakespeare was 'evidently in love, and his problem in November was to arrange for his future as quickly as he could' (81).

Building on his construction of an amiable marriage between childhood friends, Honan extends this interpretation throughout the poet's life: 'his apparently regular visits to Stratford, his investments and care to establish himself there, do not suggest he found Anne immaterial to his welfare' (87). Further, Honan turns to evidence from the first biographers of Shakespeare (Rowe and Theobald), both of whom 'imply [Shakespeare] chose marriage, not that he was trapped' (87). This Shakespeare sought a playwriting career not as an escape from his wife, but rather as the best way to support his family: 'The birth of twins virtually assured that Shakespeare's future would be more problematic, that he would be concerned to make up for lost time in a calling, and would undertake nearly anything required of him to get money. He would also know, surely, the pain of separation for long periods from a substantial and consoling family' (91).

In Honan's account, Shakespeare reluctantly left his support network in Stratford to 'better himself' and 'serve his family best' (91). The 'Shakespeare' that Honan thus constructs is both a successful artist and a responsible family man, whose 'complex evolution' (xii) did not necessitate rejecting his Warwickshire domestic life or discarding his wife, a woman with whom he was 'in love'.

Katherine Duncan-Jones, *Ungentle Shakespeare: Scenes from his Life* (2001)

In her quest to construct an 'ungentle Shakespeare', where she demotes Shakespeare 'from the lofty isolation to which he has been customarily elevated', Katherine Duncan-Jones's biography works against the tendency to see Shakespeare as 'liberal, unprejudiced, unselfish', or in other words, 'nice' (x). She accordingly fits the courtship/marriage piece into this paradigm. In Duncan-Jones's account, Hathaway was a 'free and independent' woman as a result of her father's death, which left her 'without much parental care or control' (17). This situation encouraged her to be 'a mature and spirited country girl' who 'exploited her freedom to consort with the local youth' (17). Richard Hathaway's death is translated in Duncan-Jones's account not as an opportunity for maturity or agency for Anne Hathaway, but rather for sexual looseness.

In contrast to the scenario of 'lovers' that we see in Honan's version, Duncan-Jones casts off the Shakespeare union as a 'dalliance' arising from a 'combination of boredom with the sexual curiosity natural to [Shakespeare's] years' and likely 'his first experience of sex' (17). In this story there is no courtship per se; Duncan-Jones uses the evidence of the lull in the harvest season to support her thesis of Shakespeare's 'boredom': 'sometime during this agricultural lull sexual relations began between the orphaned husbandman's daughter and the glover's eldest son' (17). The late summer also contributes to her scenario of Shakespeare's surging hormones: 'In the stickily hot August of 1582 Shakespeare was probably changing from boy into man, and experiencing the uncontrollable surges of testosterone accompanying that stage of development' (17). This was not the consummation of a relationship born of long-familiar families: Shakespeare was simply 'sowing wild oats', and instead of expressing an enduring affection for Hathaway, his sexual dalliances showed 'little or no thought to the lifelong problems he would reap' (17). Though Duncan-Jones admits that the Shakespeares could be a 'lovematch', she nevertheless reverts to the 'boredom' thesis of a Shakespeare 'stuck in uncongenial employment with no prospects' who found 'an outlet in sex' (18). In the 'ungentle' version of Shakespeare as lover, Anne Hathaway is not the object of courtship, but instead serves as relief for the 'boy' Shakespeare's surging sexual desire: 'the boy was grateful to Anne for her compliance, and persuaded himself that he loved her' (18).[6] The use of the term 'boy' here is key; Germaine Greer uses a similar term ('boy husband') to denigrate Shakespeare as a 'layabout husband good for nothing but spinning verses' (162). Shakespeare's relationship with Hathaway was simply a 'dalliance' arising from 'boredom', resulting in a 'compelled marriage' that 'had to be arranged in a hurry by Anne's kinsmen because of her pregnancy' (Duncan-Jones, 19, 17).

In this version, Stratford becomes a place where one passes the time with either physical labour or sex. Presumably, then, once Shakespeare discovers his artistic calling and matures sexually, he has no need to sow his wild oats or bother having sex with a 'spirited country girl' (17). There is virtually no courtship in this account; only a 'lifelong problem' the great poet must purge on his course to artistic success.

Stephen Greenblatt, *Will in the World: How Shakespeare Became Shakespeare* (2004)

The trajectory of artistic success, or 'how Shakespeare became Shakespeare', provides a framework for Stephen Greenblatt's best-selling biography *Will in the World*. As I have argued elsewhere, Greenblatt assembles perhaps the most uncomplimentary account of Shakespeare's marriage written in that decade.[7] Throughout *Will in the World*, Greenblatt marshals evidence to support an extended narrative of Shakespeare as an artist trapped in a loveless marriage, miserably yoked to a woman who cannot share his art, from whom he must eventually escape to find love, success, and sexual satisfaction. Greenblatt headlines his discussion of Shakespeare's marriage with the foreboding chapter title 'Wooing, Wedding, and Repenting'. Although this Shakespeare may have been sexually attracted to Anne, his parents objected to the marriage because he 'was not making a great match' (121); a reluctant and unwilling Shakespeare was thus 'dragged to the altar' to marry a woman he viewed with 'distaste, and contempt' and who 'filled him with revulsion' (124, 123, 129).[8] Indeed, in this tale, there was no courtship based on love, but instead just a 'fumbling adolescent effort' (120) resulting in the fateful conception of daughter Susanna and in much 'repenting'.

Like Duncan-Jones's 'ungentle' construction of Shakespeare, which demotes Anne Hathaway to a 'dalliance' with a 'spirited country girl' inspired by a combination of boredom, summer heat, and teenage hormones, Greenblatt constructs a narrative of a 'disastrous mistake' that Shakespeare must abandon in order to attain his 'amazing success story' (12). As a woman who could neither read nor write, this Anne Hathaway had no connection with this Shakespeare, who felt the 'frustrated longing for spousal intimacy' (129).[9] As well as the separation inherent in a forced union between a poetic genius and an illiterate Midlands woman, Greenblatt also secures his view of Shakespeare the 'repentant' groom by making a case for the religious differences between the Shakespeares, who 'almost certainly leaned toward Catholicism', and the Hathaways, who 'almost certainly leaned in the opposite direction' (118). Given the vast divide between hero and heroine in this tale, it makes sense that in planning for his burial, 'the last thing [Shakespeare] wanted was to be mingled with the woman he married' (147). The main flaw for the hero Shakespeare in this story is his return to Stratford, which does not allow for a full-scale obliteration of his sexual 'mistake'.

Peter Ackroyd, *Shakespeare: The Biography* (2005)

Departing from Greenblatt's narrative, Peter Ackroyd maintains that 'far from being a *mésalliance* or forced marriage ... the partnership of William Shakespeare and Anne Hathaway could have been an eminently sensible arrangement' (88). Inspired by Shakespeare's successful record as a savvy businessman, Ackroyd reads this quality back into the courtship, arguing that Shakespeare 'may even have exercised a good deal of caution, or common sense, in his choice of lifelong partner. This was thoroughly in keeping with his practical and business-like approach to all of the affairs of the world' (88). Ackroyd's terms are important here: this shrewdly intelligent Shakespeare would choose a 'lifelong partner' and would not be subject to the 'urges of testosterone' that characterize Duncan-Jones's Shakespeare, nor would Ackroyd's Shakespeare make the 'disastrous mistake' of Greenblatt's hero.

For Ackroyd, the courtship and subsequent marriage are part of Shakespeare's adroit business acumen; as such, the poet does not need to jettison his wife en route to London success. This account of the Shakespeare courtship shows a Shakespeare cognizant of the practical problems of wooing indoors at the Hathaway cottage, since its 'timber construction' made it 'a box of noise, so courtship would have been untenable as well as uncomfortable' (91). Ackroyd's clever Shakespeare would be too astute to carry on a courtship in these conditions, since 'from the upstairs bedchambers you can hear everything in the rooms below and, through the cracks in the floorboards, see everything as well' (91). Instead, the courtship is relocated in the full natural splendour of the Warwickshire countryside, again showing a poet who leverages his assets (a pastoral setting) to achieve his desired outcome (a lifelong partnership). A man of 'judgement and intelligence', this savvy Shakespeare would not be so reckless as to copulate in a 'stickily hot August' with 'little or no thought to his future', as the Shakespeare of Duncan-Jones does.

Yet even so, one cannot get around the fact that Shakespeare was only eighteen when daughter Susanna's conception occurred. Ackroyd's solution to this is to suggest that the age difference between the Shakespeares could imply 'sexual self-confidence on Shakespeare's part', rather than carelessness or imprudence, and to affirm that accounts of the Shakespeare courtship must do 'justice to Shakespeare's judgment and intelligence which, even at the age of eighteen, might have been acute' (88).

René Weis, *Shakespeare Revealed: A Biography* (2007)

In *Shakespeare Revealed*, René Weis's account of Shakespeare's life is a story that 'begins and ends in a Midlands market town' (3), with a focus on 'the material reality of sixteenth-century Stratford' (4–5). Because Weis's goal is to emphasize the Stratford parts of Shakespeare's biography, it is logical that he would give the Warwickshire components (and the marriage being one of the most prominent aspects of this piece) a positive interpretation, unlike Greenblatt's narrative, which constructs Stratford and Hathaway as something Shakespeare could not wait to escape on his journey to the metropolis of London, where he sought sexual and artistic satisfaction.

To help equalize the Shakespeares, instead of providing an older, perhaps domineering Anne Hathaway, and a younger, innocent 'boy' Shakespeare, Weis offers the possibility that the Shakespeares were closer in age, which would defuse the 'predatory older woman' myth. The only evidence for the eight-year gap between William and Anne is the inscription on her tombstone, which states she was 67 when she died; Weis proposes that 'the numbers 1 and 7 are easily confused in inscriptions', so perhaps there is only a two-year gap between husband and wife (51). Though Weis admits that it is impossible to know how William and Anne met, or how they 'found the opportunity' to have sex, he uses Ophelia's lines ('Young men will do't if they come to't' and 'Before you tumbled me, / You promised me to wed') to argue that in *Hamlet* Shakespeare was 'recalling his own teenage sexual encounters', but in real life he 'honour[ed] his commitment to Anne, and married her' (52).[10]

Proposing that Anne Hathaway's mother was a Whateley of Temple Grafton, and that Anne returned there after her father's death, Weis sees Anne Hathaway and Anna Whateley as one and the same (54–55, 58). He further suggests that perhaps Anne was related to the Whateley family living in Stratford, and 'in the months between her father's death in September 1581 and November 1582 she was in the habit of visiting her relatives in Henley Street' (58).

The fact that the Shakespeare and Hathaway families knew each other is fodder for imagining a scenario for their relationship. Weis offers an intriguing possibility for 'the odd business of Shakespeare's father dragging himself out of retirement from the town council to vote just at the time when his son was having sex with Anne Hathaway' (57). Weis also suggests that the coincidence between the town council meeting of 2 September 1582 and the conception of Susanna Shakespeare, may have involved a Verona-like feud between the Shakespeares and the Whateleys:

> John Shakespeare's vote against Whateley [for mayor] appears to have been a hostile act, confirming that Anne was indeed related to this family, and that the two Henley Street clans had come to grief over the love affair between her and Will ... John Shakespeare rejoined the council briefly and voted as he did to remind Whateley of his status before all assembled peers. (60)

Like Romeo and Juliet, William and Anne marry despite the tension between these 'Henley Street clans'.

Because Shakespeare's Warwickshire is central to Weis's conception of the poet, he thus maintains that Shakespeare's 'life in Henley Street may have been happier than has sometimes been assumed', on the basis of depictions of home life in the plays and poems, such as the 'wonderful portrayals of children', including little Macduff, Juliet, Mamillius, and Perdita (66–67). He contends that 'there is no reason to think that Shakespeare did not love Anne Hathaway at this time, that he and she did not have many intimate conversations, and particularly about the rearing of their children', also on the basis of sonnet 143 and because he was 'bewitched by his twins', as seen in *The Comedy of Errors* and *Twelfth Night* (66–67).

Jonathan Bate, *Soul of the Age: A Biography of the Mind of William Shakespeare* (2009)

Jonathan Bate's *Soul of the Age* places much emphasis on the Warwickshire components, due in part to his structural plan for the biography. Rather than writing a linear narrative (a 'deadening march of chronological sequence', in his words), Bate instead 'loop[s] backward and forward through his life' to illustrate his conception of Shakespeare's life as 'cyclical, not sequential', since 'the influence of our early childhood stays with us all our lives' (xviii). This format thus precipitates a weight given to the Warwickshire pieces of the biography throughout the narrative, not just in chapters focusing on the 1580s and 1610s.

Bate admits that it is 'impossible to unearth the significance' of the age difference between the Shakespeares, but he offers a variety of possibilities: 'Sexual precocity? Passionate ardor? A cunning way with seductive words? Carelessness when it came to the moment?' (150). To solve the Anne Hathaway/Anna Whateley conundrum, he suggests an answer which both explains the two names and situates Anne Hathaway in a position of power. Anne Hathaway may have married a Whateley in Temple Grafton, and then may have been widowed, 'giving young Will the opportunity to move in swiftly with the offer of sexual solace and the hope of a widow's ample marriage portion' (152). In this narrative, Anne Hathaway has something to offer beyond the seductress characterized by Anthony Burgess in *Nothing Like the Sun* (1964).[11] She is a desirable woman because of her financial security, not just an outlet to satisfy teenage lust.

In keeping with this narrative, Bate asserts that 'It is a biographical myth to suppose that Will was marched off to a shotgun wedding by friends of the Hathaways who were incensed at hearing that Miss Anne was in the family way' (152), in contrast to Duncan-Jones and Greenblatt.[12] Bate suggests two examples from Shakespeare's canon which may account for this type of 'distorting lens' often used by biographers: *Venus and Adonis*, 'in which an innocent boy is seduced by a sexually voracious older woman (or rather goddess)' and *The Taming of the Shrew*, where 'it has too often been assumed that because Shakespeare wrote [*Shrew*], his wife must have been one' (152–53).

Rejecting both of these models, he offers his own version of Shakespeare as wooer – Bassanio from *The Merchant of Venice*, who is 'clever but cold, an adventurer and a wordsmith who always looks after himself, a man on the lookout for a wealthy woman to help him out of a financial crisis and who has the good fortune to find one who is also beautiful, ultraintelligent, and attracted to him' (153). By extension, Anne Hathaway is then Portia, a literate, witty, and intelligent counterpart to Bassanio, but as Bate readily admits, 'there is no more evidence for this fancy' than for the Adonis or *Shrew* arguments (153). Even so, the imaginary narrative he suggests through the Portia/Bassanio relationship is strikingly more generous to Anne Hathaway than many other biographers have been.

Bate resists the temptation to construct one narrative for the Shakespeare marriage, offering instead two interpretations: 'a grand passion prematurely consummated' or 'an arranged union between two families who knew each other well' (153). Either option presumes a connection between the Shakespeares, either based on 'passion' or on family connections. Like Peter Ackroyd, Bate also uses Shakespeare's financial acumen as evidence for his mature attitude to love: 'making enough money to keep the family going, and sustaining a marriage for well over thirty years' were 'not the achievements of the romantic lover', but rather 'manifestations of love' (161).

Conclusion

The recent interest in the Stratford pieces of Shakespeare's life has brought prominence to the depiction of Anne Hathaway as part of the biography over the last few decades. Departing from Duncan-Jones's 'ungentle' poet and Greenblatt's tortured artist who cannot wait to escape his Stratford life and the stifling wife who dominates it, these biographies seem to offer a redemptive view of Shakespeare's Stratford life. The more desperate, haphazard, and spurious the relationship with Anne Hathaway, the more weight the biographer seems to put on the London aspects of the biography. In contrast, the more emphasis is placed on the Warwickshire components of Shakespeare's life, the more crucial it is to construct a positive, productive, and supportive version of Shakespeare the wooer, suitor and husband. We may point to a number of factors that prompted such a shift: the desire to create a unified 'Shakespeare the poet' / 'Shakespeare the man from Stratford', Greer's polemical biography of Hathaway and feminist scholarship in general, domestic studies that have re-imagined the value of the early modern home, and perhaps even contemporary debates over motherhood and the re-evaluation of 'women's work'.[13] In fact, Paul Edmondson's work on the significance of the archaeological dig at New Place, Shakespeare's last home, suggests a more crucial role for both Stratford and for Anne Hathaway in Shakespeare's life. According to estimates, New Place had ten fireplaces (possibly up to twenty rooms), and an entourage of servants; as Edmondson points out, such an estate makes it unlikely that Shakespeare would spend more time than necessary away in rented lodgings in London.[14] In turn, biographers might reinvest the Shakespeare courtship and marriage with a more permanent and meaningful history, given this new evidence about Shakespeare's life in Stratford.

Katherine Scheil is Professor of English at the University of Minnesota. She is the author of *The Taste of the Town: Shakespearian Comedy and the Early Eighteenth-Century Theatre* (2003), *She Hath Been Reading: Women and Shakespeare Clubs in America* (2012) and *Imagining Shakespeare's Wife: The Afterlife of Anne Hathaway* (2018).

Notes

1. The licence issued on 27 November 1582 in the diocese of Worcester lists 'William Shaxpere and Anna Whateley of Temple Grafton', and the marriage bond of 28 November 1582 in the Worcester registry lists 'William Shagspere and Anne Hathwey of Stratford'. The two women's names provide the inspiration for two separate characters in Laurie Lawlor's teen novel *The Two Loves of William Shakespeare* (New York: Holiday House, 2006), one of many imaginative reworkings of this material. See also Graham Holderness, *Nine Lives of William Shakespeare* (London: Continuum, 2011), 98–99.
2. For a discussion of the interplay between biographical accounts and critical accounts of the courtship and marriage story, see my *Imagining Shakespeare's Wife: The Afterlife of Anne Hathaway* (Cambridge: Cambridge University Press, 2018), 89–169. David Bevington provides a brief discussion of the problematic relationship between the life and the works in his chapter entitled 'Sex'. See *Shakespeare and Biography* (Oxford: Oxford University Press, 2010), 31–51.

3. As Barbara Everett remarked (*Times Literary Supplement*, 17 August 2007), 'of Shakespearian biography in particular there has been a flood over the last few decades, good, bad and indifferent'. Similarly, Anne Barton writes that biographies of Shakespeare are 'alarmingly on the increase', and she counts at least one biography every year between 1996 and 2006. See 'The One and Only', *The New York Review of Books*, 11 May 2006. Both Barton and Everett do not account for biographies by Greer, Bate, Weis, Holderness and Potter.
4. Parenthetical citations throughout this chapter come from the following editions: Park Honan, *Shakespeare: A Life* (Oxford: Oxford University Press, 1998); Katherine Duncan-Jones, *Ungentle Shakespeare: Scenes from his Life* (London: Arden Shakespeare, 2001); Stephen Greenblatt, *Will in the World: How Shakespeare Became Shakespeare* (New York: W. W. Norton, 2004); Peter Ackroyd, *Shakespeare: The Biography* (New York: Nan A. Talese, Doubleday, 2005); René Weis, *Shakespeare Revealed: A Biography* (London: John Murray, 2007); Jonathan Bate, *Soul of the Age: A Biography of the Mind of William Shakespeare* (New York: Random House, 2009); and Germaine Greer, *Shakespeare's Wife* (London: Bloomsbury, 2007).
5. 'Shakespeare as lover' is one of Douglas Lanier's 'interlocking mythic narratives' for Shakespeare biography. See *Shakespeare and Modern Popular Culture* (Oxford: Oxford University Press, 2002), 150. As Graham Holderness has pointed out, 'the erotic adventures of Shakespeare "in love" [is] something we literally know nothing whatsoever about'. *Nine Lives of William Shakespeare*, 96. See Holderness's chapter 'Shakespeare in Love: "Husband I come"' (96–105). Perhaps the most extreme imagining of 'Shakespeare as lover' comes from Erica Jong's novel *Serenissima*, where the central character, Hollywood actress Jessica Pruitt, goes back in time to sleep with Shakespeare:
    After all, who would dare describe love with the greatest poet the world has ever known, the poet who himself defined love? To detail organs, motions, sheets, wet spots, would be too gross, too literal, too finally deflating! It is quite one thing to imagine the poet of poets abed with his convent Juliet or his bisexual earl – but for a mere player like myself to go back in time, bed him, and then tell tales out of school? Fie on't! Was Will Shakespeare good in bed? Let the reader judge!
    Erica Jong, *Serenissima* (New York: Dell, 1987), 295–96.
    The consummation is successful, as the novel ends with 'a bassinet trimmed with blue and silver ribbons, the baby, my little lion, cries' (381).
6. In an interview with Arthur Maltby, Duncan-Jones elaborates on the summer sex scene she constructs for the Shakespeares:
    But as for the conception of Susanna, all I was doing was assuming a normal period of gestation, combining that with the known (young) age of the father, plus the climatic conditions and rural activities normal to the time of year when conception took place. I also start from the premise that making Anne Hathaway pregnant, given that she was not, economically or socially, a hugely desirable bride, and with John Shakespeare practically bankrupt, was not at all a prudent procedure. It seems to me reasonable to presume that the pregnancy was the outcome of impulse without foresight. This would also explain what appears to have been her husband's later indifference to her ... [where] she was occasionally left short of money even around 1600 when her husband had become a very wealthy man.

Duncan-Jones adds that 'As for overdoing the imaginative element: I was not writing a doctoral thesis, but a book that ... was aimed at a popular market, albeit grounded in traditional scholarship'. *Shakespeare as a Challenge for Literary Biography: A History of Biographies of Shakespeare since 1898* (Lewiston, NY: Edwin Mellen Press, 2009), 227–28.

7. In 'Filling in the "Wife-Shaped Void": The Contemporary Afterlife of Anne Hathaway', *Shakespeare Survey* 63 (2010), 433–45, I discuss Greenblatt's strikingly derogatory interpretation of Hathaway.

8. Germaine Greer challenges this story; she asserts that Anne 'was a spinster and at her own disposal, but only misogyny would assume on the available evidence that she was pushing for the marriage and Will was resisting' (*Shakespeare's Wife*, 73).

9. In contrast to Greenblatt's argument that the Shakespeares had no intimate connection, Lois Potter suggests that they may have 'met in a theatrical context' and courted during the 'highly erotic' atmosphere of theatrical productions for Whitsuntide in Stratford. *The Life of William Shakespeare: A Critical Biography* (Hoboken, New Jersey: John Wiley and Sons, 2012), 56.

10. Like several biographers, Honan sees a relationship between Shakespeare's own life and his 'sympathetic' attitude to Claudio and Julietta in *Measure for Measure* (52).

11. In his often maligned novel *Nothing Like the Sun* (1964), Anthony Burgess creates an Anne Hathaway whom he describes as 'a young country woman as a sort of sexual monster' in order to produce a Shakespeare that was 'very heavily seduced and, eventually, rendered sick ... of the varied patterns of heterosexual lust'. Anthony Burgess, 'Genesis and Headache', in *Afterwords*, ed. Thomas McCormack (New York: Harper and Row, 1969), 36.

12. Lois Potter similarly doubts the shotgun wedding model: 'While Shakespeare's wedding may have been a shotgun affair, it is equally possible that he and Anne had been planning marriage for some time, or that, if their parents were reluctant to approve, the couple deliberately forced the issue' (56–57). Potter points out that the choice of Susanna's name, with its 'association with injured innocence ... might suggest an element of defiance on the part of the young couple' (58).

13. Here I am thinking of works such as Catherine Richardson's *Domestic Life and Domestic Tragedy in Early Modern England: The Material Life of the Household* (Manchester: Manchester University Press, 2006) and Wendy Wall's *Staging Domesticity: Household Work and English Identity in Early Modern Drama* (Cambridge: Cambridge University Press, 2002).

14. See Paul Edmondson, Kevin Colls and William Mitchell, *Finding Shakespeare's New Place: An Archaeological Biography* (Manchester: Manchester University Press, 2016).

Chapter 6
Biographical Aftershocks
Shakespeare and Marlowe in the Wake of 9/11

Robert Sawyer

As Ben Jonson seems to have correctly predicted in his poem attached to the First Folio of 1623, Shakespeare's works were destined not only to surpass those of his numerous contemporaries, such as Thomas Kyd, John Lyly, and Marlowe and his 'mighty line', but also those of earlier English writers, including Chaucer and Spenser.[1] Yet of all the English playwrights, only Christopher Marlowe remains a true 'rival' for Shakespeare's predominance as an author.

This chapter examines the relationship between Shakespeare and Marlowe as it has been portrayed in biographical forms in the early twenty-first century. I hope to demonstrate how present historical and aesthetical pressures, particularly the events following 9/11, shape the literary relationship between the two playwrights. The biographers who write about the rivalry are equally ripe for examination, for as Terence Hawkes reminds us, it is these critics who 'choose the facts ... and texts' and also 'do the perceiving'.[2]

Notes for this section begin on page 117.

As I have argued elsewhere, Marlowe was often portrayed in the twentieth century, particularly during the Cold War, as the 'evil and racy rival of the gentle and honest Shakespeare'.[3] Just six months before the 9/11 attacks on the World Trade Center and the Pentagon, however, Katherine Duncan-Jones's biography of Shakespeare burst on the scene and the political landscape was as altered as the biographical renderings of the two playwrights.[4] While I begin my survey with a brief review of Duncan-Jones's *Ungentle Shakespeare*, I focus more on biographical works which followed hers to show how twenty-first-century biography has already re-written the relationship.

Earliest Accounts

Although the facts are sparse in the earliest biographical accounts of the rivalry, we do know that Shakespeare and Marlowe were prominent figures in the London theatres between 1590 and 1593, and we can also be certain that both produced plays at the Rose. Perhaps even more significantly, both wrote history plays performed by Pembroke's Men and Lord Strange's Men.[5] The enclosed world of the London theatre, in fact, allows critics and biographers to speculate, as Juliet Dusinberre has, that the two 'were probably acquainted', while Stanley Wells goes one step further, positing that it is 'quite likely' that the two 'were friends'.[6] Robert Logan concludes that 'it would be less conceivable that they did not meet than that they did'.[7] As we know from the work of Andrew Gurr and others, the theatrical world Shakespeare and Marlowe inhabited was as intimate as it was innovative.[8]

Textual evidence also suggests some relationship between the two. For example, Shakespeare was almost certainly alluding to Marlowe as 'the dead shepherd' in *As You Like It*, when Phoebe quotes the line, 'Who ever loved that loved not at first sight?' (3.5.82), a phrase from Marlowe's *Hero and Leander* printed shortly before Shakespeare's play was first performed.[9] In Act 3, Touchstone the clown claims, 'When a man's verses cannot be understood, nor a man's good wit seconded with the forward child, understanding, it strikes a man more dead than a great reckoning in a little room' (3.3.10–13), probably an allusion to Marlowe's murder, which may have been the result of an argument over the 'reckoning', or bar bill, in Eleanor Bull's rooming house and tavern in Deptford.

Before moving to the twenty-first-century biographical renderings, it is worth looking at the origins of the so-called rivalry. One of the earliest published biographical accounts of the two playwrights set the stage for centuries to follow by contrasting Shakespeare with Marlowe. In 1592, Greene lay on his deathbed suffering from a 'banquet of Rhenish wine and pickled herring', according to Thomas Nashe (1.287–88), and seems to have completed his infamous *Groats-worth of Wit* at this same time.[10] This is the pamphlet with a letter attached referring to Shakespeare as an 'upstart Crow, beautified with our feathers', possessing a 'Tygers hart wrapt in a Players hyde' (12:144).[11] Even worse, Greene continues, this amateur from the country 'supposes he is as well able to bombast out a blank verse as the best of you', referring to actors performing the plays composed by three 'fellow scholars about this city', including Marlowe, and, in all likelihood, Thomas Nashe and George Peele.[12] As James Shapiro has noted, though the tract was 'intended as invective', the very mention of Shakespeare shows just 'how great a threat the young actor was becoming to the leading dramatists of the day', including Marlowe. Indeed, as Shapiro concludes, the work 'nicely illustrates the way in which parodic attempts [Greene's single line adaptation of Queen Margaret's speech in *3 Henry VI*] to contain a rival can boomerang, serving instead to confirm and legitimate the target of parody'.[13] Greene was obviously no Shakespeare, but the idea of parody, imitation, and even emulation would colour many contemporaries' comparisons when surveying the significant playwrights of the day.

After Greene's death, Henry Chettle produced a fair copy of the pamphlet for printing; his role in the production and editing of Greene's work is important for a number of reasons. In the 'Preface' to his next work, *Kind-Heart's Dream*, published shortly after Greene's work (1592), he not only identifies the aggrieved parties, but he also characterizes the playwrights who may have been offended, specifically Marlowe and Shakespeare.[14] First, Chettle denies responsibility for *Groatsworth*, but he also offers an apology (although a muted one in Marlowe's case), for printing the work. He begins by declaring that Greene, who had died just three months earlier, had left 'many papers in sundry Booke sellers hands', including his *Groatsworth*. Chettle then explains his role in the work: 'To be briefe, I writ it over, and, as neare as I could, followed the copy [of Greene's handwritten version], onely in that letter I put something out, but in the whole booke not a word in, for I protest it was all Green's'.[15] What this seems to suggest is that while Chettle admits to having had a hand in censoring part of the attached letter, he protests that he did not compose or alter a single word of the pamphlet itself.[16]

In addition to the personal disclaimer, Chettle apologizes to any writers that may have been offended by the letter attached to *Groatsworth*, the one addressed 'to divers play-makers'.[17] It has come to his attention, Chettle explains, that the note was 'offensively by one or two of them taken', almost certainly referring to Shakespeare and Marlowe. But at this point, he makes a clear distinction between the two playwrights' personal lives, concluding that although he was not 'acquainted' with either of the writers 'that take offence', he adds that 'with one of them [he] care[s] not if [he] never be'. Later in the passage, he even defends Shakespeare's personal character because numerous people 'have reported his uprightness of dealing'.[18]

This opposition between 'gentle' Will Shakespeare and 'blasphemous' Kit Marlowe began almost immediately following this document, heightened perhaps by the controversial death of Marlowe in May of 1593. But this very distinction, so often seen in the *sympathy* exhibited for Shakespeare and the *antipathy* toward Marlowe, may be an essential aspect of any theoretical understanding of the biographical similitude between the playwrights. As Michel Foucault explains: 'Sympathy is an instance of the *Same* so strong and so insistent that it will not rest content to be merely one of the forms of likeness; it has the dangerous power of assimilating, of rendering things identical to one another, of mingling them, of causing their individuality to disappear'.[19] That is 'why sympathy is compensated for by its twin, antipathy', which 'maintains the isolation of things and prevents their assimilation'. In other words, if the transgressive Marlowe did not exist, seen in such biographical inventions as the Baines Note,[20] it seems it was necessary to invent him as a foil to the kinder, gentler Shakespeare.

Twenty-First Century

If Marlowe was usually characterized in the twentieth century as the sexier and somewhat seamier *doppelgänger* to Shakespeare, that thread of thought began to unravel with the publication of Duncan-Jones's biography of Shakespeare in 2001. Her book challenged all the conventional wisdom in Shakespeare biography, for in her reading Shakespeare was not only mean-spirited and vain, but also a social climber, a sort of 'mushroom gentleman' who had 'risen too far, too fast', and worse, had achieved his status by profiting from a 'morally dubious profession'.[21] In addition, according to Duncan-Jones, the local population in Stratford 'may have felt that the wealthy Shakespeares were doing far too little for the poor and homeless', and, therefore, were 'resolutely evad[ing] civic responsibilities'. Reviews of her book were impassioned on both sides; some called it 'engrossing' and 'courageous';[22] others thought it 'single-minded' and 'sometimes distorted'.[23]

The publicity over the book, however, only seemed to swell the tide of Shakespearean biography based on conjecture. While the limits of this chapter will only allow me to consider a few post-9/11 biographies of the two playwrights, I hope to show how their take on the 'rivalry' reflects their own moment in history. I would like to look at four chronological responses to the 9/11 catastrophe and then pair them with the biographical versions of the rivalry which appeared at approximately the same time. Taking them in order, I will categorize them as follows: crisis, credibility, conjecture, and conspiracy.

Crisis

While I understand the peril of making connections between an internationally tragic event such as 9/11 and literary biography, I think it is possible to see how in some ways the assault forced Americans to break through their illusion of safety, finally to find themselves, according to Slavoj Žižek, in 'the desert of the real', as the American 'holiday from history' suddenly ended.[24] That the destruction wrought by the terrorist attack immediately became a worldwide phenomenon is suggested by Jacques Derrida's claim, just two months later, that the event had 'taken over our public space and our private lives'[25] after the twin towers – 'the capital of capital' – were destroyed.[26]

Although it would be four more years before London experienced its own version of 9/11 (on 7/7/2005), Tony Blair (recorded in the *Guardian* on 2 October 2001) seemed confident in asserting the shared Anglo-American response in times of crisis: 'We were with you at the first. We will stay with you to the last'.[27] George Bush's poodle or not, he was probably correct in proclaiming that '[t]here is a coming together' and that the 'power of community is asserting itself', for if 'order and stability' do not 'exist elsewhere', Blair continued, 'it is unlikely to exist here'.[28]

The relationship between artistic production and 9/11 (and, perhaps by extension, 7/7) in both countries has also been hotly debated. For instance, Herbert Blau, writing in 2003, felt comfortable in claiming that '[i]f the fall of the Iron Curtain seemed for some years to open things up, Homeland Security ... is closing things down'.[29] And while he admits that art may depict terrorists and terrorism 'with harrowing accuracy', he poignantly adds that art 'hasn't much to tell us, at this baffling historical moment, about how to turn the others off'.[30] He concludes on a somewhat ambiguous note: 'The fact is that no immediate change of heart will diminish the perilous threat of multitudinous others who look upon us as a menace to what they believe' or those who portray the West as 'a domineering power without the capacity ... to feel their pain' due to our 'moral blindness'.[31] Still, Blau concedes, since '[m]oral blindness' and 'spiritual blindness' are 'traditional concerns of art, particularly tragic drama', then perhaps 'the crisis, if irreparable, is so painfully explored as to bring wisdom from suffering'[32] or at the very least an 'aestheticizing of the apocalypse', for better or for worse.[33] Perhaps the world would end with a bang instead of a whimper after all.[34]

It is also worth remembering that, in E. Ann Kaplan's terms, 'trauma produces new subjects, that the political-ideological context within which traumatic events occur shapes their impact, and that it is hard to separate individual and collective trauma'.[35] Thus the response to 9/11 across the artistic spectrum and across the sea was both personal and profound.[36] So, it only makes sense that some of the 'quiet trauma' produced by 9/11 would seep into new biographical presentations of the Marlowe and Shakespeare connection.[37]

Credibility

The 9/11 attacks, and the incredulity they engendered, led to a series of charges of cover-up and conspiracy (a point we will return to shortly), and responses to these charges. In this heated time, at least one biographer of Marlowe urged caution and restraint in depicting the relationship between the two playwrights, just as sensible politicians urged a similar measured response to the attacks in New York and Washington. Constance Kuriyama's book (mentioned above) grew, in part, out of an earlier essay she had written urging caution in biographical speculation about either playwright *or* the relationship between them. In her essay, 'Marlowe, Shakespeare, and the Nature of Biographical Evidence', Kuriyama posits that while legal documents are the most useful of sources, this type of 'evidence, while quite direct and generally reliable, is rarely exciting or illuminating'.[38] She then asks how we should deal with a 'body of lore' which she describes as 'contentious hearsay evidence'.[39] The question for biographers then becomes, in her legal phrasing, 'what criteria do we use to distinguish between admissible and inadmissible hearsay evidence' when trying to present a portrait of either playwright or their relationship?[40] She proposes three questions that must be asked of each piece: 'First of all, how inherently probable is the hearsay evidence? Second, is the hearsay evidence supported by other evidence, preferably evidence of a more substantial sort? Finally, how much credibility can we assign to the source or sources of the hearsay?'[41]

In the wake of the 9/11 attacks such careful consideration of evidence dominated the investigation into the bombings and the terrorists, and it seems to have influenced her reading of the Marlowe–Shakespeare relationship as well. For in her Marlowe biography she avoids all speculation about the two playwrights, even concluding that Marlowe's death resulted from no more than he and Ingram Frizer 'quarreling over the bill', as this is 'perfectly consistent with what we know about Marlowe', rather than an attempt by the Privy Council to hush him up.[42] Her 'just the facts, Ma'am' approach seemed balanced and fair, a solid corrective to the speculation that was about to run rampant not only in the case of 9/11, but also for literary biography generally, and the rivalry between the two playwrights specifically.[43]

Conjecture

The response to 9/11 as noted above, and particularly the media coverage, was filled with pointed fingers, sabre rattling, sweeping generalizations, and incorrect 'conjectures' which ultimately led to the second Gulf War. The Bush administration's conjecture (and I use the word cautiously here) that somehow Iraq initiated or abetted the bombings was the most dominant instance of such thinking, but a host of other regrettable conjectures followed.

At about the same time, Lois Potter, in an essay entitled 'Having Our Will: Imagination in Recent Shakespeare Biographies' noted that many of the recent books on Shakespeare, but most specifically Stephen Greenblatt's *Will in the World* (2004), amounted to 'interpretation more than biography ... achiev[ing] clarity in part through omission'.[44] This point parallels well with Hawkes' reminder that so-called New Historicists may be guilty of 'discount[ing] the nature of the choosing and the omission, the selections and suppressions that determine' their take on a given subject.[45] Potter later concedes that contemporary 'biographers of Shakespeare would be lost if they were not allowed to ask unanswerable questions', and she goes on to suggest, in a more materialist moment, that the marketplace also influences the content of such works: 'I would guess', she conjectures, 'that most biographies are the product of a publisher's desire for a book that will supersede, rather than complement, all previous ones'.[46]

In Greenblatt's reading of the Shakespeare–Marlowe rivalry we see his 'imagination' and conjecture writ large. For example, the biography speculates that Shakespeare 'almost certainly' saw *Tamburlaine* at the Rose Theatre, and 'he probably went back again and again'. The performance 'may indeed have been one of the first' Shakespeare ever saw in London, 'perhaps *the* first' (italics in the original) according to Greenblatt, and he concludes that 'it appears to have had upon him an intense, visceral, indeed life-transforming impact'.[47]

Greenblatt goes on to suggest that after hearing Edward Alleyn reciting Marlowe's mighty lines, Shakespeare 'must have said to himself something like, "You are not in Stratford anymore"' as 'the rhetoric of triumph' in the play became 'ever more intoxicating'.[48] This alleged encounter with Marlowe's work was, Greenblatt conjectures, 'a crucial experience for Shakespeare, a challenge to all of his aesthetic and moral and professional assumptions'.[49] He later proclaims that if 'Marlowe [had] not existed' Shakespeare would have 'written plays, but those plays would have been decisively different'. According to Greenblatt, this experience even changed Shakespeare's career path: 'the decision not to make his living as an actor alone but to try also to write for the stage on which he performed' came via 'Marlowe's influence'. While all this may be somewhat true, like the historical fiction that came to dominate the best-seller list following 9/11, none of it is based in fact. But facts did not get in the way of Greenblatt any more than they did the 'truthers',[50] the still active group that believes a conspiracy, and nothing but a conspiracy, could have caused 9/11.

Conspiracy

The notion of a conspiracy causing or aiding 9/11 has been so thoroughly investigated and repeated that I do not need to rehash these imaginative notions here, but it may be worth remembering that in 2005 both the *Scientific American* (February) and *Popular Mechanics* (March) felt the need to devote cover stories to debunking such theories. As the editor of *Popular Mechanics* explained, 'Sadly, the noble search for truth is now being hijacked by a growing army of conspiracy theorists', in part, he believes, because in a 'culture shaped by Oliver Stone movies and "X-Files" episodes, it is apparently getting harder for simple, hard facts to hold their own against elaborate, shadowing theorizing'.[51]

I would propose that this same culture of conspiracy infected the world of Marlowe and Shakespearean studies. For instance, in 2004, Shakespeare's Globe Theatre in London held an 'authorship conference' widely reported in newspapers such as *The New York Times*. In an article entitled 'To Be or Not to Be ... Shakespeare', the author interviewed the director of the Globe at the time, Mark Rylance, who claimed that the 'candidacy of Marlowe was ... interesting to [him]', but Rylance also thought there were multiple candidates, and added that there is 'just so much evidence that you cannot write Bacon out of these plays' either. He concluded that he presented a 'particular difficulty for a lot of scholars'. Rylance's suppositions were countered by Brian Vickers, who in an email exchange with the author of the article, responded that '[n]o serious scholar I know of bothers with the doubters'.[52]

This counterthrust by many in the academic community, however, did nothing to quell the clamour of the anti-Stratfordians, our own version of the 9/11 'Truthers'. For instance, the following year, Rodney Bolt published *History Play: The Lives and Afterlife of Christopher Marlowe*.[53] This work at least wore its fiction on its dust jacket; one critic called it 'bold and wickedly fun new fictional biography', while making sure it was not mistaken for 'another standard anti-Stratfordian tract attempting to settle the authorship debate' because 'Bolt freely admits he's making this up'. The book also garnered decent reviews in *The Times Literary Supplement* and *The Kirkus Review*.[54] I see this book, however, as a bridge from the Greenblatt biography to a rash of books that do *not* admit to the fiction of Marlowe's 'authorship' of Shakespeare's plays. These include, but are not limited to, *The Shakespeare Enigma* (Polair 2004); *The Truth Will Out: Unmasking the Real Shakespeare* (Harper Perennial 2007); *Marlowe's Ghost: the Blacklisting of the Man who was Shakespeare* by Daryl Pinksen (iUniverse 2008); *The Marlowe-Shakespeare Connection: A New Study of the Authorship Question* (McFarland 2008); and *The Shakespeare Controversy: An Analysis of the Authorship Theories* (McFarland 2009). While conceding that these presses are not the most scholarly, and one was even self-published, the conspiracy theory movement was strong enough to prompt James Shapiro, one of our more judicious Shakespearean critics, to respond with *Contested Will: Who Wrote Shakespeare?*, published in 2010 by Simon and Schuster.

Conclusion

The proliferation of conspiracy theories since 9/11 regarding Shakespeare has now spread to the world of popular culture, in part, by moving from print circles to cinematic 'exposés'. In Roland Emmerich's film, *Anonymous: William Shakespeare Revealed* (2011), the promotional material asks in bold letters, 'Was Shakespeare a Fraud?', and the movie answers that question by trotting out that old standby candidate, the Earl of Oxford as the real author of the plays.[55] While the rivalry with Marlowe is not a central feature of the movie, wild conjecture is. As Douglas Lanier has posited, the movie displays a 'pile-up of factual errors', borrowing more from a long 'list of intercinematic' references rather than any reliance on 'fidelity to the verifiable historical record'.[56] While the anti-Stratfordian movement has a long, albeit dubious, history, it seems that it is only in a post-9/11 climate that such a film could have been so widely circulated. As Stephen Marche explains, the film gets the 'Oliver Stone/Da Vinci Code treatment', a comment that sounds very similar to the editorial characterization of 9/11 conspiracy theorists mentioned above in relation to the 'Truthers'.[57]

Crises, conjecture, conspiracy, controversy – such stuff as dreams (and nightmares) are made on. While we can never really 'capture' the past, as Hawkes reminds us,[58] we can at least examine the ways in which the present shapes our version of the past; and the Shakespeare–Marlowe connection, as I hope I have shown, is certainly not immune to such re-presentations in the early twenty-first-century biographies. In doing so, we learn as much about the critics, and the present in which they are situated, as we do about any so-called rivalry between the playwrights.

Acknowledgements

Part of this work was completed thanks to funding by the Marco Institute at the University of Tennessee in the form of a Lindsay Young Visiting Faculty Fellow. I want to thank the director, Heather Hirschfeld, for her generous support.

Robert Sawyer is Professor of English at East Tennessee State University, where he teaches Shakespeare, Victorian Literature and Literary Criticism. He is the author of *Victorian Appropriations of Shakespeare* (Fairleigh Dickinson UP, 2003), *Marlowe and Shakespeare: The Critical Rivalry* (Palgrave, 2017), and *Shakespeare Between the World Wars* (Palgrave, 2019). He is also co-editor of *Shakespeare and Appropriation* (Routledge, 1999) and *Harold Bloom's Shakespeare* (Palgrave, 2001).

Notes

1. Charlton Hinman and Peter W. M. Blayney, eds, *The First Folio of Shakespeare* (New York: W. W. Norton, 1968, 1996), 9.
2. Terence Hawkes, *Shakespeare in the Present* (London and New York: Routledge, 2002), 3. For more on the so-called 'rivalry' between Marlowe and Shakespeare, see my *Marlowe and Shakespeare: The Critical Rivalry* (Houndmills, Basingstoke: Palgrave, 2017).
3. Robert Sawyer, 'Shakespeare and Marlowe: Re-Writing the Relationship', *Critical Survey* 21.3 (2009), 41–58; 53.
4. Katherine Duncan-Jones, *Ungentle Shakespeare: Scenes from his Life* (London: Arden, 2001).
5. Lawrence Manley posits that Strange's Men 'may have been the first company to attempt permanent residence in London', and, unlike the Queen's Men, this company 'courted controversy' with their 'innovative plays by a new generation of playwrights, among them Kyd, Marlowe, and Shakespeare' (254). See Lawrence Manley, 'From Strange's Men to Pembroke's Men: *2 Henry VI* and *The First Part of the Contention*', *Shakespeare Quarterly* 54.3 (2003), 253–87.

6. Juliet Dusinberre, introduction to *As You Like It*, ed. Juliet Dusinberre (London: Arden, 2006), 81; Stanley Wells, *Shakespeare and Co.* (New York: Pantheon Books, 2006), 77.
7. Robert Logan, *Shakespeare's Marlowe: The Influence of Christopher Marlowe on Shakespeare's Artistry* (Aldershot, England: Ashgate, 2007), 3.
8. See Andrew Gurr, *The Shakespearean Stage: 1574–1642* (Cambridge: Cambridge University Press, 2009).
9. All quotations refer to Juliet Dusinberre, ed., *As You Like It*.
10. Thomas Nashe, *The Works of Thomas Nashe*, vol. 1, ed. R. B. McKerrow, rev. F. P. Wilson (Oxford: Oxford University Press, 1958).
11. *The Life and Complete Works in Prose and Verse of Robert Greene*, ed. A. B. Grosart, 15 vols (London, 1881–86). F. E. Halliday suggests that Greene's 'outburst becomes comprehensible if Shakespeare was an actor' with a 'company to which Greene sold most of his plays'. While the reference may suggest that Shakespeare was a good actor, Halliday goes on to conclude that he was 'merely a hireling ... strutting in the feathers of Greene's poetry as if it were his own'. See F. E. Halliday, *The Life of Shakespeare* (Kelly Bray, Cornwall: House of Stratus, 2001), 107.
12. S. Schoenbaum, *Shakespeare's Lives* (Oxford: Clarendon Press, 1970), 50.
13. James Shapiro, *Rival Playwrights: Marlowe, Jonson, Shakespeare* (New York: Columbia University Press, 1991), 5.
14. Nashe called the tract 'a scald trivial lying pamphlet', and went on to protest, too much some think, in the following declaration: 'God never have care of my soule, but utterly renounce me, if the least word or sillable in it proceeded from my pen, or if I were any way prive to the writing or printing of it'. See Thomas Nashe, *The Works of Thomas Nashe*, vol. 1, 154.
15. Henry Chettle, *Kind-Heart's Dream*, ed. Edward F. Rimbault (London: The Percy Society, 1841), v.
16. Schoenbaum speculates that the line Chettle blotted out may have been a reference to Marlowe's alleged homosexuality, a possibility as intriguing as it is unverifiable. See Schoenbaum, *Shakespeare's Lives*, 52.
17. All quotes in the paragraph refer to Chettle, *Kind-Heart's Dream*, iv.
18. According to David George, this means that 'Chettle has seen Shakespeare act ..., but he has heard only *by report* of his honesty and his happy fluency in composing plays'. See David George, 'Shakespeare and Pembroke's Men', *Shakespeare Quarterly* 32.3 (1981), 320.
19. Both quotes refer to Michel Foucault, 'The Prose of the World', in *The Order of Things* (New York: Random House, 1970), 24.
20. This is the document produced by Richard Baines which characterizes Marlowe as an atheist, sodomite and counterfeiter. The most detailed account of the relationship between the two can be found in Roy Kendall, *Christopher Marlowe and Richard Baines: Journeys Through the Elizabethan Underground* (Cranbury, NJ: Fairleigh Dickinson University Press, 2004).
21. Both quotes refer to Katherine Duncan-Jones, *Ungentle Shakespeare*, 259.
22. David Riggs, 'Review of *Ungentle Shakespeare: Scenes from His Life*', *Shakespeare Quarterly* 53.4 (Winter 2002), 550–53; 551, 553.
23. Bridget Gellert Lyons, 'Review of *Ungentle Shakespeare: Scenes from His Life*', *Renaissance Quarterly* 56.2 (Summer 2003), 553–56; 554.

24. Slavoj Žižek, 'Welcome to the Desert of the Real', *Re:Constructions blog*, 15 September 2001, http://web.mit.edu/cms/reconstructions/interpretations/desertreal.html.
25. Jacques Derrida, interview by Giovanna Borradori, '9/11 and Global Terrorism: A Dialogue with Jacques Derrida', University of Chicago Press, 2003, http://www.press.uchicago.edu/books/derrida/derrida911.html.
26. Martin McQuillen, *Deconstruction after 9/11* (London: Routledge, 2009), 4.
27. Tony Blair, 'Speech to the Labour Party Conference', *The Guardian*, 2 October 2001, http://www.guardian.co.uk/politics/2001/oct/02/labourconference.labour6.
28. Part of my point here is that the UK authors I cite may have been equally affected by the events of 9/11 as were American critics, although I am aware of the differences in the response of the UK (see McQuillen, *Deconstruction after 9/11*, 12) and the fact that many older London residents could still recall the Second World War attacks on their homeland, a point Kaplan makes vis-a-vis her own experience as an expatriate living in New York at the time of the bombings. See E. Ann Kaplan, *Trauma Culture: The Politics of Terror and Loss in Media and Literature* (New Jersey: Rutgers University Press, 2005), 3–4, 9. See also Tony Blair, 'Speech to the Labour Party Conference'.
29. Herbert Blau, 'Art and Crisis: Homeland Security and the Noble Savage', *PAJ* 25.3 (2003), 6–19; 6.
30. Ibid., 8.
31. Ibid., 9.
32. Ibid., 9.
33. Ibid., 18.
34. For a dramatic essay on how aesthetics and terrorism might collide, see Graham Holderness and Bryan Loughrey, '"Rudely Interrupted": Shakespeare and Terrorism', *Critical Survey* 19.3 (2007), 107–23.
35. Kaplan, *Trauma Culture*, 1.
36. As Julia Kristeva claims, both personal and public trauma do 'damage' to our 'systems of perception and representation'. See Julia Kristeva and Leon S. Roudiez, *Black Sun: Depression and Melancholia* (New York: Columbia University Press, 1992), 223.
37. The term 'quiet trauma' is borrowed from T. M. Luhrman in *Cultures Under Siege*, ed. Antonius C. G. M. Robben and Marcelo M. Suárez-Orozco (Cambridge: Cambridge University Press, 2000), 158ff, to indicate a vicarious suffering felt by those close to, but not actual, victims of a traumatic event.
38. Of course, as Kuriyama admits, legal documents on Marlowe's arrests and other alleged transgressions run counter to this point. See Constance Kuriyama, 'Marlowe, Shakespeare, and the Nature of Biographical Evidence', *Studies in Literature* 20.1 (1988), 1–12; 1.
39. Ibid., 2.
40. Ibid., 2.
41. Ibid., 3.
42. Ibid., 137.
43. See Robert Sawyer, 'Christopher Marlowe: A Renaissance Life', *South Atlantic Review* 68.3 (Summer 2003), 154–58.
44. Lois Potter, 'Having Our Will: Imagination in Recent Biographies', *Shakespeare Survey* 58 (2005), 1–8; 8.

45. Hawkes, *Shakespeare in the Present*, 2.
46. Potter, 'Having Our Will', 8. Potter's own biography of Shakespeare was published in 2012: *The Life of William Shakespeare: A Critical Biography* (Malden, MA: Wiley-Blackwell, 2012).
47. Stephen Greenblatt, *Will in the World: How Shakespeare Became Shakespeare* (New York: Norton, 2004), 189.
48. Ibid., 191.
49. This quote and the following two quotes refer to Greenblatt, *Will in the World*, 192.
50. These so-called 'Truthers' have not yet been appeased. *The National Geographic* TV channel ran an episode on 31 May 2011 entitled '9/11: Science and Conspiracy'. According to a 2018 BBC report on conspiracy theories about 9/11, a '2016 study from Chapman University in California, found more than half of Americans believe the government is concealing information about the 9/11 attacks'. See https://www.bbc.com/news/blogs-trending-42195513.
51. James Meigs, 'The Lies Are Out There', *Popular Mechanics* 182.3 (2005), 1.
52. William S. Niederkorn, 'To Be or Not to Be ... Shakespeare', *The New York Times*, 21 August 2004.
53. Rodney Bolt, *History Play: The Lives and Afterlife of Christopher Marlowe* (New York: Harper, 2005).
54. See reviews of Rodney Bolt, *History Play*, Amazon.com, http://www.amazon.com/History-Play-Afterlife-Christopher-Marlowe/dp/1596910208.
55. *Anonymous*, directed by Roland Emmerich (Brandenburg, Germany: Columbia Pictures, 2011).
56. Douglas Lanier, '"There Won't Be Puppets, Will there?": "Heroic" Authorship and the Cultural Politics of *Anonymous*', in *Shakespeare Beyond Doubt: Evidence, Argument, Controversy*, ed. Paul Edmondson and Stanley Wells (Cambridge: Cambridge University Press, 2013), 215–24; 215.
57. Stephen Marche, 'Wouldn't It Be Cool if Shakespeare Wasn't Shakespeare?' *The New York Times*, 21 October 2011.
58. Hawkes, *Shakespeare in the Present*, 2.

Fiction

Chapter 7
Performance and Life Analogies in Shakespeare Novels for Young Readers

Marga Munkelt

Introduction

The two most extremely opposed orientations in Shakespeare criticism focusing on Shakespeare's biography, personality, and creativity are represented by doubts concerning his authorship, on the one hand, and by bardolatry, i.e., 'uncritical worship'[1] of his genius, on the other. Among the features used for arguments in favour of both stances are Shakespeare's upbringing in the country, the absence of a university education, his so-called lost years, and the incompatibility of his two lives in Stratford and London. In the selected novels for young readers discussed here, doubters and worshippers alike are offered fictional solutions, even though playfully simplified for the intended readership, to some of the biographical uncertainties. Following Paul Franssen's distinction between 'literary biography

Notes for this section begin on page 136.

proper' and 'frankly fictional accounts',[2] the novels investigated here are in the second category and do not try to prove 'hard facts' but only utilize 'some well-known data' about Shakespeare's time.[3]

The discussion will be concerned with the way in which fiction and the assumption of a historical reality are merged,[4] and, by sharing the perspectives of teenaged protagonists who are in interaction with Shakespeare and his theatre, with how life and the world of the theatre are related to each other. The intention is not to contribute to the history of children as readers,[5] but rather to uncover in the novels what seems to be common ground in the re-creation of Shakespeare's theatre environment and acting or writing conditions. Their impact on the protagonists' lives will be explored as well as the way in which play-acting and playwriting are essential to each other. Whereas Heminges and Condell's praise in *The First Folio* 'paved the way for the later apotheosis of Shakespeare as pure genius',[6] their appearance in these novels, by contrast, contributes to a 'de-mythologisation' of Shakespeare as they share with him and the young protagonists work and business in the theatre.[7]

The choice of the ten novels is based on an attempt to present a variety of young protagonists and points of view. The majority of the novels are narrated in the first person by male protagonists, who come into contact with Shakespeare.[8] In two novels, Shakespeare's wife and his daughter Judith are first-person narrators,[9] and one narrative, although written in the third person, is presented from the confines of what is perceived by Shakespeare's daughter Susanna.[10] The only novel with Shakespeare himself as protagonist[11] is likewise narrated in the third person, but interrupts the omniscient perspective with personal letters written by the teenaged Will to his parents. Four of the novels (by Harris, Hassinger, Meyer, and Tiffany) are, thus, directly concerned with persons from Shakespeare's family, but Shakespeare himself is not used as homodiegetic or autodiegetic narrator.[12] In addition to enhancing the tales' subjectivity, this characteristic may be an expression of respect for the many-sidedness of Shakespeare's world and the complexity of its interpretations: there cannot be a claim of presenting a first-hand truth.

Performance Patterns

In Shakespeare's *As You Like It*, Jacques says that

> All the world's a stage
> And all the men and women merely players;
> They have their exits and their entrances,
> And one man in his time plays many parts. (2.7.139–42)

This famous statement is explicitly and implicitly applied, with variations, to all the novels. The fact that Shakespeare's phrase 'one man in his time plays many parts' is modified in Harris's novel as 'over Time a man must playe many parts' (*Pirate's Fire*, 283) foregrounds the inevitability of life as play.[13] One may want to remember, at this point, that *player* is 'the usual term until the seventeenth century'[14] for *actor*, that *act* means both 'to carry out an action' and 'to perform a role in a play',[15] and that *perform* and *performance* denote a personal achievement, on the one hand, and a public (artistic) activity, on the other.[16] Widge, the protagonist of Gary Blackwood's *Shakespeare's Scribe*, begins his first-person narration with reflections on his life as an actor: 'Acting seems, ... after all, but an elaborate form of lying – pretending to be someone you are not' (*Shakespeare's Scribe*, 3). But he also finds it impossible to separate acting in the theatre from everyday performing. In a silent moment of self-recognition he admits to himself: 'I was an admirable liar. I had even lied myself into the most successful company of players in London, the Lord Chamberlain's Men. It stood to reason that I would be an admirable actor as well' (*Shakespeare's Scribe,* 3). The boy-actor Sal Pavy in Blackwood's *Shakespeare's Spy*, however, tries to differentiate stage-acting from life-acting: 'we're not really *doing* anything, are we? We're just *pretending* to do things. Sometimes I could do with a bit less acting and a bit more action, that's all' (*Shakespeare's Spy,* 19).

In one way or other, all the novels establish connections between life and performance and support the idea that human beings construct who they are by continuous performance[17] – utilizing, as it seems, the ambiguity of *actor*, who was, before acting became a profession, simply 'one who acts, ... a doer.'[18]

The Model: Geoffrey Trease, *Cue for Treason*

Geoffrey Trease's novel is the earliest (1940) of its kind.[19] The novel yokes life and theatre (as the title-word *cue* already indicates)[20] and explores themes that are picked up in most of the other Shakespeare novels for young readers.[21] Erica Hateley, accordingly, calls Gary Blackwood the 'inheritor of Trease'.[22]

In Trease's novel, Peter Brownrigg, son of a Cumberland farmer, is on the run from legal persecution and is saved by a company of travelling players in need of a boy-actor who can sing. Another young actor named Kit also joins the company, and ultimately both children end up among the Lord Chamberlain's Men as Shakespeare's apprentices. Eventually it is found out that Kit is a girl (Katherine) who has disguised herself as a boy to run away from an unwanted marriage. As a 'boy'-actor, she plays girls like Peter does, but is much more convincing in her movements and display of emotions.[23] Shakespeare suspects that Kit is a girl but he pretends, for professional reasons, not to know.

Two forms of disguise, 'to conceal and to reveal',[24] are illustrated by Kit and Peter in a performance of *Romeo and Juliet*. With Sir Philip Morton, her unwanted fiancé, who also happens to be Peter's pursuer, in the audience, Kit is afraid of being detected: although made up as Juliet, she looks much the same as in real life. Peter is, however, unnecessarily afraid of being detected, because costumed as a girl he remains unrecognized.

By eavesdropping, Peter and Kit uncover a conspiracy to murder the queen during a performance of *Henry V*, which involves communicating the cue by means of the play-text. Both children find out that not only Sir Philip is involved in the conspiracy but also another Member of Parliament and even an actor-colleague: nobody is who he seems to be. However, when the queen thanks them personally for preventing her assassination, Kit appears undisguised because 'Her Majesty [...] would] be furious if she found out afterwards' about her cross-dressing (*Cue for Treason*, 235). Elizabeth I is interested in a traditional future for the girl, and eventually Kit happily marries Peter.[25]

The types of performance patterns used in Trease's novel can be classified into six categories: (1) escape, (2) disguise, (3) spying, (4) improvisation, (5) performance and personal identity, and (6) performing public identity.

Variations of the Model

All the novels present young protagonists in search of an orientation in their lives, and the performance categories in Trease apply (with variations) to all of them. The characters' quest is sometimes based on a probing into the past, but more often it is initiated and supported by encounters with and in the theatre. Their personal goal is gradually developed and refined by means of their theatrical experience. As stage-actors they learn that as life-actors they must 'believe in the impression fostered by their own performance' and be 'sincere'.[26]

Escape

All the novels are about escape, whether from pursuit by the law, from the limitations of country life or simply one's home; whether running away from violent superiors; escape for religious reasons; in search of one's origin and family, or, as a woman in men's clothes, striving for independence. Escape implies liberty but also the need for shelter (as the etymological connection with *cap* and *cape* indicates).

In Trease's *Cue for Treason*, the theatre company is a place of refuge. The same is true in Robert Harris's novel *Will Shakespeare and the Pirate's Fire*, when Shakespeare's father saves his teenage son Will from the legal threats of Sir Thomas Lucy by pushing him onto the stage in a performance of *Cambyses*.[27] Thus, Will Shakespeare, like Peter Brownrigg, gets in touch with the theatre entirely coincidentally. In Gary Blackwood's trilogy, the protagonist Widge, who originally comes to the theatre in order to steal a copy of *Hamlet* for his master, ultimately finds protection among the actors. In the same story, the Jesuit Priest Father Garrett[28] hides in the theatre from religious pursuit. Also Richard Malory in J. B. Cheaney's *The Playmaker* comes to the theatre because he needs a place to stay.

The plot element of escape is elaborated metaphorically in all the novels and is redefined, with positive connotations, as a kind of quest – particularly in Cheaney's *The Playmaker* and Blackwood's *Shakespeare Stealer* trilogy. The protagonists realize that knowing where they come from does not mean they have to return to their roots, but that they have a choice. Both 'escape' from their origins and choose new 'fathers': in Cheaney, this is Shakespeare himself;

in Blackwood, it is Shakespeare's colleague, Thomas Pope, whose apprentice he is, in whose house he lives, and whose family name he adopts in the end.

Although, in Harris's novel, the teenager Will Shakespeare escapes with the assistance of his father, his father's dangerous (i.e., Catholic) religious orientation is built up as a constant threat, and the impending necessity for further escapes or cover-ups for their Catholic family members is an ongoing theme, as it is in *The Playmaker*. The connotations of the theatre – both the building and the institution – as a liberal and humane sanctuary establish a counterbalance to its being morally branded by the Puritans as a place of 'ill repute'.[29] In *Loving Will Shakespeare*, for example, the danger for actors to go astray as 'vagabonds' is maintained in the admonitions of the Stratford community (e.g., 95, 217, 220), but in the protagonists' reality, the theatre enables them to work out their problems.

Disguise

The strategy of disguise is particularly pursued by women in a society with severe gender restrictions. Like Kit in *Cue for Treason*, women in the other novels cross-dress as boys in order to be able to move about freely and pursue their goals. Thus, in Blackwood's trilogy, Julian, who turns out to be Julia, has the typical career of many Shakespearean heroines who cross-dress as boys in order to then play women.[30] At the end of the trilogy, Julia returns from professional acting as a woman abroad, again in the guise of a boy, because 'most of the public still regarded female players as degraded and immoral' (*Shakespeare's Spy*, 248–49). And though Julian's part of the story may be 'historically unlikely, this character does remind modern audiences of the tremendous gaps between the opportunities available to boys and girls in the period.'[31]

Pretence and cross-dressing are not exclusively associated with the professional theatre. In Harris's novel, Will Shakespeare escapes from prison in women's clothes (*Pirate's Fire*, 242–44, like Falstaff in *The Merry Wives of Windsor*), but often 'disguise' is accomplished by role-playing, independent of costume. Will Shakespeare, in *Pirate's Fire*, anachronistically drawing on plot elements from *The Tempest*, invents a creative biography for himself as a strategy for not being identified as a spy; and Thomas Cole, in Hassinger's *Shakespeare's Daughter*, avoids being prosecuted as a Catholic for a while by being a member of the St. Paul's boys' choir. In the same novel, Susanna Shakespeare pretends to be Emilia Lanier's maid on her way to London. Several of the other minor characters likewise play carefully designed roles (e.g., in *The Playmaker*, Richard Malory's aunt, a Catholic nun, pretends that her convent is an orphanage). A greater challenge than these temporary 'disguises' is Anne Hathaway's effort in Meyer's novel to avoid an unwanted marriage (*Loving Will Shakespeare*, 35, 121, 133–34). In order to find temporary relief from parental and social pressure (e.g., 179 ff.), she falsely agrees to marry the man who has been chosen for her, but repeatedly invents reasons for postponing the banns. His urging her to have sex with him before the wedding ultimately provides her with a reason to stop pretending and to call off the wedding (202–7).

Generally, Iago's form of role-playing, 'I am not that I am', is utilized in all the novels. However, sometimes the fact that one is exactly who one is appears to work as deception, too: Will Shakespeare, in Harris's novel, is not recognized by his pursuer because Sir Thomas Lucy does not expect him on the stage in mid-performance. By contrast, Kit as Juliet is recognized only because she stands out as female in an all-male cast.

Spying

In practically all the novels, the historical context is characterized by social, political and religious manipulation and control. Varying Trease's plot element of a crime prevented by inadvertent spying, Harris's novel has Will Shakespeare (together with Walter Raleigh and Edward de Vere, of all people) actively spy for the English Crown against Ireland and Spain. In other novels, the overall atmosphere of suspicion during Elizabeth's reign is extended to the rivalry between professional acting companies and theatres contending for commercial supremacy: In *Shakespeare's Spy*, Widge works as a spy for the Lord Chamberlain's Men (203–20), whereas Shakespeare's brother Edmund, on the payroll of the Admiral's Men, turns out to be a spy against them (220–22).

Due to a fear of losing their preferred positions in the company, Widge and his friend in Blackwood's novels spy on their co-apprentice Sal, whom they suspect to be a cross-dressed girl. It even seems that Sal intentionally contributes to this impression – perhaps to increase his professional attraction.[32] Thus, the action of spying on Sal when he takes a bath clarifies not only the gender facts in the novel but also that he deceives by pretending to pretend.[33]

Knowing that one is spied upon can entail either fear or triumph. Spying and eavesdropping are forms of social pressure in *Loving Will Shakespeare*, where Anne is in an almost permanent fear of being seen with a man or, worse, kissing Will and ultimately of being indicted by the 'bawdy court' (e.g., 220, 223). Quite differently, Sal, in *Shakespeare's Scribe*, utilizes his awareness of being observed for profit: he pretends that he diligently fulfils his chores as a prentice whenever one of the sharers is watching (50).

Improvisation

In the context of professional acting, *improvisation* indicates actors' 'capacities to say the right sort of thing in their own words'[34] during a performance, and the necessity to improvise is most often caused by a mishap. As an emergency practice, this style is utilized in most of the novels. In Blackwood's *Shakespeare's Scribe*, the boy-actors are praised for their versatility in 'thribbling'[35] whenever another player has forgotten his text (20). In Meyer's novel, Will Shakespeare is appreciated in one of his early acting employments for exactly this ability, but the enjoyment of creativity is also implied: 'If a player forgot his lines', he tells Anne, 'I improvised speeches to lead him back to his proper place. Anne it was splendid!' (*Loving Will Shakespeare*, 189).

The non-theatrical sense of improvisation, that is, the 'execution of anything off-hand',[36] is generally applicable to a host of situations in most people's everyday lives. A form of improvising between extemporizing in life and thribbling on stage is the observation of (religious) ceremony and (social) rituals where, despite a prescriptive frame, individual spontaneity is called for. Examples are sheep-shearing festivals and Twelfth-Night celebrations, with men cross-dressing as women and a queen and king of misrule 'elected' (see *Loving Will Shakespeare*, chapters 5, 8, 11). This form of entertainment is contrasted by the enforced counterfeit observance of social conventions in order to protect one's own or someone else's integrity. Anne, for example, improvises a public show of unfelt penance when her friend Emma is accused of an illicit sexual encounter (*Loving Will Shakespeare*, 56–59).

In several novels, the characters adapt the skills they have acquired on the professional stage to crises and challenges outside the theatre. Moreover, the actors' access to theatre equipment is a valuable aid to improvisation in critical situations. Lives are saved, for example, when, in Trease's novel (and similarly in Blackwood's), bandits attack the company's vehicles and the actors quickly present themselves as soldiers, using the uniforms they have among their stage-costumes as well as the property weapons. Being trained in stage-fights turns out to be useful on the road (*Cue for Treason*, 223–25; *Shakespeare's Scribe*, 59–63), and Will, in Meyer's novel, improvises a show of versatility in sword-fighting (*Loving Will Shakespeare*, 151–52). For private excitement, Judith Shakespeare uses costumes of the Globe theatre for a dinner in the Earl of Southampton's home (*My Father Had a Daughter*, 244). Even more creatively, the apprentice Sam uses stage make-up to suggest symptoms of the bubonic plague – convincing enough to drive bandits away but also to scare his fellow-actors (*Shakespeare's Scribe*, 144–45).

Performance and Personal Identity

The intertextual reference to life as a play in *As You Like It* is omnipresent. Paradoxically, 'pretending to be someone you are not', as Widge defines *performance* (*Shakespeare's Scribe*, 3), entails recognition and self-knowledge. Widge's career in the *Shakespeare Stealer* trilogy is a 'personal trajectory of Shakespearean maturation that takes him from spectator, to actor, to author',[37] and Richard Malory in *The Playmaker* profits from theatrical performance strategies for coming to terms with his own emotions, but, inversely, also carries his sad personal experiences into the parts for which he is cast (*Playmaker*, 112–13).[38] The role in which, for Richard, life and theatre become nearly inseparable is that of Perdita in *The Winter's Tale*,[39] but the departure of his just-found father marks a caesura in his life: 'You are at the beginning of your own play, and free to make of it what you will', says his father (*Playmaker*, 289). The title of the novel, *The Playmaker*, carries multiple meanings, however: Richard calls his father 'the playmaker' of his life (*Playmaker*, 291); he recognizes Shakespeare as the playmaker in the theatre; but he himself becomes the playmaker of his own future.

In *Loving Will Shakespeare*, Anne and Will together 'perform' their identity as a couple in a makeshift private world where public conventions are suspended. But whereas Will pursues his individual quest by leaving for London (251), Anne suppresses hers in order to 'keep his love' when she agrees 'that he must go' (252). She uses a 'counterfeit smile' (257), 'pretending that all was well' (257) but aware of her pretence at this moment (258).

Special attention must be paid to Cooper's *King of Shadows*. This time-slip novel has the American boy-actor Nat Field, who lives in the twentieth century, change places with the boy-actor Nathaniel Field of the Lord Chamberlain's Men in the sixteenth century.[40] The young protagonist learns to accept his past and his identity by playing Puck in *A Midsummer Night's Dream* to Shakespeare's Oberon.[41] The title of the novel, *King of Shadows*, hints at the dual role of Oberon as king of fairies by means of a textual echo (5.1.423) and as 'king' of actors, i.e., Shakespeare, with *shadow* implying the additional meaning of player or impersonator.[42] The entire novel advocates the idea that performing as an actor has a lasting influence on the actor as a person.[43]

Performing Public Identity

The two basic meanings of *identity* are 'absolute or essential sameness; oneness' and 'individuality, personality'.[44] As has been shown, in theatrical performance, a vital characteristic is the absence of 'absolute or essential sameness' or 'oneness', because one only pretends to be someone else – even someone of a different gender. The idea of a public 'doer', the presentation of a self-image for the public that suppresses all other possible identities, is illustrated in the appearances of Queen Elizabeth I. In several of the novels, the idea of the 'king's two bodies',[45] the body politic and the body natural that are separate and yet ought to be united, is apparent in the portrayal of the queen.

In all the novels in which Elizabeth I appears, she becomes the most constant spectacle of an actress whose self-constructed image has smothered the person underneath. Thus, when, in Meyer's *Loving Will Shakespeare*, she passes through Warwickshire, the citizens of Stratford are satisfied to notice that she looks like her pictures (50). Several of the other young protagonists are, however, disappointed to find that the 'real' Queen Elizabeth does, at a closer look, not correspond with Gloriana (*King of Shadows*, 137). Elizabeth's public performances as a monarch, meant to act out the essence of king- or queenship, are limited by time and reality. The children notice that in her 'peacock glory' (*Cue for Treason*, 233) and her make-up resembling a 'ghastly mask' (*Shakespeare Stealer*, 182) the queen looks like a piece of art, and especially that her teeth are rotten (*King of Shadows*, 137; *The Shakespeare Stealer*, 182). In Blackwood's *Shakespeare's Spy*, Elizabeth's poor hearing is exposed and initiates humorous misunderstandings (10), causing Widge to realize with sadness 'that Her Majesty was mortal' (11).

How much Queen Elizabeth prioritizes public performance is narrated in Blackwood's *The Shakespeare Stealer*. After having seen the Lord Chamberlain's Men's *Hamlet*, she praises Widge's Ophelia and asks his name. When Widge admits that he does not know his real proper name, she promises: 'Well, Widge, if you go on performing as admirably as you did for us, you'll make a name for yourself' (182). Earning a public name by merit and desert, also in acting, can cure a dubious origin, as demonstrated by the 'performance' of her public name, Queen Elizabeth.

Conclusion

The most consistent analogy of life and stage is created by the time-slip strategy of Cooper's *King of Shadows* in which *A Midsummer Night's Dream* is the thematic and structural background. As Linda Hall points out, this narrative device is a means of getting young readers interested in history, because it is 'a story with its feet in the present but its head and heart in the past.'[46] The emotional closeness of Nat and Shakespeare is present in both centuries and on both continents due to the 'flexibility' of the genre,[47] and it is additionally documented by the material availability of Shakespeare's gift to Nat, a version of Sonnet 116.

In all the novels, parallels between Shakespeare's plays and the protagonists' lives are indicated – often by means of intertextual references. In *Loving Will Shakespeare*, for instance, Will's invitation 'Kiss me, Anne' becomes almost a leitmotif (e.g., 233, 239, 241, 254), and it conjures up the love of Kate and Petruchio, which is as unlikely as that of Anne and Will. Also, Shakespeare's *The Two Gentlemen of Verona* and *Twelfth Night* are foregrounded in several of the novels, perhaps owing to their emphasis on cross-dressing, because gender roles cause great differences in female or male acting in life and on the stage.

Indirectly, all the novels confirm the many parallels between Shakespeare's life and his plays as they have been unearthed and discussed by critics and biographers for some time.[48] The narratives indirectly suggest that the young protagonists, as stage-actors and as life-performers, possibly relive experiences that can be ascribed also to Shakespeare. In Trease's novel, Peter even imagines direct parallels between Shakespeare's past (for example, as a possible runaway) and his own biography (*Cue for Treason*, 79).

A certain readiness in the fictional Shakespeare to cross legal and social boundaries becomes generally noticeable. By accommodating girls in his theatre, he reduces the degree of 'pretence'. Shakespeare's decision in *Cue for Treason* to allow Kit, a girl, to play Juliet in *Romeo and Juliet* (78), is particularly innovative and rebellious, since 'the companies themselves did not consider actresses the equal of actors' (*Shakespeare's Spy*, 248–49).[49] Moreover, the Shakespeare in Tiffany's novel lets his daughter continue to 'boy' her hair and remain in the company for a while even after he has recognized her (*My Father Had a Daughter*, 177).

Above all, Shakespeare as seen with the eyes of his juvenile friends and co-actors contradicts the expectations of bard-worshippers – especially because the life-and-theatre analogies are extended not only to his personal life but also to his working methods as a poet and playwright. There is nothing magical about his creations, because he educates himself (e.g., *Pirate's Fire*, 41, 116), adopts ideas from reality (e.g., *Scribe*, 148), admits borrowing and stealing plots from other writers (e.g., *Spy*, 122–23), amends plays composed by others (e.g., *Pirate's Fire*, chapter 9), employs his apprentices to make politically correct adjustments in his plays (e.g., *Spy*, 78–79), collaborates (in Blackwood's novels) with a boy-actor on *The Two Gentlemen of Verona* and *All's Well That Ends Well*, and even allows him to finish *Timon of Athens* under his own name.

The fact that the Shakespeare for young readers conducts professional discussions with Ben Jonson about the skill of playwriting (*Playmaker*, 304–5) and with equal seriousness with the boy-actor Widge (*Scribe*, chapter 21) testifies to his openness to the ideas of others, which he picks up as long as they seem 'real'. He rejects Aristotle's 'unities' because 'life is not like that' (*Playmaker*, 304). In other words, the novels portray Shakespeare's plays as manifestations of human experience rather than as creations of a genius. Shakespeare is 'de-bardolatrized' and transformed into an ordinary human being with a good sense of humour, one who is a friend of the young people,[50] and who merges life and play like the protagonists depicted in the novels.

From the ten novels discussed here Shakespeare emerges as representing performance on all levels of his existence. He writes about observed life-performances; his own 'performance' is one of parallel acting; his 'presentation of self in everyday life' (to use the phrasing in Goffman's book title[51]) coincides with the transformed quotation from *As You Like It* stating that 'over Time a man must playe many parts' (2.7.142; see *Pirate's Fire*, 283) as well as with the practice in his time of doubling or tripling parts. Shakespeare's two lives are linked by performance: his existence in Stratford reflecting a *life as performance* whereas his professional career in London is a *life of performance* or *for performance*.

Marga Munkelt, in addition to teaching English language and literature at the University of Münster, was a Visiting Professor in the Department of English at the University of New Mexico for several years. Her teaching experience includes all fields of English literature as well as selected aspects of American literature and (post)colonial studies. Her main research interests are drama, Shakespeare studies and Chicano/a studies. Among her publications are the co-edited New Variorum *Antony and Cleopatra* (1990) and the New Cambridge *Julius Caesar* (updated edition, 2004), an edition of *Mexican-American Short Stories* (revised edition, 2012) and the co-edited anthology *Postcolonial Translocations* (2013). Her articles have appeared in such journals as *Analytical and Enumerative Bibliography, Critical Survey, Romanische Studien, Shakespeare Studies, Studies in the Western* and *Theatre History Studies* along with multiple anthologies and encyclopaedias.

Notes

1. John Lennard and Mary Luckhurst, *The Drama Handbook* (Oxford: Oxford University Press, 2002), 320.
2. Paul J. C. M. Franssen, 'The Life and Opinions of William Shakespeare, Gentleman: Biography between Fact and Fiction', in *Literature as History / History as Literature: Fact and Fiction in Medieval to Eighteenth-Century British Literature*, ed. Sonja Fielitz (Frankfurt: Peter Lang, 2007), 63–77; 63.
3. Ibid., 64.
4. A few of the authors provide notes explaining which characters and dates are facts and where they intentionally deviate from the known chronology. For example, 'Author's Note' in Gary Blackwood, *Shakespeare's Scribe* (New York: Dutton Children's Books, 2000), v–vi, and *Shakespeare's Spy* (New York: Dutton Children's Books, 2006), 280–81; 'Historical Note' in J. B. Cheaney, *The Playmaker* (New York: Alfred A. Knopf, 2000), 306–7; 'Afterword' in Robert J. Harris, *Will Shakespeare and the Pirate's Fire* (London: HarperCollins Children's Books, 2006), 286–88, and 'Author's Note' in Carolyn Meyer, *Loving Will Shakespeare* (Orlando: Harcourt, 2006), 263–65.
5. For a history of children as readers, see Kathleen McDowell, 'Toward a History of Children as Readers, 1890–1930', *Book History* 12 (2009), 240–65.
6. Jonathan Bate, *The Genius of Shakespeare* (London: Picador, 1997), 29.
7. Sidney Lee, who liked to stress Shakespeare's 'sobriety' and 'sanity of ... mental attitude toward life's ordinary incidents' was criticized by S. Schoenbaum for this 'highest praise' of 'the supreme artificer'. See Schoenbaum, *Shakespeare's Lives* (Oxford: Oxford University Press, 1991), 373.
8. These novels are Gary Blackwood, *The Shakespeare Stealer Series* (New York: Dutton Children's Books, 1998–2003) consisting of: *The Shakespeare Stealer* (1998), *Shakespeare's Scribe* (2000) and *Shakespeare's Spy* (2006); J. B. Cheaney, *The Playmaker* (New York: Alfred A. Knopf, 2000); Susan Cooper, *King of Shadows* (New York: Margaret K. McElderry Books, 1999); and Geoffrey Trease, *Cue for Treason* (1940; Harmondsworth: Penguin Books / Puffin Books, 1949).
9. Meyer, *Loving Will Shakespeare* and Grace Tiffany, *My Father Had a Daughter: Judith Shakespeare's Tale* (New York: Berkley Books, 2003). Tiffany's novel is not marked as being expressly for young readers.
10. Peter W. Hassinger, *Shakespeare's Daughter* (New York: Laura Geringer Books / HarperCollins, 2004). As Erica Hateley points out, novels with female narrators or protagonists are the exception. See 'Author(is)ing the Child: Shakespeare as Character', *Shakespeare in Children's Literature: Gender and Cultural Capital* (New York and London: Routledge, 2009), 49–81.
11. Harris, *Will Shakespeare and the Pirate's Fire*.
12. Nor, for that matter, is his daughter Susanna.
13. The phrase is quoted by Will in a letter to his parents which credits Henry Beeston, the manager of Lord Strange's Men (perhaps a confusion with the historical Christopher Beeston).
14. Lennard and Luckhurst, *The Drama Handbook*, 353.
15. Ibid., 317.
16. According to the *Oxford English Dictionary* definition.

Performance and Life Analogies in Shakespeare Novels for Young Readers 137

17. See Erving Goffman, *The Presentation of Self in Everyday Life* (Harmondsworth: Penguin, 1959) and Judith Butler, *Bodies That Matter: On the Discursive Limits of 'Sex'* (New York: Routledge, 1993).
18. Lennard and Luckhurst, *The Drama Handbook*, 173.
19. Critics emphasize that it was written during the war and has a nationalistic tenor. See, for example, Pat Pinsent, '"Not for an Age but for all Time": The Depiction of Shakespeare in a Selection of Children's Fiction', *New Review of Children's Literature and Librarianship* 10.2 (2004), 115–26; 118, and Hateley, 'Author(is)ing the Child', 53.
20. See also Trease, *Cue for Treason*, 227, 231, 235.
21. The term 'Shakespeare novel' is used here in the broadest sense of a novel set in Shakespeare's time.
22. Hateley, 'Author(is)ing the Child', 54. It is hard to assess the other novels' intentional adoption of ideas and themes from Trease, but the similarities are obvious. Another possible model for the way in which life as performance is explored fictionally, would be Marc Norman and Tom Stoppard's *Shakespeare in Love* (1999). Hateley reminds us that Peter W. Hassinger sued Miramax over *Shakespeare in Love* (Hateley, 'Author(is)ing the Child', 199). See 'Shakespeare Film Studios "Face Trial"', BBC News, 11 October 2006.
23. Although Hateley observes that this fact 'undermines her acting abilities' (see Hateley, 'Author(is)ing the Child', 53), it may instead stress the limitations of female characters being enacted by boys. In Blackwood's *Shakespeare Stealer*, for example, Julia teaches Widge how to play Ophelia (*Shakespeare Stealer*, 176).
24. Martin Meisel, *How Plays Work: Reading and Performance* (Oxford: Oxford University Press, 2007), 60.
25. This narrative element of unquestionable gender roles definitely dates the novel in the *early* twentieth century.
26. Goffman, *The Presentation of Self*, 28.
27. It is not the goal of this chapter to examine systematically the degree of the novels' historical correctness.
28. He is later identified in the novel as Father Gerard (see, for example, chapters 7–8, 14, 18–21, 30) and is possibly (con)fused with the historical Father Garnet.
29. Tanya Pollard, *Shakespeare's Theater: A Sourcebook* (Oxford: Blackwell, 2004), xii.
30. The ramifications of this phenomenon then and now are explored from various angles in James C. Bulman, ed., *Shakespeare Re-Dressed: Cross-Gender Casting in Contemporary Performance* (Madison, WI: Fairleigh Dickinson University Press, 2008).
31. Megan Lynn Isaac, *Heirs to Shakespeare: Reinventing the Bard in Young Adult Literature* (Portsmouth, NH: Boynton/Cook, 2000), 40.
32. For boy-actors as rivals, see Stanley Wells, *Shakespeare & Co.* (London: Penguin Books, 2006), 53–58.
33. This boy-actor is historically documented to have acted at Blackfriars, although he 'may never have acted with the Chamberlain's Men'. See Blackwood, 'Author's Note', *Shakespeare's Spy*, 280, and Wells, *Shakespeare & Co.*, 56 and 171.
34. Lennard and Luckhurst, *The Drama Handbook*, 126.

35. Blackwood uses 'thribbling (through)' repeatedly and defines it as 'improvising when another player falters' (see *Shakespeare's Scribe*, 20); *thribbling* (with a similar definition) is also used by the narrator in Cooper's *King of Shadows*, who rejoices: 'isn't it a great word?' (89). According to Lennard and Luckhurst (*The Drama Handbook*, 335 and 126), the seventeenth-century term is *fribbling*. The possible confusion of the two words may be due to their phonetic similarity.
36. See *Oxford English Dictionary* definition.
37. Hateley, 'Author(is)ing the Child', 54. If one recalls the career of the boy-actor Nathaniel Field, who became a playwright later in his life, Widge's development is not at all implausible. See Wells, *Shakespeare & Co.*, 56–59, and note 38.
38. The order of the kinds of roles which the boy-actors are trained to play in the novels seems to correspond with the training in Shakespeare's time (see Wells, *Shakespeare & Co.*, 57). Thus, Richard Malory first fills in for a sick member of the Lord Chamberlain's Men. Then he is asked to play small roles in *Henry VI* or Nerissa in *The Merchant of Venice* and moves on to larger parts.
39. For the fragile margin between life and stage, see *The Playmaker*, 178; for the fusion of Richard's and Perdita's biographies, see *The Playmaker*, 210.
40. This boy-actor is also a character in Tiffany's *My Father Had a Daughter*, where he even becomes the lover of Judith Shakespeare. About the historical Nathaniel Field, see Wells, *Shakespeare & Co.*, 56–59.
41. That Shakespeare may have played Oberon is a well-known conjecture, as is his having played Prospero in *The Tempest*. See Wells, *Shakespeare & Co.*, 29.
42. *Oxford English Dictionary*: 'an unreal appearance; a delusive semblance or image' (Shadow sb. II.3).
43. The fact that, in this novel, the twentieth-century director of *A Midsummer Night's Dream* is called Richard Babbage contributes humorously to the general validity of Nat's experience. For details on acting styles, see Tiffany A. Conroy, 'Presenting Shakespeare's Life and Times for Young People', *Reimagining Shakespeare for Children and Young Adults*, ed. Naomi J. Miller (New York and London: Routledge, 2003), 239–51; 249.
44. See *Oxford English Dictionary* (Identity 1 and 2).
45. See Ernst H. Kantorowicz, *The King's Two Bodies: A Study in Mediaeval Political Theology* (Princeton: Princeton University Press, 1957).
46. Linda Hall, '"Time no Longer" – History, Enchantment and the Classic Time-Slip Story', *Historical Fiction for Children: Capturing the Past*, ed. Fiona M. Collins and Judith Graham (London: David Fulton, 2001), 43–53; 46.
47. Ibid., 52.
48. See David Bevington, *Shakespeare and Biography*, Oxford Shakespeare Topics (Oxford: Oxford University Press, 2010), esp. 99–154 (chapters 6 and 7).
49. Erica Hateley criticizes Blackwood for favouring male protagonists and excluding the 'feminine characters ... from symbolic relationships with the playwright' ('Author(is)ing the Child', 50).
50. Hateley's opinion about the novels by Hassinger, Blackwood, and Tiffany draws a parallel between Shakespeare's 'acting as father to child protagonists' and his 'playtexts as artefacts of paternal advice from the Father of Western Culture' ('Author(is)ing the Child', 50).
51. Goffman, *The Presentation of Self in Everyday Life*.

Chapter 8
Shakespeare as Character in Two Works by José Carlos Somoza

Ángel-Luis Pujante and Noemí Vera

> Mais, chère Clarence, pardonnez, ne faites
> pas attention à toutes mes extravagances;
> toujours la tête remplie de mes ouvrages...
> Alexandre Duval, *Shakespeare amoureux*
>
> Perhaps if we should meet Shakspeare, we should not
> be conscious of any steep inferiority; no: but of a great
> equality, – only that he possessed a strange skill of
> using, of classifying, his facts, which we lacked.
> Ralph Waldo Emerson, 'Intellect'

Shakespeare's earliest manifestations as a fictional character date back to the eighteenth century, when he featured as a ghost,[1] but his presence as a fully-fledged fictional character did not occur until the beginning of the nineteenth century. One of the most characteristic appearances then took place on the European stage, with *Shakespeare amoureux*, a comedy by Alexandre Duval (1803).[2] Then

Notes for this section begin on page 148.

a free Spanish version by Ventura de la Vega entitled *Shakespeare enamorado*, staged in Madrid in 1828,[3] gave rise to a stream of revivals with distinguished actors, and became the first of a series which has continued up to the present day featuring Shakespeare as a character in Spanish drama, and more recently in fiction and the cinema.[4] The resulting images of Shakespeare the man have already been discussed,[5] with the exception of those created by writer José Carlos Somoza in his play *Miguel Will* (1999)[6] and his short story 'Hamlet' (2008).[7] Our main aim in this chapter is to present and examine these two works, paying special attention to the image of Shakespeare that emerges in them.

José Carlos Somoza is an established name in contemporary Spanish fiction. Born in Havana, Cuba, in 1959, he came to Spain at the age of one as the only thing his parents were allowed to take with them when they were unexpectedly and summarily ordered to leave their country for political reasons. He studied Medicine and Psychiatry and worked as a psychiatrist for a short while before deciding to become a full-time writer – which he did after his first novel was awarded a literary prize. Then, the international success of his fifth novel, *La caverna de las ideas* (English title: *The Athenian Murders*), confirmed that his decision had been the right one. So far he has written a dozen novels, three of which have been translated into several European languages, and three are being adapted for the cinema.[8]

Somoza's interest in Shakespeare has also been expressed in other works. His recent *El cebo* [*The Bait*][9] is a thriller focused on desire, in which a deep knowledge of Shakespeare's plays is a key element and forms the basis of a psychological theory applied by the police in trapping criminals. He has also published three articles on Shakespeare. In his 'Shakespeare is Legion',[10] he explains how he got to know the work of Shakespeare, who, he confesses, is the author who has most 'possessed' him – a possession which continued at the time of writing the article. In 'Remordimientos de una reina' [A Queen's Remorse],[11] Somoza explores evil in Lady Macbeth in association with the famous invocation 'Unsex me here', the implications of which he tentatively explores. Nevertheless, his concern with evil in Shakespeare is best found in a previous article, 'La maldad es silencio (Shakespeare y los personajes malvados)' [Evil is silence (Shakespeare and evil characters)],[12] in which – centring on the character of Macbeth – he shows how speech (and occasionally excess of speech) enhances the evil of Shakespeare's villains.

It will be useful to begin with the shorter and more recent of the two works. 'Hamlet', a whimsical short story about Shakespeare being compelled to write a play by a mysterious member of 'the Corporation', was Somoza's contribution to a collection of stories written expressly about the dealings and manoeuvres of this secret society.

'The Corporation', first mentioned in Fernando Marías' 1996 novel *Esta noche moriré* [*Tonight I Will Die*], is conceived of as a clandestine organization devoted to the collection of works produced under their coercion by some of the greatest artists and writers in history as long-term investments. Coinciding with the reissue of Marías' novel, the idea of this Corporation and its dealings was used by seven Spanish writers of mystery novels, including Somoza, as the basis for different short stories. The volume, edited by Fernando Marías himself, shows the various ways in which this secret association managed to pressurize creators as renowned as Shakespeare, Dostoyevsky, or Kafka. Once obtained, these works would be preserved by the society as long as necessary till they decided to sell them at the highest market price: one of them is Kafka's last chapter of his 'unfinished' *The Castle*, which, according to their plans, is to see the light in 2024, the first centenary of Kafka's death.

In 'Hamlet', Shakespeare is visited in his Stratford home by a member of the Corporation who blackmails him into writing an 'alternative' version of the play he is about to finish: *Hamlet*. Narrated from the viewpoint of 'Hamlet' (a stray dog Shakespeare brings home from the graveyard where he and his wife are mourning their son's death), this short story tells of the curious writing process by which the Bard struggles to finish the play he is forced to write within the stipulated time, while secretly taking revenge on the Corporation.

Shakespeare assigns each of the characters in *Hamlet* to one of his dog's body parts (his tongue becomes Claudius, his left leg Ophelia, Hamlet is his skull, etc.) and asks 'Hamlet' to move them at his pleasure: this way, the dog 'dictates' to him the plot of this new play. But, not content with this, Shakespeare also devises a plan to unmask the Corporation when the second coerced *Hamlet* comes out: he buries a manuscript by an oak tree explaining the true story of the Corporation, and tries to ensure that someone will find it in the future; to this end, he makes one of the characters in this revised *Hamlet* hint at searching for an oak tree near the churchyard when he leaves his wife his second best bed – assuming, on the one hand, that somebody will be interested in reading his Last Will and Testament many years after his death and that the person in question will be capable of linking his will to the quotation in the play – and, on the other hand, that nobody would seriously believe that he was leaving only a second best bed to his wife. The story finishes with the dog regretting having eaten the piece of paper containing Shakespeare's denunciation of the Corporation's intrigues.

'Hamlet' presents a Shakespeare in his thirties, living in London but visiting his family in Stratford 'almost every month', and reasonably concerned about their welfare. Immediately after his son's death, Shakespeare has to face this blatant threat by the Corporation: 'our business is very simple: you agree to our request, and times of comedy will come. You do not, and tragedies might be performed again in your home' (126).[13] As Shakespeare tells his dog, this man and his Corporation make him shudder. However, far from showing himself weak or even begging for mercy, he attempts to appear calm in front of him: 'My master was pale' says Hamlet, 'And he smelled of fear: thin but sharp, like a stiletto. However, he tried not to show it' (126). Despite the seriousness of the matter and the fact that he is really frightened, Shakespeare displays defiance towards the Corporation, even daring to insult its representative. Though he immediately expresses his intention to take revenge on them, he is intelligent and cool enough to avoid a direct confrontation.

Somoza also offers a glimpse of Shakespeare's family life in Stratford. Shakespeare's dog describes Anne Hathaway as 'a severe, dark peasant woman with richly sharp cheekbones' (122), in whose hands the money her husband brings home disappears. The relationship between the couple often seems strained, and Anne shows herself to be bad-tempered and rather bossy. However, the recent loss of her son also contributes to a less unpleasant image of her. She bursts into tears when she wrongly thinks that her husband was calling the dog 'Hamnet', and does not show any interest in it because dogs cannot fill the emptiness left by people, to which Shakespeare replies that some people are emptier than dogs. Despite the fact that he is equally affected – the dog-narrator talks about 'that strange habit they both had of not forgetting their son's death and staying sad' (123) – Shakespeare's attitude is quite different from that of his wife, and he relies on his own talent and sense of humour to overcome the hardest situations.

This glimpse of Shakespeare's family life would make the story fall into the category of 'Domestics', which O'Sullivan proposes for Shakespeare's 'other lives' depicting the Bard's life at home and his relationship with his wife (2). However, this image appears to be complementary to that which tends to dominate in the story; that of a Shakespeare at work, for whom writing is a way of escape: he seems to enjoy the process of creation even under the most adverse conditions. Despite his huge creativity, he is very down-to-earth as regards his work, too: 'I must admit, Hamlet, that I am bad at plots. I can put myself in my characters' place and make them speak as if they were alive, but I copy what happens to them from the books I read. I cannot make up another plot for my *Hamlet* in one month' (129). Shakespeare is able to accept his limitations, and for him writing is something that requires time and effort. He is quite methodical about his work, and always writes in a locked study where nobody can disturb him.

However, when he begins to write for the Corporation, he decides to resort to what he calls '*dramatis canae*' [the dogs of the play], turning an almost ritualistic process into a surrealist game (remember that his main intention was both to avoid trouble and to mock the Corporation). Through this 'innovative' writing method, Shakespeare shows that anyone (even a dog) can be the author of a play considered a work of art by some people – the man from the Corporation among them. As it happens, when Shakespeare shows him the alternative *Hamlet*, he says: 'It is a stroke of genius. ... It is clear that you were inspired by the careful observation of human beings' (134), showing up both himself and the Corporation's authority or capacity for recognizing a real work of art, and maybe also drawing attention to the fact that some people tend to overestimate certain works just because their authors have a good reputation. Hamlet the dog mentions that Shakespeare used to burst out laughing every time he remembered the man's comment after skimming through the play. And the man, when hearing Shakespeare call his dog 'Hamlet', exclaims, 'You are obsessed with your work!' In a way this may be true: the dog comments that his master never became discouraged while writing the play and that his enthusiasm made him look 'as if he were infected by the bubonic plague' (132).

The depiction of Shakespeare as a fictional character becomes more interesting and complex in Somoza's *Miguel Will*, a semi-Pirandellian play which explores the spiritual relationship between Miguel de Cervantes and William Shakespeare. In it Shakespeare, at the end of his career, appears obsessed with the writing of *Cardenio* as he stumbles on the difficulty of dealing with the character of Don Quixote, whom he wants to incorporate into the play. For him the problem lies in creating a stage character who is both a noble man and a buffoon, a man of high ideals and a fool who cannot stop making stupid mistakes. As a result, Shakespeare becomes so engrossed with this problem that he himself begins to go through a process of 'quixotization', often being incapable of distinguishing reality from fiction. Once more, the image that emerges here is that of Shakespeare at work, which seems to be in line with those fictions categorized by O'Sullivan as 'Players' (2), i.e., those attempting to identify 'the essential man' in his theatre milieu.[14]

Somoza's Shakespeare, however, is a psychologically complex actor-writer. His physical and mental states deteriorate. When he starts working on the production of *Cardenio*, he begins to leave aside not only all his hobbies, but also his other plays, as he can hardly remember that he and Fletcher were also working on their *Henry VIII*. Shakespeare's transformation is also reflected in his physical appearance and even in his health: he is pale, sweaty, has dark circles under his eyes and shaky hands, and looks as if he were ill. Denis Rafter, the Irish theatre director based in Madrid who staged *Miguel Will*, summarized the character of Shakespeare in his director's notes as: 'Neurotic – Bundle of nerves – Tired – 48 years old. Not as tall as Burbage'.[15]

One consequence of Shakespeare's fixation is his decision to play the role himself, changing his name to Miguel Will and wearing a basin on his head for a costume. Unfortunately, Miguel Will-Shakespeare faints during the performance and, despite the fact that Burbage stands in for him, the audience does not seem to understand the character. It is then that John Fletcher intervenes and tells Shakespeare that he has modified the play, deleting the character of Miguel Will. Disappointed, Shakespeare reacts by throwing the manuscript into the fire. At the end of the play, an 'oneiric-Cervantes' makes his appearance to congratulate Shakespeare on his particular treatment of Don Quixote, and forecasts their recognition as the best writers in the history of literature.

Some years after directing *Miguel Will*, Denis Rafter commented on Burbage's change of approach to his playing of Don Quixote:

> Burbage, following Shakespeare's instructions, becomes a buffoon and plays his part looking for laughs. But this second attempt is even less successful; therefore, the prolific author keeps searching until he enters a kind of madness that makes him exclaim: 'Pray, Muses: leave me alone! I have to live! I am not only my characters'.[16]

However, Rafter omits the closing words: 'Or am I?' In what Somoza calls the Bard's 'Pirandellian doubt', Shakespeare is not even sure of his own identity. In any case, he is aware of his neurosis, and somehow even accepts it as part of his job: 'We writers, engrossed in the problem of a play, tend to see it everywhere. We do not see friends, but characters. We writers are like Don Quixote: we have to go mad to manage to produce something really good'. This 'madness' extends to Shakespeare's confusion between reality and fiction in his daily life: he mistakes his servants for the actors of his company, and his maid says that he has even called his dog 'Burbage'.

Mirrors, for this Shakespeare, are a sort of magical door through which he can contact all the people he is obsessed with, namely his actors and Cervantes. He looks at himself in a mirror and instead of his own reflection he suddenly sees Burbage, who complains that he feels used by him. 'I am the brains. You are my shadow. My reflection', Shakespeare replies. And shortly afterwards: 'Shut up! You are nothing! You are there because I am here! ... I am the only one who matters. I am the writer. You are nobody' (55). However, when the rest of the actors in his company also appear in order to support Burbage and vindicate their importance, Shakespeare gives in and apologizes.

This scene exemplifies one of the main features of Shakespeare's character in *Miguel Will*: he is a mixture of pride and humility, arrogance and modesty. On the one hand, although he feels 'an urgent need of writing' with *Cardenio*, he also admits there are times when writers sit in front of a sheet of paper and have no inspiration. Despite the fact that he is not only the director, but also the author of *Cardenio*, Shakespeare consults the actors about how to stage the play and tries to listen to their opinions – though eventually his huge involvement in the project makes him turn a deaf ear to their comments. On the other hand, he cannot help showing himself rather conceited: when Condell – who plays Nicholas the barber in *Cardenio* – tries to remind him that there are certain conventions in the theatre other than those in the novel which he should take into account, Shakespeare interrupts him in a sarcastic tone: 'Are you giving me lessons in drama, Henry?' (28).

This arrogance of Shakespeare's is clearly shown at the end of the play, when he decides to burn the manuscript modified by Fletcher. As Susan Fischer points out, in Somoza's play Shakespeare is not able to cope with the idea of having a rival like Fletcher, 'less subtle but more to the fore theatrically speaking, whose philosophy was always "if the character gets complicated, omit it"'.[17] Indeed, the Shakespeare in *Miguel Will* had acidly complained of this rival: 'I'm tired of seeing how a play written by a good-for-nothing, arselicker like Fletcher becomes the king's favourite' (84). However, though levelled at Fletcher, Shakespeare's frustration does not come from jealousy, but rather from the fact that he has not been able to make the audience understand his interpretation of Don Quixote despite his huge personal effort and involvement.

José Carlos Somoza thinks that fictions like his 'Hamlet' or *Miguel Will* cannot make any contribution to Shakespeare's biography proper, but they can, however, awaken in the reader an interest in him as a human being and in what little is known about his life. In this respect, Somoza refuses to present Shakespeare as an extraordinary figure above or unlike us mere mortals – in fact, his Shakespeare even complains that the terrible fate of good writers is to be more mediocre than their inventions. Besides, in neither of these two works did Somoza intend to present a 'historical' Shakespeare, even if both works are studded with real or near-real facts about him, which are there as literary asides to the reader. For Somoza it is the gaps and ambiguities in the life and works of such a profound and imaginative author that tempt the inventiveness of so many contemporary writers and that also tempted his.[18]

However, these gaps and ambiguities place the fiction writer in a position which is not too dissimilar from that of the biographer, who, faced with the scarcity of facts, is forced to speculate. And, one way or another, speculation is geared towards an image of Shakespeare the man, his personality, his character, his habits. It is here that, despite his fictionalization and the biographical liberties taken, Somoza's approach to the Bard can coincide with that of a biographer who, like him, has decided to focus on Shakespeare the writer. In neither his *Miguel Will* nor his 'Hamlet' are we presented with images of Shakespeare *amoureux*, as in the early plays or the contemporary film on him, or of a Shakespeare in anger, as in Edward Bond's *Bingo*, but of Shakespeare the professional – 'less a Shakespeare in Love than a Shakespeare at Work'.[19]

Somoza's Shakespeare 'sweats' and strikes 'the second heat / Upon the Muses' anvil', as Jonson put it, to such an extent that he implores the muses to leave him alone. Whether at the Globe or in his Stratford home, the Shakespeare in *Miguel Will* is so engrossed in the creation of a complex character that he is pushed to the brink of derangement. In Somoza's 'Hamlet', writing helps him overcome the sorrow for his recently lost son: there he is also obsessed with his work, and needs to work in isolation. Moreover, it is his downright professional dedication that brings out some features of a strong, even unpleasant Shakespeare. Despite his admiration for the Bard, Somoza does not avoid aspects of an 'ungentle' Shakespeare, 'a man among men, a writer among writers'.[20] The Shakespeare in *Miguel Will* clashes many a time with his colleagues at the Globe, despises Fletcher, and behaves proudly. The one in 'Hamlet' has to yield to the demands of the Corporation, but does not do so passively: he is defiant and insults its representative, mocks them in his working method and the resulting play, and vindictively buries a secret message to unmask and denounce them in due course.

In other words, Shakespeare, for Somoza, is certainly the author who has most 'possessed' him, but his Shakespeare is also a man, with his weaknesses and foibles like any other, brought down from the pedestal to which critics and biographers had elevated him for so long – or simply, and in the words of his contemporary Thomas Heywood, Shakespeare the human being who 'was but Will' for all his 'enchanting Quill'.

Acknowledgements

This chapter is part of Research Project FFI2008-01969/FILO, funded by the Spanish Ministry of Science and Innovation.

Ángel-Luis Pujante is Emeritus Professor of English at the University of Murcia. He has written mainly on English Renaissance drama (Middleton and Shakespeare) and literary translation. He has co-edited, among others, *Four Hundred Years of Shakespeare in Europe* (with Ton Hoenselaars, 2003) and *Shakespeare in Spain. An Annotated Bilingual Bibliography* (with Juan Francisco Cerdá, 2014), and has published *Shakespeare llega a España. Ilustración y Romanticismo* (2019), a critical study of the early reception of Shakespeare in Spain. His main current area of research is the reception of Shakespeare in Spain and Europe. From 2000 to 2008 he was the head of the research project 'The presence of Shakespeare in Spain in the Framework of Europe Culture', in which he still collaborates. He is honorary president of ESRA.

Noemí Vera is a PhD candidate in Arts and Humanities at the University of Murcia. Her research focuses on Spanish biographies of Shakespeare and the study of Shakespeare as a character in Spanish fiction.

Notes

1. See the chapter on Shakespeare's ghosts in this volume, and Michael Dobson, *The Making of the National Poet: Shakespeare, Adaptation, and Authorship, 1660–1769* (Oxford: Oxford University Press, 1992), 140. See also Maurice J. O'Sullivan, Jr., ed., *Shakespeare's Other Lives. An Anthology of Fictional Depictions of the Bard* (Jefferson, North Carolina, and London: McFarland, 1997), 11. For the fictional treatment of authors in general, see *The Author as Character: Representing Historical Writers in Western Literature*, ed. Paul Franssen and Ton Hoenselaars (Madison, NJ: Fairleigh Dickinson University Press; London: Associated University Presses, May 1999).
2. Alexandre Duval, *Oeuvres complètes d'Alexandre Duval*, tome 5 (Paris: J.-Barba, 1822).
3. Alexandre Duval, *Shakespeare enamorado*, trans. Ventura de la Vega (Madrid: Repullés, 1831).
4. A paper on the 2007 Spanish film *Miguel y William* ('Inés París' *Miguel y William*: Shakespeare's Spanish shipwreck') was presented by Noemí Vera at the joint ESRA / German Shakespeare Society conferences in Weimar, April 2011.
5. See Keith Gregor and Encarna Vidal, 'The "Other" William and the Question of Authority in Spanish Stage Depictions of Shakespeare', *Sederi* 12 (2002), 237–46, and Keith Gregor, 'Shakespeare as Character on the Spanish Stage: A Metaphysics of Bardic Presence', in *Four Hundred Years of Shakespeare in Europe*, ed. A. Luis Pujante and Ton Hoenselaars (Newark and London: University of Delaware Press & Associated University Presses, 2003), 43–53.

6. José Carlos Somoza, *Miguel Will* (Madrid: SGAE, 1999; repr. Barcelona: Random House Mondadori, 2006). An English translation by Keith Gregor is pending publication. References are to the 1999 edition.
7. José Carlos Somoza, 'Hamlet', in *Historia secreta de la Corporación*, ed. Fernando Marías (Madrid: 451 Editores, 2008), 119–36.
8. More information, both in Spanish and English, can be obtained from Somoza's webpage: www.clubcultura.com/clubliteratura/clubescritores/somoza/home.htm
9. José Carlos Somoza, *El cebo* (Barcelona: Plaza y Janés, 2010). After *El cebo*, Somoza has continued to seek inspiration in Shakespeare's plays. As he has informed us in a private communication, his recent novel *El origen del mal* [The origin of evil] (Barcelona: B, 2018), based on the case of a real spy of Franco's, was inspired by *Macbeth*.
10. José Carlos Somoza, 'Shakespeare is Legion', in *Shakespeare and Spain*, ed. José Manuel González and Holger Klein (Lewiston, Queenston & Lampeter: The Edwin Mellen Press, 2002), 267–77.
11. José Carlos Somoza, 'Remordimientos de una reina', *El País Semanal* , 22 May 2005. www.elpais.com/articulo/portada/Remordimientos/reina/elpeputec/20050522elpepspor_17/Tes
12. José Carlos Somoza, 'La maldad es silencio (Shakespeare y los personajes malvados)', *Frenia* 2.1 (2002), 109–121.
13. This and all the subsequent translations into English are our own.
14. See also Douglas Lanier, *Shakespeare and Modern Popular Culture* (Oxford: Oxford University Press, 2002), 119–27.
15. Denis Rafter, 'Cuaderno de dirección', in *Miguel Will*, 105.
16. Denis Rafter, '*Miguel Will*. Un encuentro entre dos genios', *ADE Teatro* 107 (2005), 200.
17. Susan Fisher, 'Cervantes sobre las tablas: *Miguel Will*, de José Carlos Somoza', *Theatralia: revista poética del teatro* 5 (2003), 247–60; 255.
18. Somoza, email message to Ángel-Luis Pujante, 26 April 2011.
19. James Shapiro, *1599. A Year in the Life of William Shakespeare* (London: Faber and Faber, 2005), xxiii.
20. Katherine Duncan-Jones, *Ungentle Shakespeare: Scenes from his Life* (London: Arden Shakespeare, 2001), x.

Chapter 9

The Bard-Baiting Model in *Upstart Crow* and *Something Rotten*

Richard O'Brien

In their introduction to the *New Oxford Shakespeare,* Gary Taylor and Terri Bourus argue that all anti-Stratfordian conspiracy theories are a kind of 'fan fiction: dissatisfied with the dull documented life of their favorite author, his fans write for him a new biography in order to provide a better, more satisfying plot.'[1] Pop culture narratives like *Anonymous* are not, of course, Shakespeare fan fiction in its truest sense: a medium encountered largely online which is dialogic both between networks of contemporary authors, and between those authors and the Shakespearan *ur*-text. Each, however, participates in aspects of what Valerie Fazel and Louise Geddes identify as the domain of fanfic, as a 'document of reception that uses and recognizes Shakespeare's place in an ever-changing world'.[2]

Fazel and Geddes's description of fanfic as 'a free-roaming, self-reflexive examination of its source material' which 'playfully interrogates the genres that it exploits, and in doing so, exists as

Notes for this section begin on page 171.

a type of screenshot of Shakespeare's place in the popular imagination' might, furthermore, help us to understand an emerging counter-trend in contemporary fictionalizations of Shakespearean biography (277). Some biofictions afford Shakespeare a less desirable cultural place than what Taylor and Bourus call the 'fancy frocks and stately homes' of aspirational myth (12). This trend sometimes dovetails with the authorship 'controversy' in separating the man from the work. Authors in this model, which I call 'Bard-baiting', gleefully denigrate the man Shakespeare while frequently reserving some degree of qualified praise for his writing.

In what follows, I define this paradigm, suggest cultural parallels for the approach to Shakespearean authority it foregrounds, and observe its operation across two key texts: the BBC sitcom *Upstart Crow* (2016–18) and the Broadway musical *Something Rotten,* which premiered in 2015. These texts offer a counterpoint to the paradigm of 'meet[ing] the author', recently adduced by Janice Wardle within biofictions such as *Shakespeare in Love* and seen in the glossy TNT series *Will*, which, despite substantial Bard-baiting elements in the latter, primarily take 'conventional' and 'partial' stances on Shakespeare-as-character.[3] I conclude with a broader reflection on the purposes and effects of this emerging narrative trope.

What's at Stake, or Defining Bard-Baiting

A definition of Bard-baiting requires an understanding of what forces in biofiction it ranges itself against. Many trends in recent pop presentations of Shakespearean biography have been clarified by Wardle, who describes how the 1998 biopic *Shakespeare in Love* explicitly 'encouraged engagement and assessment of the premise that Shakespeare was like us, which we might say is a rather teleological reduction of the idea that he might be for all time'.[4] The narrative of *Shakespeare in Love* is driven by a 'frustrated' character who, like his real-life analogue, is also already a married father, cheating on his wife left behind in Stratford.

The film's Shakespeare is, however, not presented as morally dubious. *Shakespeare in Love* remains, as Wardle notes, a conservative biographical portrait largely in line with the traditional sentimental view of the playwright's moral character mocked by Edward Bond: 'Orthodox critics usually assume that Shakespeare would have driven a car so well that he'd never have an accident'.[5] As such, despite his infidelity – of which Katherine West Scheil has suggested that 'millennial audiences are willing to overlook an adulterous Shakespeare if it means that they can experience a love story that explains his creative process' – this orthodox biographical Shakespeare still unproblematically functions as a 'source of moral authority' which, like other kinds of authority, might be bestowed by his 'material presence alone'.[6]

Other recent pop culture narratives follow on from Madden's Shakespeare. TNT's *Will* posits the author as a youthful sex symbol, drawing on a punk-inspired musical and visual aesthetic to eschew the pitfalls of a musty schoolroom Shakespeare. In the DVD 'Making Of' featurette accompanying the 2015 film *Bill*, writer Ben Willbond introduces his comic take on the 'lost years' of a young 'loser' Shakespeare, who will, but crucially has not *yet*, become 'the guy who wrote these amazing works of art'. Both pursue a model emphasizing the twinned journeys of artistic development and personal growth, which I term the 'Bill-dungsroman'. The fledging playwright confronts various obstacles including 'destructive' marital infidelity (*Will*, Episode 9), creative immaturity, and his own selfishness and arrogance, which he must overcome to emerge as a recognizably 'great poet' (*Will*, Episode 5) into a world which is 'ready for Shakespeare' (*Bill*) – once Shakespeare himself has become 'ready' to inhabit his own iconic status.

True Bard-baiting is, at least superficially, more iconoclastic. If, as Scheil notes, 'few works construct a negative image of Shakespeare, likely so as not to alienate a potential audience seeking stories of Shakespeare's private life', works which do advance such an image seem to speak to an audience seeking something rather more adversarial (99). Narratives in this mode depict a Shakespeare who is to varying extents corrupt, cowardly, squalid and morally flawed; furthermore, they stage attacks by other characters, with whom the audience is guided to identify, on Shakespeare's personal life and literary choices. *Upstart Crow* and *Something Rotten* pursue the implications of an immoral or unpleasant Shakespeare significantly further than *Bill* or *Will*, allowing the playwright to fail in love and art, to be meaningfully bested by others, and to be knocked down to size.

Apparent vitriol towards both man and work might be what most separates Bard-baiting as a category of biofiction from more light-hearted, joshingly anachronistic jokes around the iconicity of a figure whose status is, for the audience, already assured. Andreas Höfele notes how in bear-baiting spectacles, 'the bear would have been perceived as the more human-like creature, yet it fell to the dogs to execute the violent impulses of the human audience by proxy'.[7] How much more might these impulses arise in relation to the figure whose 'greatest legacy', according to *Will*'s showrunner Craig Pearce, and to Harold Bloom, is 'teaching us what it is to be human'?[8]

The 'violent impulses' of these texts share a certain tonal quality with the performances of the Scottish theatre company Shit-faced Shakespeare, who offer heavily-abridged versions of Shakespearean plays with the rogue element of one actor in the company arriving drunk and continuing to drink throughout the presentation. This format's subversive decentring of textual authority is nonetheless entirely temporary: Jennifer Holl, describing an American equivalent, Drunk Shakespeare, detects 'a shared spirit of spontaneous communitas that playfully dismantles traditional theatrical structures'.[9] The texts produced are brought low through the anti-iconic, unpredictable clowning of these boozy interventions but, in the paradigm of Bakhtin's carnivalesque, emerge on the other side of this collision with their hierarchical position intact and even, through repeat performance, reinvested with social and cultural meaning.

Bard-baiting fictions, I argue, pursue a similar dialectic between a mocking subversion which at times tips into conscious degradation of Shakespeare, and a tempered but continued 'reverence' (Holl) for the texts disseminated under his name. Biofictions of authors often foreground, in terms increasingly familiar from contemporary conversations about what Claire Dederer calls 'the art of monstrous men', the question of whether 'we believe genius gets special dispensation, a behavioral hall pass'.[10] Despite their apparent challenges to his authority, Bard-baiting works tend to grant Shakespeare such a pass, if only after subjecting him to heavy scrutiny. Like the captive bear my chosen descriptor references, Shakespeare – or a version of his work, separated from his tainted biography – demonstrates his superior vigour and lives on to fight another day.

'You're showing a very unpleasant side': *Upstart Crow* and *Something Rotten*

Premiering in 2015 and 2016 respectively, the Broadway musical *Something Rotten* and the BBC sitcom *Upstart Crow* each present the critical view of both Shakespeare's composition process and his moral character which exemplifies what I call 'Bard-baiting'. *Upstart Crow's* creator, Ben Elton, was nonetheless involved in the more traditionally Bardolatrous 2018 biopic *All Is True,* in which Shakespeare is called 'the most beautiful mind ... that ever existed in this world', praise which we are not invited to question. The existence of this companion piece supports an argument that Elton's Bard-baiting series, as it develops, shows itself more deeply invested in the Shakespeare myth than might initially appear.[11] As the earlier musical takes greater liberties with the concept of authorship (and views its relation to morality more sternly) than the sitcom, I discuss the two works out of chronological order.

Almost every episode of *Upstart Crow* ends with David Mitchell's Shakespeare being fed an idea by his wife Anne which will go on to define some of his most enduring works: she even coins 'all's the world's a stage', only to be told it is a 'bit of a tortured image' (2.5). Elsewhere, entire speeches from *Othello* (2.1) and *Henry IV Part Two* (2.2) are transcribed verbatim from the conversation of supporting characters, and Susanna suggests the entire plot, and title, of *Love's Labours' Lost* (3.2). Though Shakespeare's acquaintances furnishing him with material is not a new concept in biofiction, Mitchell's character demonstrates a particularly obtuse lack of imagination:

> Here am I, trying to conjure up a brilliant plot involving parted lovers in an exotic foreign location, and there you are making it impossible for me to think because you're parted from your lover who's gone to an exotic foreign location ... Hang on! (2.3)

Shakespeare is not only reliant on significant prompting from others for some of his best ideas, but is also devoid of generic sense – those around him frequently interpret his tragic plots, notably that of *Hamlet*, as funny, identifying *avant la lettre* what Susan Snyder called 'the comic matrix of Shakespeare's tragedies'.[12] When he fails to credit his servant, Bottom, for providing one of the most enduring images of *Romeo and Juliet* once it has been admired by the Earl of Southampton, Bottom tellingly comments: 'You're showing a very unpleasant side, if you don't mind me saying, Master' (2.6).

Despite frequently critiquing the English class system which he feels is keeping him down, this Shakespeare also actively pursues fame and social status as a gentleman. An occasional anti-elitist strain – 'what I have, I have by merit' (2.4) – is undercut by his unconcealed desire to mingle with the wealthy and powerful, a theme to which Elton's later film *All Is True* returns in a more melancholic key. On finally receiving his family coat-of-arms, Will renounces his previous iconoclasm: 'Now I'm posh myself, I see the English class system is entirely appropriate, my own elevation wholly merited' (3.2). Will treats his servant rudely, and espouses anti-working class sentiments: he believes that 'all people of lowly birth are inherently hilarious, because of their pathetic stupidity and delusions of grandeur', and that 'servants go in the stage directions' (3.1). In a satirical flight alluding to recent industrial action by British railway workers, Will admits that his support of the striking coachmen is tempered by a selfish wish that they would 'burn in hell till the end of time' (2.3).

The series also repeatedly foregrounds Shakespeare's ironic inability to predict future social and artistic developments: 'Sonnets are what the kids are digging and ever shall' (1.4); 'fact-averse' conspiracy theorists will 'never wield political influence' (2.5). For Sarah Dustagheer, such moments invite us 'to laugh at our inherent belief in our modern sophistication and sense of historic progress', but notably it is Shakespeare himself rather than the supporting characters who is most commonly on the wrong side of history.[13] His rarely-accurate predictions often allude to the prophecy of Lear's fool through variations of the phrase 'there will come in a time in Albion, when ...'. Frequently devolving into critiques of modern mass culture tropes, including reality television and binge-drinking among young women 'staggering from tavern to tavern' (2.3), they represent a distinctly middle-aged and small-c conservative attitude to twenty-first-century cultural politics.

His physical appearance contributes to the overall effect. Unlike the urbane young gun of *Shakespeare in Love,* here Shakespeare does not even *look* young: he is styled with the receding hairline of the 1623 Droeshout engraving. Within the show's somewhat chronologically-fluid world, Shakespeare – played by David Mitchell, aged 41 when it premiered – has yet to write *The Taming of the Shrew*, *The Comedy of Errors*, and *The Two Gentlemen of Verona*, texts which most scholarship agrees were all extant by the time the historical Shakespeare was 30.[14]

Illustrations 9.1 and 9.2. Laurie Davidson (above) and David Mitchell (below), playing Shakespeares of roughly equivalent ages in *Will* and *Upstart Crow*. Screen capture by author.

An anachronistically old 'young Shakespeare' – by contrast to a 'Shakespeare made fit', such as the handsome and conventionally-hirsute Laurie Davidson, aged 24–25 during the shooting of the 1589-set *Will* – helps to suggest that Shakespeare himself is, and always has been, superannuated and tedious.[15] His rants about failures to follow rules and procedure have low stakes, as Marlowe points out: 'tell it to a leper' (3.6). When castigating the 'mooching hooligans' (2.6) who should not have been allowed onto a delayed coach because they arrived after its stated departure time, this Shakespeare comes across as more reactionary than revolutionary.

Indeed, far from being politically radical (as his Catholicism serves to make him in *Will*), Mitchell's playwright cravenly serves the demands of power. His life is threatened by association with a houseguest, his former schoolmaster Simon Hunt, who turns out to be a 'Jesuit terrorist' sent from Douai (2.2). When told 'you will burn for it' (2.2), rather than defending a persecuted co-religionist, Will kicks the priest out of his house, eventually exposing him to a martyr's death, to save his own skin.[16] Christopher Marlowe, present in Warwickshire as a government agent, fudges the issue so that Shakespeare is not suspected, but hailed as 'a hero' who 'entrapped the traitorous Hunt' (2.2): there is no suggestion that Shakespeare feels any compunction about a Catholic, with close religious ties to his mother, being handed over to state torturers, or that he might wish to participate in political resistance.

Will's moral weakness for political gain also extends to a gleeful admission that his portrayal of Richard III was a series of 'alternative fact[s]' which 'the Queen loved' sufficiently that 'lies become truth'. Rather than causing him to reflect on the dangers of art becoming propaganda, this outcome inspires Shakespeare to produce a flattering portrait of the queen's father with 'redeeming features'. He agrees, without shame, when asked by his landlady's daughter, Kate, if he truly intends to 'sanitize the reputation of the meanest, cruelest monarch that ever lived' (2.2). There are *some* limits to Shakespeare's toadying: on winning the queen's favour, he asks in return not for his own advancement, but for his friend Marlowe's release from the Tower (2.7).

A lack of artistic integrity is foregrounded elsewhere, however, when he proposes to 'crush, abuse, and humiliate' Kate in *The Taming of the Shrew*, designed as a strong woman to appeal to women audiences, in order to also please the 'men who pay for entry' (2.5). Furthermore, he uses explicitly racist language, describing a visiting African prince, Otello, before he has even met him, as 'wild and passionate ... primal, organic' and 'untouched by the example of ancient civilizations'. This is forcibly challenged by Kate, who points to the cultural achievements of the ancient Egyptians, Carthaginians and Numidians: this Shakespeare, in his belief that Jesus Christ was also 'blond, with blue eyes', is thus critiqued for his racial ignorance within his own time (2.1).

Besides frequently diverging from twenty-first-century mores with regard to race and gender, Shakespeare is also thoughtless and insensitive on an interpersonal level. He offers both his house and wife as surety for a loan towards investment in the Theatre (1.6) and uncaringly takes down notes for the plot of *The Two Gentlemen of Verona* while watching Kate have her heart broken (2.3). He even plucks quills from the family chicken, rendering it too scared to lay for their food supply ('Whenever you come home with the muse upon you, we get no eggs for a week'), in what might be an occluded play on Greene's reference to a feather-pinching bird who thinks far too highly of himself to care from whom he steals (1.2).

The show also musters a broad range of insults against Shakespeare's dramaturgy. Left to his own devices, Shakespeare is prolix to the point of incomprehensibility – 'you come up with a brilliant one-liner and then ruin it by going on and on and on' (2.4) – and prone to 'overcomplicate' his plots with 'your usual rubbish of mistaken identities' (2.5) such that they become 'a farrago of nonsense' (2.7). His plays are undesirably 'very long' (2.4), with the soliloquies in particular forcing the 'mob players' to stand silently 'for many hours, pretending to understand' (3.5). His rhymes do not work (the show wilfully ignores historical pronunciation change), his jokes are far too complex, and many of what will become his best-known lines are met with confusion and boredom. His daughter takes him to task for putting words in the wrong order because 'no one talks like that' (1.1).

Shakespeare himself, meanwhile, naively praises his own 'incomprehensible subplots and pointless minor characters' as an element of his work which he 'only expect[s] to get more popular over the years … particularly with schoolchildren' (3.2). *Upstart Crow* does give him a contemporary admirer in the shape of Kate, who calls elements of his writing 'perfect' (2.3, 2.4), but she also attempts in vain to counsel him to make his scripts less misogynist. Her accusation that the drugging in *Dream* constitutes 'sexual assault' is dismissed by Shakespeare as part of a 'joyless sociopolitical agenda' (3.1), because calling attention to characters 'obtaining sexual favours by deception' would involve 'criminalizing half the plays I ever wrote' (3.4).

Taken as a whole, these factors imply not an ingrained ignorance on the part of Shakespeare's contemporaries, but a fundamental backwardness in Shakespeare's own non-mimetic, language-driven and of course, male-centric dramaturgy, which invites our laughter. This Shakespeare is entirely of an age, rather than for all time, with none of the claims on proto-modern prescience or contemporaneity advanced by *Bill* or *Will*. By contrast, the largely uneducated supporting characters who critique his aesthetic choices are often far closer to twenty-first-century speech and attitudes regarding both gender politics and aesthetic norms, making Shakespeare seem conservative and outmoded even in his own milieu.

But this barrage of criticism is tempered, not least by the existence of the show: having aired three series and two Christmas specials, *Upstart Crow* implies that how these plays and poems came to be written is worth knowing. The show's class politics also position us against its main antagonist, Greene, and his doomed plots to destroy the man he calls the Crow on the wholly mistaken assumption that 'fortune favours the Cambridge man' (2.7). His one successful scheme, the initiation of the authorship conspiracy, is explicitly a classist attempt to make people believe 'some educated posh boy had writ his plays in secret' (3.3). Greene is also rendered even more linguistically distant from contemporary comprehensibility than Shakespeare himself: his *Friar Bacon and Friar Bungay* is repeatedly dismissed as an 'appalling old chestnut' (2.7), and actor Mark Heap pronounces every '-èd' and disyllabic 'i-on' in his lines in a knowing pastiche of sixteenth-century 'Original Pronunciation'.

Despite Greene's machinations against him, the people around Will continue to support and assist him, thereby shoring up his strong sense of his own talent even as they chip away at many of its elements. Bottom reifies at the same time as he punctures Shakespeare's inflated sense of self when he comments 'For a genius you don't know much about human nature' (1.3). When Anne saves the sonnets from the family fire in 1.4, her actions are still coded as worthwhile rather than creating an incomprehensible burden for future readers (as the poems are implied to be earlier in the episode). Will is told he has to 'stop taking well-known sayings and claiming you wrote them', undermining his claim to singular creative ability, but in the same sentence the show has it both ways, praising him for his skill: 'you're better than that, you know you are' (2.2).

Shakespeare himself consistently invokes an arrogant self-belief which is expressed in the language of later Bardolatry, usually when (like Elton's well-known earlier character, Blackadder) his plans have been waylaid by petty frustrations. *Richard III* is 'all perfect, all four hours of it' (2.3); Titania waking to see Bottom in *Dream* is the 'most celebrated comic moment in the entire history of English theatre' (3.1). Shakespeare agrees with Kate that it is his 'dream ... to be recognized now and for all time as indisputably the greatest writer that ever lived' (2.5). At one point, he launches into a flurry of phrases familiar from Bernard Levin's 'Quoting Shakespeare', which he is (we know, deservedly) 'confident will enter the common idiom', to be told 'You're very clever Mr. Shakespeare, but you can be an awful show-off' (2.5); in comparison, one of the quoted terms, 'bedazzle', becomes the focus of unself-conscious praise in *Will*.

At times, the Crow overreaches – for instance, in the blinkered liberal assumption that his writing a 'slightly sympathetic Jew' in *The Merchant of Venice* has 'set humanity upon a path which must lead inevitably to a world of universal tolerance, peace, love and understanding' (3.3) – but broadly, the teleology of Shakespeare's future importance allows for circular reasoning around his apparent failings. An obscure speech is explained away with the idea that 'future generations, trusting in my genius, will just think they're being stupid and have missed something' (2.5). Future generations trusting in his genius is, indeed, the safety net which makes possible Elton's critique both of Shakespeare's dramaturgy and his morality.

Three further factors help to shore up the show's heavily-hedged claims of greatness. Firstly, the first two series present the writer as perpetually on the cusp of completing *Romeo and Juliet*, framed as his potential breakout hit, which suggests that many of the lines we are hearing – even those that make it into later scripts – exist at an early stage of his authorial development in which, despite Mitchell being visibly older, his flaws can be partly forgiven as the work of an 'apprentice' (as Wardle writes of *Bill*). His moral compass also seems to be undergoing its own apprenticeship, particularly around issues of gender. Given her rare belief in him, it is striking that Shakespeare at first continually underrates Kate's worth because it is 'illegal for girls to do anything interesting' (1.1). However, the experience of writing *Shrew* leads him to realize his misogyny has 'lost [him] the good opinion of two women whose respect' he values (2.5). In response, Kate lets him partially off the hook, echoing modern liberal humanist scholars' attempts to rehabilitate Shakespeare's depiction of apparently prejudiced attitudes:

> I still respect you, Mr Shakespeare, for, although I think your play doth sorely insult women, you are a creature of your times, and in truth, even now your misogyny be less offensive than most. At least you take trouble to write your women some fine verse. (2.5)

When *Romeo and Juliet* does emerge, it is to make amends to his teenage daughter for the acknowledged mistakes of *Shrew,* and even the typically dismissive Susanna declares it a 'beautiful' and 'eternally sad' (2.5) work, which 'if you really read it ... and come back to it quite a few times ... you can start to sort of enjoy' (2.6). Indeed, as time goes on, Susanna offers a growing if tentative recognition of Shakespeare's skill within a show which has thus far broadly disparaged it, noting that *Hamlet* will eventually 'make a great tragedy' (3.2), and that Shylock's 'Hath not a Jew eyes' speech might be used to encourage her students – she has begun teaching in a dame school – to treat a classmate with a disability more empathetically (3.3).

Romeo and Juliet also allows Shakespeare to display a new-found respect for Kate and her dreams: having found he 'could hear my Juliet in no other voice but thine', he tries to cast her, in disguise, in the role, because 'you deserved it. If anyone had a right to play a star-crossed lover, it was you' (2.6). This realization leads him to the most progressive statement yet: 'I, for one, hope that one day lady-acting will be made legal' (2.6). Shakespeare's developing open-mindedness is also, somewhat ham-fistedly, extended to trans people. He decides to shelve *Twelfth Night* 'for a few years' because he is not 'sure the world's ready for a non-gender-specific trans comedy yet'; Anne calls this concept 'ahead of [its] time' (2.7). But as with the show's representation of people of colour – via Otello and a tavern-keeper character modelled on the historical 'Lucy Negro' – other jokes on the subject make it doubtful whether *Upstart Crow* is in fact undermining or merely reiterating reductive clichés.

The second 'pass' given to this morally-questionable Shakespeare is, paradoxically, his aforementioned tendency to borrow ideas from those around him. The supporting cast's contributions partially dismantle what Dustagheer calls 'the myth of the playwright divinely inspired, writing virtuoso works in isolation'. Instead, his work emerges as a common property, diffused between multiple creators, many of whom we can recognize as avatars of our own ordinariness even as they ghost-write the speeches of kings. This decentralized, common ownership of a 'Popular Shakespeare' seems to 'force the audience into a playful reassessment of their relationship with the text'; this might be one logical end-point of earlier efforts to market the plays to 'increasingly large readerships, driven by the growth in popular education as part of the high-Victorian drive for self-improvement'.[17] The work, though destabilizingly mocked by other characters, retains its aura of significance, but in some surrogated and vicarious sense now belongs to us all rather than to one incomparable being.

The third, and the most emotive, way in which the show salvages Shakespeare from his own questionable youthful conduct is through the introduction of personal tragedy. Douglas Lanier reminds us how

> [T]he principle of authorial biographicality, the notion that the art is fundamentally expressive of, or at least deeply co-extensive with, the author's life ... is often positioned against rival models of authorship that the writer must reject to become 'authentic'.[18]

Shakespeare's development is thus inextricably linked to biographical suffering. Over the course of the series, the Crow demonstrates an ongoing neglect of what Dustagheer calls his 'long-suffering wife, children and parents', including a failure to come to Hamnet's school Latin recitation even though, as Anne puts it, 'the other dads come ... a father should take an interest in his children' (2.4). This fits into a wider pattern whereby Shakespeare is presented as a negligent husband and father, fulfilling the 'myth of a libertine Shakespeare' which Scheil notes dates back to Shakespeare's own lifetime and features various 'anti-Annes ... proposed as substitute love interests' (21). Sometimes, as in *Shakespeare in Love*, this comes with no significant consequences; at the other end of the spectrum, in Jude Morgan's 2012 novel *The Secret Life of William Shakespeare*, the title character, having moved his family to London, is held responsible for his son's death from an urban plague outbreak (Scheil notes 'there is no evidence that Anne ever set foot in London', 91).[19]

In *Upstart Crow*, despite the occasional suggestion of infidelity ('the dark lady episode' is invoked, with reference to Emilia Lanier, in 3.1), this failing is partially recuperated. The second season Christmas special and the third season opener both turn on mutual declarations of love between husband and wife ('Will, I don't deserve you';

'Anne, I don't deserve you' – 2.7). Lanier does, however, reappear as Will's preferred companion for the London Theatre Awards ceremony in the final 'regular' episode of the series; an event Will chooses to attend rather than 'the most important day of [his son's] life', his christening, which Anne portentously calls an 'appointment with God' (3.6). This decision sees Will branded a 'horrible, selfish man', who continues to pursue fame and glory, and who dismisses his own wife behind her back as a 'milkmaid' and so 'not fitting company' for his attempt 'to get in with the pamperloins' (3.6).

Having asserted that life 'does not get any better than this', Will's plans crumble in quick succession: his wife enters, disrupting his intended adultery, and is subsequently called home by a letter informing her Susanna and Judith are 'a bit feverish' (3.6). Though the show stops short of blaming Will for the events that follow, when he comes home to Stratford complaining that he has not won any prizes, he discovers that something rather more serious requires his attention: the episode, and season, ends with a tragic turn in the death of his son Hamnet, which will implicitly colour Shakespeare's subsequent writing. This is a moment *Upstart Crow* repeatedly telegraphs, beginning with Susanna's suggestion in 3.2 that Shakespeare might be 'too comfortable and content' to get inside 'the heart of Hamlet's agony'. Anne responds that 'if personal tragedy is what it takes ... I hope your Danish play be never finished' (3.2).

A compensatory equation is thus established between the artistic success of *Hamlet* and the human loss of Hamnet; Dederer's concept of 'special dispensation' raises the question of whether the latter is somehow worth the former. At any rate, the death calls forth a certain humility from Elton's Shakespeare – 'for all that [Anne] says I'm the clever one, in my experience, she's right about most things' (3.6) – and an acknowledgement of profound work yet to come, in Hamnet's reported dying words that his father should not 'rush' to heaven because 'he knew how busy you are' (3.6). The season concludes with the Shakespeares in silence as David Mitchell, in voiceover, recites the lines from *King John* frequently associated with Hamnet's death, beginning 'Grief fills the room up of my absent child'. The use of this speech, not widely familiar and here unattributed, at the end of three series which have primarily presented Shakespeare as an author of histories and comedies, is *Upstart Crow*'s strongest single gesture to the idea that Shakespeare's poetry has inherent value as a potent commentary on the (tragic) human condition.

This poignant final act recalls Elton's earlier First World War-set comedy, *Blackadder Goes Forth*, the final episode of which sees its lead characters – twentieth-century versions of the cast of the time-hopping show's more frivolous earlier iterations – 'climb out of the trenches and charge into German machinegun fire' in what Tom Fordy describes as 'the dramatic equivalent of [a] bayonet to the heart'.[20] Before his death from plague, Hamnet himself attempts to risk his life in military service due to Will's 'stupid' *Henry V* 'exciting the boy about war'; Anne's stern comment, 'young men might die because of your plays', points obliquely forward to *Blackadder's* conclusion (3.4).

Upstart Crow does, however, continue beyond Hamnet's death. A somewhat unusual second Christmas episode sees Shakespeare 'mourn [his] son' and attempt to 'heal' and 'redeem [his] own sou[l]' by inspiring Greene to change his 'heartless' and 'sanctimonious' ways in a plot modelled on Dickens's 'A Christmas Carol' (3.7). This first departure from the Shakespeare corpus suggests a need for breathing space immediately after Hamnet's death, where satire on another plot might seem simply inappropriate. This final instalment doubles down on the power of the *King John* speech, which Anne quotes to her husband as profound wisdom; it also, perhaps, functions as a bridge towards the more sustained mourning of Hamnet's loss which informs the central emotional arc of Elton's second, near-contemporaneous Shakespearean biofiction, the 2018 film *All Is True*.

The Stranger who offers Will, in a kind of dream vision, the 'Christmas Carol' material in the *Upstart Crow* special is played by Kenneth Branagh, emphasizing the link between the end of the comedy series and Branagh's starring appearance in the later film biopic he also directed. *All Is True*, despite strong elements of moral critique, centres on Shakespeare's reconciliation with his estranged family, a 'victorious' homecoming which Ben Jonson ruefully asserts that the author of 'the greatest body of plays that ever were or will be ... deserved'. The assault on conventional Shakespearean biography begun in Elton's scripts for *Upstart Crow* thus seems, three seasons and one film later, to have given way to an unadulterated assertion of Shakespeare's supreme merit in the most conventional sense possible.

This eventual vindication could not be further from the treatment offered Shakespeare in my final case study, *Something Rotten*. This Broadway musical, with music and lyrics by Wayne and Karey Kirkpatrick and a book by John O'Farrell, insists on an extreme separation of work and author. Shakespeare appears here in a double perspective: as a widely beloved Elizabethan rock star, and as an egotist and plagiarist who, like Greene's upstart crow, achieves his greatest successes by stealing from other authors.

On the one hand, Shakespeare's iconic centrality to his own culture seems assured: the playwright himself appears at mass public performances, where he performs sonnets and famous speeches while holding out a microphone for responses from an adoring crowd: 'Let me hear you say now is...'[21] This is an individualistic cult of the author rather than the playing company, in which what one song names 'Will Power' is drawn from the collective force of his fanbase: 'I am the will of the people now'. One fan even makes a positive out of a trait *Upstart Crow* frames as desperately dusty and passé, declaring 'I love how he puts words in the wrong order!'[22]

Shakespeare inspires an anachronistic fervour over first editions and signed sonnets, and is near-overwhelmed by the trappings of twenty-first-century literary celebrity, a context within which Wardle argues historical fiction authors find it necessary to 'resurrect the idea of the author': 'There's lunches and meetings and poetry readings / and endless interviews'. But this already-assured celebrity status only induces what can be described as the anxiety of his own influence: Christian Borle's narcissistic Shakespeare laments in 'Hard to be the Bard' that it is 'Hard to do something as good as the last thing I did that was already great'. As regards dramaturgical technique, this unnatural elevation creates an effect similar to that described by Douglas Bruster whereby Shakespeare becomes 'a figure in whom the precedents of his craft and the efforts of his contemporaries have been collapsed' – as an offstage announcer puts it before the 'Will Power' concert, we are about to meet the man who 'puts the "I am" in iambic pentameter'.[23]

This alignment of poetic form with personal brand, however, inspires an equal and opposite reaction from rival playwright Nick Bottom. Nick's poetic brother Nigel, an avowed Shakespeare aficionado, fiercely believes in the work's literary qualities as well as its popular appeal; but Nick seems to hate even the suggestion that poetry and the theatre might ever come into contact, asking 'Why can't we just write like we speak?' He tells Nigel to 'take all the poetry energy and channel it into something that people might actually *pay* to see', and is deeply sceptical of his brother's vague defence of 'the beauty and the poetry of lyrical language': 'I don't know, I haven't understood a single word in our last three plays'. This parallels the thread in *Upstart Crow* where Shakespeare's language, particularly his verse, is deemed unrealistic, obscure and tedious: the sitcom also features the premature invention of the musical, a form of 'joyful, uplifting, popular entertainment' which is appealing precisely because it might mean that 'instead of opening with five pages of' implicitly dull 'blank verse', *Henry VI Part One* might begin with the popular madrigal 'Now Is The Month Of Maying' (2.6).

Something Rotten's Nick is, however, an iconoclast within his own time for this particular preference – unlike the chorus of critics in *Upstart Crow,* his distaste for Shakespeare's verse makes him definitively an outlier. The critiques of Shakespeare he offers speak to modern audiences, while distancing Nick from his early modern contemporaries. Nick's critiques once again constitute a dog-whistle appeal to twenty-first-century perceptions: Shakespeare is attacked not only for his jokes not landing, but also for wearing 'that silly, frilly collar round his throat', a phrase suggesting ruffs were not in common usage. *Something Rotten* finds space for the entire company to agree that the opening dialogue of *Romeo and Juliet* is intrinsically unfunny: a point also made in *Upstart Crow*. Still, though Nick's dismissal of Shakespeare, on the grounds of a preference for mimetic realism, seeks our approval as a modern audience, it has less traction for his peers, as is clear from their reactions in the raucous 'God, I Hate Shakespeare':

NICK:
>Oh, God, I hate Shakespeare
>His plays are wordy, but
>Oh, no, the great Shakespeare
>That little turd, he has no
>Sense about the audience
>He makes them feel so dumb
>The bastard doesn't care that my
>Poor ass is getting numb

MALE ENSEMBLE:
>How can you say that? How can you say that?

NICK:
>It's easy, I can say it cause it's absolutely true

MALE ENSEMBLE:
>Don't be a penis, the man is a genius

NICK:
>His genius is he's fooling all of you.

Even Nick's hatred is, however, finally folded into a form of admiration for the author's artistic achievement, in which Shakespeare performs his traditional role of encouraging the auditor to reflect on his own humanity:

> God, I hate Shakespeare
> But when I sit and really contemplate Shakespeare
> I guess I hate the fact that he is everything I ever dreamed that I could be
> I mostly hate the way he makes me feel about me

This admission paves the way for the musical's rejection of Shakespeare to shift from the work to the man. To summarize a complex plot: having heard garbled reports from a soothsayer about the content of Shakespeare's next play, Nick Bottom attempts to pre-empt its success by developing a musical theatre piece entitled *Omelette*. Nigel, meanwhile, works on an alternative script about a Prince suffering 'anguish' over a 'great loss' when his 'true love' is 'forced into religious exile' (Nigel's own Puritan love interest is currently facing the same fate). Nick rejects this script, which audience members may recognize as the text of *Hamlet,* out of hand, but when Shakespeare himself hears Nigel's lines, he recognizes their brilliance. Describing them as 'better than Shakespeare' (a name which thus already suggests iconic value), Shakespeare tries, out of professional jealousy, to dissuade their author from using them. He describes 'to be or not to be' and 'to thine own self be true', here newly-minted, as 'overused clichés' from which Nigel needs to be steered away, before declaring:

> Nigel, listen to me, you're good, quite good. Luckily I caught this before you embarrassed yourself in public, and as your friend I will read this to see if there's anything here that can be salvaged, but I don't want to see this with your name on it.

In a final trial scene, after accusing the Bottom brothers of theft, Shakespeare delivers a number of 'his' most famous speeches, and Nigel realizes that they have all been stolen from his notebook. A deal is struck to avoid execution (for which crime it is somewhat unclear): Nick and Nigel (like Viola de Lessups at the end of *Shakespeare in Love,* and perhaps Alice Burbage in *Will*) are exiled to the New World, where they will found the tradition of American musical theatre, and in return Shakespeare is allowed to continue profiting from Nigel's ideas under his own name. The closing song sees the ghost-written *Hamlet* acknowledged as a 'masterpiece', but we know that it is Nigel's masterpiece, not Shakespeare's, which the brothers, now reunited, can now celebrate together.

Despite partially dismantling the biofictional Shakespeare monolith, the musical thus evokes from its audience a tacit agreement about the quality of Shakespeare's writing. The show is still, after all, largely parasitic on Shakespeare. To sing along with 'I Hate Shakespeare', for instance, you have to produce the name 'Shakespeare' no less than fourteen times. Plot elements come from *The Merchant of Venice*, *Romeo and Juliet* and *Macbeth*; rehearsals of *Omelette* are interrupted by Nigel stating: 'something about it just doesn't feel right', playing to an audience familiar with particular quotes which Nick's attempt at piracy has distorted and thus aligning Shakespeare's text with rightness and inevitability.

By contrast, when Nigel himself brings into rehearsals a rag-tag collection of the most famous lines from *Hamlet*, the company love his work even though the script makes no internal narrative sense. The scene is only possible because enough of the audience identifies it *as Hamlet* and thus can attest to its prior value as lines which signify the arrival in the text of the 'powerful cultural institution, constructed around the figure of Shakespeare': onstage, it does not communicate anything in and of itself.[24] Nick's dismissal of these now-iconic speeches as Nigel's 'audience-repelling death play' is a clear sign as to which character we ought to be backing: despite his biographical baiting, Shakespeare's text helps us to tell right from wrong.

When Shakespeare is exposed in court (though not in the play's wider world) as a serial plagiarist and an unpleasant person, this false idol is toppled; but as the *Hamlet* rehearsal scene makes clear, with the Bard-baiting complete, the work itself can live on. Newly freed from the taint of Bardolatry, we can celebrate Shakespeare's words without the attendant and oppressive hero-worship. Nigel explains how *Hamlet* is 'truly expressive of what I am feeling in here'. As such, *Hamlet* is still given a compelling origin in lived experience: but as Taylor and Bourus describe, the work's biographicality is made possible by replacing Shakespeare himself as the author of the Shakespearean corpus with a different and far more sympathetic man.

Conclusion: 'Beautified with our feathers'?

Despite the varying levels of iconoclasm, mockery and critique to which they subject the biographical author, the bouts of Bard-baiting discussed above all resolve themselves into a tempered admission of the work's continued brilliance. At least four potentially overlapping impulses might underlie this curious trend.

Firstly, Emma Smith suggests that iconoclasm might have emerged as a culturally necessary counterweight to Bardolatrous tradition: she refers to calls for moratoria on Shakespeare and to the authorship controversy alike as 'gestures of iconoclastic resistance to the impossible ethical gravity with which we have charged these texts and, in particular, this author'.[25] This iconoclastic trend might, however, be understood as a more positive reclamation: by making Shakespeare a morally flawed individual, we make him like us and thus, in his flawed self, even more fully able to represent our common humanity in his role as 'the most human human there's ever been' – a process not dissimilar to the logic behind the Gnostic-derived idea of a married, sexually active Jesus in the 2003 thriller *The Da Vinci Code*.[26]

A third explanation might identify such attempts to make Shakespeare relatably human, rather than untouchably morally profound and beyond our comprehension, as in fact further reifying his iconic endurance. This argument would locate Bard-baiting narratives within Stephen Greenblatt's paradigm of containment, whereby the 'apparent production of subversion is ... the very condition of power'.[27] These challenges to Bardolatrous orthodoxy, in continuing to promulgate some form of fictionalized Shakespearean biography as a desirable product for pop culture consumption, thus align with Greenblatt's description of how powerful belief systems produce subversive challenges to order, which nonetheless 'do not undermine that order' (38). As Halsey and Vine add, 'to worry at authority (political, historical, or literary) is not the same thing as to reject it outright' (23). Thus, presentations of a biographically unpleasant or inadequate Shakespeare might function as a kind of cracked mirror for traditional Bardolatry: they disturb the assumptions of deifying biography but often end up endorsing the enduring power of the work.

A final, more optimistic account of the logic of Bard-baiting might recuperate its apparent endorsement of the plays' 'genius' – despite what such narratives represent as their sullied biographical origins – by reference to these works' recurrent, if tentative, disintegration of a hierarchical model of authorship. This is, perhaps, the version of a dethroned and available Shakespeare which emerges from recent works on fan cultures, wherein 'online users ... (re)create, collect, and share Shakespeare apart from the hegemony of the "educative and civilizing agencies" of academia and theatre': a popular 'Shakespeare as use' or 'Shakespeare network' whose words belong to all of us, having become source material for a variety of 'interpretive communities', and whose work we can thus retroactively picture ourselves as co-creating.[28] In this reading, Shakespeare the singular genius can be challenged or diminished without harming our engagement with the texts, because the corpus bearing his name no longer belongs, singularly or uncomplicatedly, to Shakespeare, but exists under a form of 'collaborative authority'.[29] In the words of *Something Rotten*, he is 'the Will of the people now'.

Richard O'Brien is an Assistant Lecturer in English at Maynooth University, focusing on early modern literature. He also contributes to teaching in Creative Writing at the University of Birmingham, where he was recently a Teaching Fellow in Shakespeare and Creativity, and received his PhD in 2017 for research into Shakespeare and the development of verse drama. His first publication on biofictions of the early modern period won the *Ben Jonson Journal* Discoveries Award in 2016. Richard's work on the creative afterlives of the early modern has also appeared in *Literature Compass*, *Shakespeare Bulletin*, *Connotations* and the Bloomsbury collection *New Places: Shakespeare and Civic Creativity* (2017), with a chapter forthcoming in a CUP volume on Ben Jonson's afterlives edited by Martin Butler and Jane Rickard. Richard won a Society of Authors Eric Gregory Award for his own poetry in 2017, and is Birmingham Poet Laureate 2018–2020.

Notes

1. Gary Taylor and Terri Bourus, 'Why Read Shakespeare's Complete Works?' in *The New Oxford Shakespeare: The Complete Works. Modern Critical Edition*, by William Shakespeare, ed. Gary Taylor, John Jowett, Terri Bourus, and Gabriel Egan (Oxford: Oxford University Press, 2016), 12.
2. Valerie M. Fazel and Louise Geddes, '"Give me your Hands if we be Friends": Collaborative Authority in Shakespeare Fan Fiction', *Shakespeare* 12.3 (2016), 283.
3. Janice Wardle, 'Time Travel and the Return of the Author: *Shakespeare in Love*, "The Shakespeare Code", and *Bill*', *Borrowers and Lenders* 12.1 (2018), http://www.borrowers.uga.edu/784111/show.
4. *Shakespeare in Love*, dir. John Madden (Miramax/United Studios, 1998/2004).
5. Edward Bond, 'Introduction' to *Bingo*, in *Plays: Three* (London: Methuen, 1987), 4.
6. Katherine West Scheil, *Imagining Shakespeare's Wife: The Afterlife of Anne Hathaway* (Cambridge: Cambridge University Press, 2018), 150; Katie Halsey and Angus Vine, '"Dressed in a Little Brief Authority": Authority Before, During, and After Shakespeare's Plays', in *Shakespeare and Authority*, ed. Halsey and Vine (London: Palgrave Macmillan, 2018), 9, 3.
7. Andreas Höfele, *Stage, Stake, and Scaffold: Humans and Animals in Shakespeare's Theatre* (Oxford: Oxford University Press, 2011), 10.
8. Interviewed for '*Will*: Extended Look' (Monumental Television/TNT, 2017), *YouTube*, https://www.youtube.com/watch?v=USKBuyvE1Yw&list=PLJ4e4Lb87XTypMEkHpwdiOJXRY1IW3MyX.
9. Jennifer Holl, '"Now 'mongst this Flock of Drunkards": Drunk Shakespeare's Polytemporal Theater', *Borrowers and Lenders* 11.2 (2018), http://www.borrowers.uga.edu/783933/show. The term 'communitas' is coined by the anthropologist Victor Turner.
10. Claire Dederer, 'What Do We Do with the Art of Monstrous Men?', *The Paris Review*, 20 Nov 2017, https://www.theparisreview.org/blog/2017/11/20/art-monstrous-men/.
11. *All Is True*, dir. Kenneth Branagh and screenplay by Ben Elton (Sony Pictures Classics, 2018).
12. Susan Snyder, *The Comic Matrix of Shakespeare's Tragedies* (Princeton, NJ: Princeton University Press, 1979).
13. Sarah Dustagheer, 'Upstart Crow: Shakespeare Sitcom is Really Quite Educational', *The Conversation*, 29 Aug. 2018, https://theconversation.com/upstart-crow-shakespeare-sitcom-is-really-quite-educational-102292.
14. *Upstart Crow* Seasons 1–3, dir. Matt Lipsey and Richard Boden, screenplay Ben Elton (BBC TV, 2016–18). All dating of plays here refers to the calculations of Martin Wiggins, in association with Catherine Richardson, *British Drama 1533–1642: A Catalogue*, vols. III and IV (Oxford: Oxford University Press, 2012–14).
15. Shakespeare's premature ageing is supported by the casting of actors as Richard Burbage and Henry Condell who are at least twice the age of their historical counterparts in the 1590s. An episode of the Comedy Central UK series *Drunk History*, featuring the 59-year-old Mark Heap as a Droeshout-styled Shakespeare whose recent *Henry VI* trilogy (complete by c.1594) is attacked as 'steaming dogshit', takes the same approach.

16. All quotations from Shakespeare's plays are taken from *The New Oxford Shakespeare: The Complete Works. Modern Critical Edition*, by William Shakespeare, ed. Gary Taylor, John Jowett, Terri Bourus, and Gabriel Egan (Oxford: Oxford University Press, 2016).
17. Stephen Purcell, *Popular Shakespeare: Simulation and Subversion on the Modern Stage* (Basingstoke: Palgrave Macmillan, 2009), 24; Stuart Sillars, *The Illustrated Shakespeare, 1709–1875* (Cambridge: Cambridge University Press, 2008), 27.
18. Douglas Lanier. '"There won't be Puppets, will there?": "Heroic" Authorship and the Cultural Politics of *Anonymous*', in *Shakespeare Beyond Doubt: Evidence, Argument, Controversy*, ed. Paul Edmondson and Stanley Wells (Cambridge: Cambridge University Press, 2013), 219.
19. Jude Morgan, *The Secret Life of William Shakespeare* (London: Headline Review, 2012).
20. Tom Fordy, 'A Bayonet to the Heart: The True History of Blackadder's Devastating Final Episode', *The Telegraph*, 27 Sep. 2019, https://www.telegraph.co.uk/tv/0/blackadder-goes-forth-ww1-history-final-episode-ending/.
21. Wayne Kirkpatrick and Karey Kirkpatrick, *Something Rotten! (Original Broadway Cast Recording)* (Sh-K-Boom Records, 2015), *Spotify*, https://open.spotify.com/album/0kOBkjePPpXZ4sZGspF0VH?si=TkwQtM3URgy3wF5ttqHp4g.
22. Quotations from the book of *Something Rotten!*, which remains unpublished, are transcribed from the St. James Theatre production, directed by Casey Nicholaw.
23. Douglas Bruster, 'Shakespeare and the End of History: Period as Brand Name', in *Shakespeare and Modernity: Early Modern to Millennium*, ed. Hugh Grady (London: Routledge, 2000), 87.
24. Graham Holderness, *Cultural Shakespeare: Essays in the Shakespeare Myth* (Hatfield: University of Hertfordshire Press, 2001), ix.
25. Emma Smith, 'Shakespeare – The Apex Predator', *Times Literary Supplement*, 4 May 2017, https://www.the-tls.co.uk/articles/public/shakespeare-apex-predator/.
26. *Doctor Who*: 'The Shakespeare Code' (BBC TV, 2007); Dan Brown, *The Da Vinci Code* (New York: Doubleday, 2003).
27. Stephen Greenblatt, 'Invisible Bullets: Renaissance Authority and its Subversion, *Henry IV* and *Henry V*', in *Political Shakespeare: Essays in Cultural Materialism*, ed. Jonathan Dollimore and Alan Sinfield, 2nd ed. (Manchester: Manchester University Press, 1994), 45.
28. Valerie M. Fazel and Louise Geddes, 'Introduction: The Shakespeare User', in *The Shakespeare User: Critical and Creative Appropriations in a Networked Culture*, ed. Fazel and Geddes (London: Palgrave Macmillan, 2017), 3, 7, 5. In the first excerpt here, Fazel and Geddes cite Tony Bennett as quoted in Abigail DeKosnik's *Rogue Archives* (Cambridge, MA: MIT Press, 2016), 1.
29. Fazel and Geddes, '"Give me your Hands"', 274.

Select Bibliography

Ackroyd, Peter. *Shakespeare: The Biography*. New York: Nan A. Talese, Doubleday, 2005.
Adam, Ch. *Commémoration de Shakespeare. Aux Universités d'Angleterre, d'Ecosse et d'Irlande*. 1916. BL Ac. 382.b (1).
Akenside, Mark. *The Poetical Works of Mark Akenside*. Edinburgh, 1781.
All Is True. Film. Dir. Kenneth Branagh. Screenplay by Ben Elton. Sony Pictures Classics, 2018.
Anonymous. Film. Dir. Roland Emmerich. Columbia Pictures, 2011.
Asimov, Isaac. 'The Immortal Bard', in his *Earth is Room Enough* (1953, rpt. St. Albans: Panther, 1960), 149–51.
Askew, Frederick, Rev. *Shakespeare Tercentenary Souvenir: England's Thoughts in Shakespeare's Words*. Lowestoft: Flood and Son, 1916.
Barton, Anne. 'The One and Only'. *The New York Review of Books*, 11 May 2006.
Bate, Jonathan. *The Genius of Shakespeare*. London: Picador, 1997.
Bate, Jonathan. *Soul of the Age: A Biography of the Mind of William Shakespeare*. New York: Random House, 2009.
Baumgartner, Alexander. 'Shakespeares Religion'. *Stimmen aus Maria Laach* 53 (1897), 487–505.
Bernays, Michael. 'Shakespeare ein katholischer Dichter'. *Shakespeare Jahrbuch* 1 (1865), 220–99.
Bevington, David. *Shakespeare and Biography*. Oxford: Oxford University Press, 2010.
Birch, W. J. *An Inquiry into the Philosophy and Religion of Shakespeare*. London, 1848.
Blackwood, Gary. *The Shakespeare Stealer*. New York: Dutton Children's Books, 1998.
Blackwood, Gary. *Shakespeare's Scribe*. New York: Dutton Children's Books, 2000.
Blackwood, Gary. *Shakespeare's Spy*. New York: Dutton Children's Books, 2006.

Bolt, Rodney. *History Play: The Lives and Afterlives of Christopher Marlowe*. New York: Bloomsbury, 2005.
Bond, Edward. *Bingo: Scenes of Money and Death*. London: Methuen, 1974.
Brandl, Alois. *Shakespeare and Germany. British Academy Third Shakespeare Annual Lecture*. London: The British Academy, 1913.
Bruster, Douglas. 'Shakespeare and the End of History: Period as Brand Name', in Hugh Grady (ed.), *Shakespeare and Modernity: Early Modern to Millennium* (London: Routledge, 2000), 168–88.
Bulman, James C. (ed.). *Shakespeare Re-Dressed: Cross-Gender Casting in Contemporary Performance*. Madison, WI: Fairleigh Dickinson University Press, 2008.
Burgess, Anthony. *Nothing Like the Sun*. 1964; London: Vintage, 1992.
Burgess, Anthony. 'Genesis and Headache', in Thomas McCormack (ed.), *Afterwords* (New York: Harper and Row, 1969), 28–47.
Calvo, Clara. 'Shakespeare and Cervantes in 1916: The Politics of Language', in L. Bezzola Lambert and Balz Engler (eds), *Shifting the Scene: Shakespeare in European Culture* (Newark, NJ: University of Delaware Press, 2004), 78–94.
Carlyle, Thomas. *On Heroes, Hero-Worship and the Heroic in History*. Ed. Michael K. Goldberg. Oxford: University of California Press, 1993.
Cartelli, Thomas. 'Shakespeare, 1916: *Caliban by the Yellow Sands* and the New Dramas of Democracy', in *Repositioning Shakespeare: National Formations, Postcolonial Appropriations* (London: Routledge, 1999), 63–83.
Chateaubriand, François-René de. *Essai sur la littérature anglaise*. Paris: Furne et Gosselin, 1836.
Cheaney, J. B. *The Playmaker*. New York: Alfred A. Knopf, 2000.
Chedgzoy, Kate. 'Strange Worship: Oscar Wilde and the Key to Shakespeare's *Sonnets*', in *Shakespeare's Queer Children: Sexual Politics and Contemporary Culture* (Manchester; New York: Manchester University Press, 1995), 135–76.
Chettle, Henry. *Kind-Heart's Dream*. Ed. Edward F. Rimbault. London: The Percy Society, 1841.
Coleridge, Samuel Taylor. *Biographia Literaria*. Ed. Adam Roberts. Edinburgh: Edinburgh University Press, 2014.
Colmer, Francis. *Shakespeare in Time of War: Excerpts from the Plays Arranged with Topical Allusion*. London: Smith, Elder & Co, 1916.
A Comparison between the Two Stages. London, 1702. Rpt. New York and London: Garland, 1973.
Conroy, Tiffany A. 'Presenting Shakespeare's Life and Times for Young People', in Naomi J. Miller (ed.), *Reimagining Shakespeare for Children and Young Adults* (New York and London: Routledge, 2003), 239–51.
Cooke, Katharine. *A. C. Bradley and his Influence in Twentieth-Century Shakespeare Criticism*. Oxford: Clarendon, 1972.

Cooper, Susan. *King of Shadows*. New York: Margaret K. McElderry Books, 1999.
Danchin, Pierre (ed.). *The Prologues and Epilogues of the Restoration, 1660–1700*. Nancy: Publications Université de Nancy II, 1981ff.
Danchin, Pierre (ed.). *The Prologues and Epilogues of the Eighteenth Century: A Complete Edition*. Nancy: Publications Université de Nancy II, 1990ff.
Danson, Lawrence. 'Oscar Wilde, W. H., and the Unspoken Name of Love'. *ELH* 58 (1991), 979–1000.
Dávidházi, Péter. *The Romantic Cult of Shakespeare: Literary Reception in Anthropological Perspective*. London: Macmillan, 1998.
Dean, Antony C., Rev. *'His Own Place'. The Tercentenary 'Shakespeare Sermon'. Preached in the Church of the Holy Trinity, Stratford-on-Avon, 30 April 1916*. Hampstead, N. W.: J. Hewetson and Son, 1916.
DiPietro, Cary. *Shakespeare and Modernism*. Cambridge; New York: Cambridge University Press, 2006.
Dobson, Michael. 'Accents Yet Unknown: Canonisation and the Claiming of *Julius Caesar*', in Jean I. Marsden (ed.), *The Appropriation of Shakespeare: Post-Renaissance Reconstructions of the Works and the Myth* (New York and London: Harvester Wheatsheaf, 1991), 11–28.
Dobson, Michael. *The Making of the National Poet: Shakespeare, Adaptation, and Authorship, 1660–1769*. Oxford: Oxford University Press, 1992.
Doctor Who: 'The Shakespeare Code'. TV series. BBC TV, 2007.
Douglas, Alfred. *The True History of Shakespeare's Sonnets*. London: M. Secker, 1933.
Duncan-Jones, Katherine (ed.). *Shakespeare's Sonnets*. Arden 3. Walton-on-Thames: Thomas Nelson & Sons, 1997.
Duncan-Jones, Katherine. *Ungentle Shakespeare: Scenes from his Life*. London: Arden Shakespeare, 2001.
Dusinberre, Juliet (ed.). *As You Like It*. London: Arden, 2006.
Dustagheer, Sarah. 'Upstart Crow: Shakespeare Sitcom is Really Quite Educational'. *The Conversation*, 29 Aug. 2018. https://theconversation.com/upstart-crow-shakespeare-sitcom-is-really-quite-educational-102292.
Duval, Alexandre. *Shakespeare amoureux. Oeuvres complètes d'Alexandre Duval*. Tome 5. Paris: J.-Barba, 1822.
Duval, Alexandre. *Shakespeare enamorado*. Tr. Ventura de la Vega. Madrid: Repullés, 1831.
Edmondson, Paul, Kevin Colls and William Mitchell. *Finding Shakespeare's New Place: An Archaeological Biography*. Manchester: Manchester University Press, 2016.
Eighteenth Century Essays on Shakespeare. Ed. D. Nichol Smith. 1903. 2nd ed. Oxford: Clarendon Press, 1963.
Elze, Karl. *William Shakespeare*. Halle: Waisenhaus, 1876.
Engler, Balz. 'Shakespeare in the Trenches'. *Shakespeare Survey* 44 (1991), 105–11.

Engler, Balz. 'Stratford and the Canonization of Shakespeare'. *European Journal of English Studies* 1 (1997), 354–66.

Everett, Barbara. 'Reade Him, Therefore'. *Times Literary Supplement*, 17 August 2007, 12–15.

Fagan, J. B. *Shakespear v. Shaw*. Unpublished typescript 1905. Spielmann Coll., University of Birmingham.

Fazel, Valerie M. and Louise Geddes. '"Give me your Hands if we be Friends": Collaborative Authority in Shakespeare Fan Fiction'. *Shakespeare* 12(3) (2016), 274–86.

Fazel, Valerie M. and Louise Geddes (eds). *The Shakespeare User: Critical and Creative Appropriations in a Networked Culture*. London: Palgrave Macmillan, 2017.

Fisher, Susan. 'Cervantes sobre las tablas: *Miguel Will*, de José Carlos Somoza'. *Theatralia: revista poética del teatro* 5 (2003), 247–60.

Foulkes, Richard. *The Shakespeare Tercentenary of 1864*. London: The Society for Theatre Research, 1984.

Foulkes, Richard. 'The Theatre of War: The 1916 Tercentenary', in *Performing Shakespeare in the Age of Empire* (Cambridge: Cambridge University Press, 2002), 180–204.

Franssen, Paul, and Ton Hoenselaars (eds). *The Author as Character: Representing Historical Writers in Western Literature*. Madison, NJ: Fairleigh Dickinson University Press; London: Associated University Presses, 1999.

Franssen, Paul. 'The Life and Opinions of William Shakespeare, Gentleman: Biography between Fact and Fiction', in Sonja Fielitz (ed.), *Literature as History / History as Literature: Fact and Fiction in Medieval to Eighteenth-Century British Literature* (Frankfurt: Peter Lang, 2007), 63–77.

Franssen, Paul. *Shakespeare's Literary Lives*. Cambridge: Cambridge University Press, 2016.

Fulda, Ludwig. *Deutsche Kultur und Ausländerei*. Leipzig: Hirzel, 1916.

Genée, Rudolph. *Shakespeare. Sein Leben und seine Werke*. Hildburghausen: Bibliographisches Institut, 1872.

George, David. 'Shakespeare and Pembroke's Men'. *Shakespeare Quarterly* 32(3) (1981), 305–23.

Gervinus, Georg Gottfried. *Shakespeare*. 2 vols. Leipzig: Engelmann, 1862.

Gervinus, Georg Gottfried. *Händel und Shakespeare. (Eine Parallele.) Zur Ästhetik der Tonkust*. Leipzig: Engelmann, 1868.

Goethe, Johann Wolfgang von. 'Shakespeare und kein Ende!' *Jubilaeumsausgabe*. Vol. 6. Frankfurt, Leipzig: Insel, 1998.

Gollancz, Israel (ed.). *A Book of Homage to Shakespeare*. London: Oxford University Press, 1916.

Greene, Robert. *The Life and Complete Works in Prose and Verse of Robert Greene*. Ed. A. B. Grosart. 15 vols. London, 1881–86.

Greenblatt, Stephen. *Shakespearean Negotiations*. Oxford: Clarendon, 1988.
Greenblatt, Stephen. 'Invisible Bullets: Renaissance Authority and its Subversion, *Henry IV* and *Henry V*', in Jonathan Dollimore and Alan Sinfield (eds), *Political Shakespeare: Essays in Cultural Materialism*, 2nd ed. (Manchester: Manchester University Press, 1994), 18–47.
Greenblatt, Stephen. *Will in the World: How Shakespeare Became Shakespeare*. New York: W. W. Norton, 2004.
Greer, Germaine. *Shakespeare's Wife*. London: Bloomsbury, 2007.
Gregor, Keith, and Encarna Vidal. 'The "Other" William and the Question of Authority in Spanish Stage Depictions of Shakespeare'. *Sederi* 12 (2002), 237–46.
Gregor, Keith. 'Shakespeare as Character on the Spanish Stage: A Metaphysics of Bardic Presence', in A. Luis Pujante and Ton Hoenselaars (eds), *Four Hundred Years of Shakespeare in Europe* (Newark and London: University of Delaware Press and Associated University Presses, 2003), 43–53.
Gross, John. *Shylock: Four Hundred Years in the Life of a Legend*. London: Chatto and Windus, 1992.
Gurr, Andrew. *The Shakespearean Stage: 1574–1642*. Cambridge: Cambridge University Press, 2009.
Habicht, Werner. *Shakespeare and the German Imagination*. International Shakespeare Association Occasional Paper No. 5. Hertford: Austin, 1994.
Habicht, Werner. 'Shakespeare Celebrations in Times of War'. *Shakespeare Quarterly* 52 (2001), 441–55.
Hall, Linda. '"Time no Longer" – History, Enchantment and the Classic Time-Slip Story', in Fiona M. Collins and Judith Graham (eds), *Historical Fiction for Children: Capturing the Past* (London: David Fulton, 2001), 43–53.
Halliday, F. E. *The Life of Shakespeare*. Kelly Bray, Cornwall: House of Stratus, 2001.
Halsey, Katie, and Angus Vine (eds). *Shakespeare and Authority*. London: Palgrave Macmillan, 2018.
Hansen, Niels Bugge. 'Something Is Rotten. . .', in Ros King and Paul Franssen (eds), *Shakespeare and War* (Houndmills, Basingstoke: Palgrave Macmillan, 2008), 153–65.
Harris, Frank. *The Man Shakespeare and his Tragic Life Story*. London: Palmer, 1909.
Harris, Frank. *Shakespeare and his Love*. London: Palmer, 1910.
Harris, Frank. *The Women of Shakespeare*. London: Methuen, 1911.
Harris, Robert J. *Will Shakespeare and the Pirate's Fire*. London: HarperCollins Children's Books, 2006.
Hassinger, Peter W. *Shakespeare's Daughter*. New York: Laura Geringer Books/ HarperCollins, 2004.

Hateley, Erica. *Shakespeare in Children's Literature: Gender and Cultural Capital*. New York and London: Routledge, 2009.

Hauptmann, Gerhart. 'Deutschland und Shakespeare'. *Shakespeare Jahrbuch* 51 (1915), 7–12.

Hawkes, Terence. 'Swisser-Swatter: Making a Man of English Letters', in John Drakakis (ed.), *Alternative Shakespeares* (London: Methuen, 1985), 26–46.

Hawkes, Terence. *That Shakespeherian Rag*. London: Methuen, 1986.

Hawkes, Terence. *Shakespeare in the Present*. London and New York: Routledge, 2002.

Hinman, Charlton, and Peter W. M. Blayney (eds). *The First Folio of Shakespeare*. New York: W. W. Norton, 1968, 1996.

Höfele, Andreas. *Stage, Stake, and Scaffold: Humans and Animals in Shakespeare's Theatre*. Oxford: Oxford University Press, 2011.

Holderness, Graham. *Cultural Shakespeare: Essays in the Shakespeare Myth*. Hatfield: University of Hertfordshire Press, 2001.

Holderness, Graham, and Bryan Loughrey. '"Rudely Interrupted": Shakespeare and Terrorism'. *Critical Survey* 19(3) (2007), 107–23.

Holderness, Graham. *Nine Lives of William Shakespeare*. London: Continuum, 2011.

Holl, Jennifer. '"Now 'mongst this Flock of Drunkards": Drunk Shakespeare's Polytemporal Theater'. *Borrowers and Lenders* 11(2) (2018). http://www.borrowers.uga.edu/783933/show.

Honan, Park. *Shakespeare: A Life*. Oxford: Oxford University Press, 1998.

Isaac, Megan Lynn. *Heirs to Shakespeare: Reinventing the Bard in Young Adult Literature*. Portsmouth, NH: Boynton/Cook, 2000.

Jones, Henry Arthur. *Shakespeare and Germany (Written during the Battle of Verdun)*. London: Chiswick Press, 1916.

Jong, Erica. *Serenissima*. New York: Dell, 1987.

Kahn, Coppélia. 'Remembering Shakespeare Imperially: The 1916 Tercentenary'. *Shakespeare Quarterly* 52 (2001), 456–78.

Kendall, Roy. *Christopher Marlowe and Richard Baines: Journeys Through the Elizabethan Underground*. Cranbury, NJ: Fairleigh Dickinson University Press, 2004.

Kenny, Thomas. *The Life and Genius of Shakespeare*. London: Longman, Green, 1864.

Kirkpatrick, Wayne, and Karey Kirkpatrick. *Something Rotten! (Original Broadway Cast Recording)*. Sh-K-Boom Records, 2015. Spotify. https://open.spotify.com/album/0kOBkjePPpXZ4sZGspF0VH?si=TkwQtM3URgy3wF5ttqHp4g.

Knapp, Mary E. *Prologues and Epilogues of the Eighteenth Century*. New Haven: Yale University Press, 1961.

Kuriyama, Constance. 'Marlowe, Shakespeare, and the Nature of Biographical Evidence'. *Studies in Literature* 20(1) (1988), 1–12.

Lanier, Douglas. *Shakespeare and Modern Popular Culture*. Oxford: Oxford University Press, 2002.
Lanier, Douglas. '"There Won't Be Puppets, Will there?": "Heroic" Authorship and the Cultural Politics of *Anonymous*', in Paul Edmondson and Stanley Wells (eds), *Shakespeare Beyond Doubt: Evidence, Argument, Controversy* (Cambridge: Cambridge University Press, 2013), 215–24.
Laroche, Rebecca. 'The Sonnets on Trial: Reconsidering "The Portrait of Mr W. H."', in James Schiffer (ed.), *Shakespeare's Sonnets: Critical Essays* (New York: Garland, 1999), 391–410.
Lawlor, Laurie. *Two Loves of William Shakespeare*. New York: Holiday House, 2006.
Lee, Sidney, Sir. *Shakespeare Tercentenary Commemoration, 1616–1916: Shakespeare Birthplace. Catalogue of an Exhibition of Original Documents of the XVIth & XVIIth Centuries Preserved in Stratford-upon-Avon, Illustrating Shakespeare's Life in the Town*. Stratford-upon-Avon: Edward Fox and Sons, 1916.
Lenz, Jakob Michael Reinhold. *Werke und Schriften*. Ed. Britta Titel and Hellmut Haug. Stuttgart: Goverts, 1966–67.
Logan, Robert. *Shakespeare's Marlowe: The Influence of Christopher Marlowe on Shakespeare's Artistry*. Aldershot, England: Ashgate, 2007.
Lyons, Bridget Gellert. 'Review of *Ungentle Shakespeare: Scenes from His Life*'. *Renaissance Quarterly* 56(2) (Summer 2003), 553–56.
Maltby, Arthur. *Shakespeare as a Challenge for Literary Biography: A History of Biographies of Shakespeare since 1898*. Lewiston, NY: Edwin Mellen Press, 2009.
Manley, Lawrence. 'From Strange's Men to Pembroke's Men: *2 Henry VI* and *The First Part of the Contention*'. *Shakespeare Quarterly* 54(3) (2003), 253–87.
Marche, Stephen. 'Wouldn't It Be Cool if Shakespeare Wasn't Shakespeare?' *The New York Times*, 21 October 2011.
McDowell, Kathleen. 'Toward a History of Children as Readers, 1890–1930'. *Book History* 12 (2009), 240–65.
Memoirs of the Shakespear's-Head in Covent Garden: By the Ghost of Shakespear. London, 1755.
Meyer, Carolyn. *Loving Will Shakespeare*. Orlando: Harcourt, 2006.
Morgan, Jude. *The Secret Life of William Shakespeare*. London: Headline Review, 2012.
Munk, Kaj. 'Kaj Munk taler med Shakespeare'. *Forum, Tidsskrift for Musik og Teater*, 3 (March 1935), 8–10.
Nashe, Thomas. *The Works of Thomas Nashe*. Vol. 1. Ed. R. B. McKerrow, rev. F. P. Wilson. Oxford: Oxford University Press, 1958.
Niederkorn, William S. 'To Be or Not to Be ... Shakespeare'. *The New York Times*, 21 August 2004.

Norrenberg, Peter. *Allgemeine Geschichte der Literatur: Ein Handbuch der Geschichte der Poesie aller Völker*. 3 vols. Münster: Russell, 1882–84.

O'Sullivan, Maurice J. (ed.). *Shakespeare's Other Lives. An Anthology of Fictional Depictions of the Bard*. Jefferson, North Carolina, and London: McFarland, 1997.

Pérez Galdós, Benito. 'La casa de Shakespeare', in *Memoranda*, rpt. in *Novelas y Miscelánea* (Madrid: Aguilar, 1973), 1196–203.

Pfister, Manfred. 'Hamlet und der deutsche Geist'. *Shakespeare Jahrbuch (West)* 1992, 13–38.

Pfister, Manfred. '"In States Unborn and Accents Yet Unknown": Shakespeare and the European Canon', in Ladina Bezzola Lambert and Balz Engler (eds), *Shifting the Scene: Shakespeare in European Culture* (Newark, NJ: Delaware University Press, 2004), 41–63.

Pinsent, Pat. '"Not for an Age but for all Time": The Depiction of Shakespeare in a Selection of Children's Fiction'. *New Review of Children's Literature and Librarianship* 10(2) (2004), 115–26.

Pollard, Tanya. *Shakespeare's Theater: A Sourcebook*. Oxford: Blackwell, 2004.

Potter, Lois. 'Having Our Will: Imagination in Recent Biographies'. *Shakespeare Survey* 58 (2005), 1–8.

Potter, Lois. *The Life of William Shakespeare: A Critical Biography*. Hoboken, New Jersey: John Wiley and Sons, 2012.

Purcell, Stephen. *Popular Shakespeare: Simulation and Subversion on the Modern Stage*. Basingstoke: Palgrave Macmillan, 2009.

Raich, J. M. *Shakespeare's Stellung zur katholischen Religion*. Mainz, 1884.

Reichensperger, August. *William Shakespeare, insbesondere sein Verhältnis zum Mittelalter und zur Gegenwart*, in Franz Hülskamp (ed.), *Zeitgemäße Broschüren*, Vol. 7, nos. 9 and 10 (Münster: Russell, 1871).

Richter, Thomas. '"Shakespeare's Katholicität" – Die Kontroverse um Shakespeares Konfession in Deutschland zur Zeit des Kulturkampfes'. *Shakespeare Jahrbuch* 136 (2000), 108–30.

Riggs, David. 'Review of *Ungentle Shakespeare: Scenes from His Life*'. *Shakespeare Quarterly* 53(4) (Winter 2002), 550–53.

Rio, Alexis François. *Shakespeare Catholique*. Paris: Charles Douniol, 1864.

Rollins, Hyder Edward (ed.). *A New Variorum Edition of Shakespeare: The Sonnets*. 2 vols. Philadelphia; London: J. B. Lippincott, 1944.

Rosenthal, Laura J. 'The Author as Ghost in the Eighteenth Century'. *1650–1850: Ideas, Aesthetics, and Inquiries in the Early Modern Era* 3 (1997), 29–56.

Rylance, Mark. 'The Big Secret Live! "I am Shakespeare" Webcam Daytime Chatroom Show!!!'. 2007. Unpublished typescript.

Salmon, Edward. *Shakespeare and Democracy*. London and New York: McBride, Nast & Co., 1916.

Sand, George. *Le Roi Attend: Prologue* (1848), in her *Théâtre Complet*, Vol. 1 (Paris: Lévy, 1876), 125–42.

Sawyer, Robert. 'Christopher Marlowe: A Renaissance Life'. *South Atlantic Review* 68(3) (Summer 2003), 154–58.
Sawyer, Robert. 'Shakespeare and Marlowe: Re-Writing the Relationship'. *Critical Survey* 21(3) (2009), 41–58.
Scheil, Katherine. 'Filling in the "Wife-Shaped Void": The Contemporary Afterlife of Anne Hathaway'. *Shakespeare Survey* 63 (2010), 433–45.
Scheil, Katherine. *Imagining Shakespeare's Wife: The Afterlife of Anne Hathaway*. Cambridge: Cambridge University Press, 2018.
Schiller, Friedrich. *Schillers Werke: Nationalausgabe*. Ed. Norbert Oellers. Weimar: Hermann Böhlaus Nachfolger, 1983.
Schink, Johann Friedrich. *Shakespeare in der Klemme* (1780), in Gerhard Müller-Schwefe (ed.), *Shakespeare im Narrenhaus: Deutschsprachige Shakespeare-Parodien aus zwei Jahrhunderten* (Tübingen: Francke Verlag, 1990), 126–34.
Schoch, Richard. 'The Birth of Shakespeare's Birthplace'. *Theatre Survey* 53 (2012), 181–201.
Schoenbaum, S. *Shakespeare's Lives*. 2nd ed. Oxford; New York: Oxford University Press, 1993.
Schroeder, Horst. *Oscar Wilde, The Portrait of Mr W. H.: Its Composition, Publication and Reception*. Braunschweig: Seminar für Anglistik und Amerikanistik, TU Braunschweig, 1984.
Shakespeare, William. *The New Oxford Shakespeare: The Complete Works. Modern Critical Edition*. Ed. Gary Taylor, John Jowett, Terri Bourus, and Gabriel Egan. Oxford: Oxford University Press, 2016.
Shakespeare in Love. Film. Dir. John Madden. Screenplay by Marc Norman and Tom Stoppard. Miramax/United Studios, 1998/2004.
Shakespeare Tercentenary Observance in the Schools and Other Institutions. London: Geo W. Jones, 1916.
Shapiro, James. *Rival Playwrights: Marlowe, Jonson, Shakespeare*. New York: Columbia University Press, 1991.
Shapiro, James. *1599. A Year in the Life of William Shakespeare*. London: Faber and Faber, 2005.
Shaw, George Bernard. *The Dark Lady of the Sonnets* (1910), in Maurice J. O'Sullivan (ed.), *Shakespeare's Other Lives. An Anthology of Fictional Depictions of the Bard* (Jefferson, North Carolina, and London: McFarland, 1997), 92–103.
Shaw, George Bernard. 'Mr Frank Harris's Shakespear', in *Nation*, 24 December 1910, rpt. in Brian Tyson (ed.), *Bernard Shaw's Book Reviews* (University Park: Pennsylvania State University Press, 1991–96), Vol. 2, 240–54.
Shawcross, J. P. *The Shakespeare Tercentenary: A Popular Address*. London: Skeffington and Son, 1916.
Sillars, Stuart. *The Illustrated Shakespeare, 1709–1875*. Cambridge: Cambridge University Press, 2008.

Sinfield, Alan. 'Shakespeare and Dissident Reading', in *Cultural Politics – Queer Reading* (London: Routledge, 1994), 3–4.

Smith, Emma. 'Shakespeare – The Apex Predator.' *Times Literary Supplement*, 4 May 2017. https://www.the-tls.co.uk/articles/public/shakespeare-apex-predator/.

Smith, Gretchen E. 'Aurore Dupin Dudevant and Jean-Baptiste Poquelin: George Sand Reconstructs Molière', in Paul Franssen and Ton Hoenselaars (eds), *The Author as Character: Representing Historical Writers in Western Literature* (Madison: Fairleigh Dickinson, 1999), 141–56.

Snyder, Susan. *The Comic Matrix of Shakespeare's Tragedies*. Princeton, NJ: Princeton University Press, 1979.

Somoza, José Carlos. *Miguel Will*. Madrid: SGAE, 1999; repr. Barcelona: Random House Mondadori, 2006.

Somoza, José Carlos. 'Shakespeare is Legion', in José Manuel González and Holger Klein (eds), *Shakespeare and Spain* (Lewiston, Queenston & Lampeter: The Edwin Mellen Press, 2002), 267–77.

Somoza, José Carlos. 'La maldad es silencio (Shakespeare y los personajes malvados)'. *Frenia* 2(1) (2002), 109–21.

Somoza, José Carlos. 'Remordimientos de una reina'. *El País Semanal* 22 May 2005. www.elpais.com/articulo/portada/Remordimientos/reina/elpeputec/20050522elpepspor_17/Tes.

Somoza, José Carlos. 'Hamlet', in Fernando Marías (ed.), *Historia secreta de la Corporación* (Madrid: 451 Editores, 2008), 119–36.

Somoza, José Carlos. *El cebo*. Barcelona: Plaza y Janés, 2010.

Somoza, José Carlos. *El origen del mal*. Barcelona: B, 2018.

Taylor, Paul. 'The Bard's Big Year: A Nation still in Love with Shakespeare'. *Independent*, Monday 24 December 2007, 8–9.

Tiffany, Grace. *My Father Had a Daughter: Judith Shakespeare's Tale*. New York: Berkley Books, 2003.

Trease, Geoffrey. *Cue for Treason*. 1940. Rpt. Harmondsworth: Penguin Books / Puffin Books, 1949.

Ulrici, Hermann. *Shakespeares dramatische Kunst*. Leipzig: T. O. Weigel, 1839.

Upstart Crow. TV series. Dir. Matt Lipsey and Richard Boden. Screenplay Ben Elton. BBC TV, 2016–18.

Van der Hoop, A., Jr. 'De Schim van Shakespear'. *De Nederlandsche Mercurius* 26 (4 March 1829), 409–10.

Vehse, Eduard. *Shakespeare als Protestant, Politiker, Psycholog, und Dichter*. Hamburg: Hoffmann, 1851.

Vera, Noemí. 'Inés París' *Miguel y William*: Shakespeare's Spanish Shipwreck'. Unpublished paper. Weimar, April 2011.

Vischer, Friedrich Theodor. *Shakespeare-Vorträge*. 6 vols. Stuttgart, Berlin: Cotta, 1899–1905.

The Visitation; or an Interview between the Ghost of Shakespear and D—v—d G—rr—ck, Esq. (1755; rpt. in Maurice J. O'Sullivan (ed.), *Shakespeare's Other Lives. An Anthology of Fictional Depictions of the Bard* (Jefferson NC and London: McFarland, 1997), 205–9.
Von Friesen, Heinrich. *Das Buch: Shakespeare von Gervinus. Ein Wort über dasselbe*. Leipzig: Baensch, 1869.
Wardle, Janice. 'Time Travel and the Return of the Author: *Shakespeare in Love*, "The Shakespeare Code", and *Bill*'. *Borrowers and Lenders* 12(1) (2018). http://www.borrowers.uga.edu/784111/show.
Watson, Nicola J. 'Kemble, Scott, and the Mantle of the Bard', in Jean I. Marsden (ed.), *The Appropriation of Shakespeare: Post-Renaissance Reconstructions of the Works and the Myth* (New York and London: Harvester Wheatsheaf, 1991), 73–92.
Watson, Nicola J. *The Literary Tourist*. London: Palgrave, 2006.
Weis, René. *Shakespeare Revealed: A Biography*. London: John Murray, 2007.
Wells, Stanley. *Shakespeare & Co*. London: Penguin Books, 2006.
Wiggins, Martin, and Catherine Richardson. *British Drama 1533–1642: A Catalogue*. Oxford: Oxford University Press, 2011–....
Wilde, Oscar. 'The Portrait of Mr. W. H.' (1889), in Ian Small (ed.), *Oscar Wilde: Complete Short Fiction* (Harmondsworth: Penguin Classics, 1994), 47–79.
Wolf, Paul. *Rufe vom anderen Ufer*. Weimar: Alexander Duncker, 1934.

Index

A
Ackroyd, Peter, 99–100
Adam, Ch., 83, 87, 92nn58–59
All Is True, 164
   bardolatry and, 154–55
Anonymous, 150
   authorship and, 116
   Lanier on, 116
   Marche on, 116
Aristotle, 134
Askew, Fred, 82
As You Like It
   Marlowe and, 108
   performance and, 125, 131, 135
authority
   Dobson on, 10–11
   ghost of Shakespeare, W., and, 7, 9–25
   Halsey and Vine on, 169
authorship, 123
   Anonymous and, 116
   Bolt on, 6–7, 115–16
   conspiracy and, 115–16, 150, 159
   Emmerich and, 116
   ghost of Shakespeare, W., and, 26n2
   Marlowe and, 6–7, 115–16
   Shapiro on, 116
   Something Rotten and, 167–68
   Tercentenary, 1916, and, 73
   Upstart Crow and, 159

autobiography
   Douglas and, 55–57
   Harris, F., and, 59
   Wilde and, 6, 49–50

B
Baines, Richard, 118n20
Baines Note, 110, 118n20
Bard-baiting, 5
   co-creation of Shakespeare, W., and, 170
   containment and, 169
   Drunk History and, 171
   Drunk Shakespeare and, 153
   Holl on, 153
   iconoclasm and, 169
   Scheil on, 152, 162
   Shit-faced Shakespeare and, 153
   Something Rotten and, 164–70
   Upstart Crow and, 151–52, 154–64
   Will and, 151
bardolatry, 5, 123
   All Is True and, 154–55
   First Folio, 1623, and, 124
   Germany and, 32
   ghost of Shakespeare, W., and, 21–22
   iconoclasm and, 169
   novels for young readers and, 134–35
   Pérez Galdós on, 71

Something Rotten and, 168
Upstart Crow and, 164
Barton, Anne, 105n3
Bate, Jonathan, 76
   courtship/marriage, Shakespeare, W., and, 102–3
Baumgartner, Alexander, 47nn31–33
   religion of Shakespeare, W., and, 42–43
bear-baiting, 153
Betterton, Thomas
   Dryden and, 11
   ghost of Shakespeare, W., and, 10–11, 13
Bill, 152
Birch, W. J., 38
Bismarck, Otto von, 40–41
Blackadder Goes Forth, 164
Blackwood, Gary
   cross-dressing and, 128
   escape and, 127
   Hateley and, 126
   improvisation and, 130–31
   novels for young readers by, 125–27, 129–31, 138n49, 138n51
   spying and, 129–30
Blair, Tony, 111–12
Blau, Herbert, 112
Boas, Guy, 20
Bolt, Rodney
   authorship and, 6–7, 115–16
   Marlowe and, 6–7, 115–16
Bond, Edward, 147, 151–52
Bouchier, Arthur, 91n26
Les Bourgeois de Calais (Rodin), 85
Bourus, Terri, 151
boy-actors, in novels for young readers, 125–26, 130, 132, 134, 137n33, 138n40, 138nn37–38
Brandl, Alois, 74–75
Brown, Dan, 169
Bruster, Douglas, 165
Burgess, Anthony, 102, 106n11
Bush, George W., 111–13
business acumen of Shakespeare, W., 99–100, 103
Butler, Samuel, 56, 58

C

Cardenio, 144–46
Carlyle, Thomas
   hero worship and, 84
   religion of Shakespeare, W., and, 39
Catholicism, 36–39, 42–43
   Bismarck and, 40–41
   Pius IX and, 40–41
Cervantes, Miguel de, 144–45
character of Shakespeare, W.
   Elze on, 34–35
   Germany and, 34–35
   Kenny on, 35
Chateaubriand, François-René de, 39
Cheaney, J. B., 127–28, 131
Chettle, Henry, 118n18
   homosexuality and, 118n16
   Marlowe and, 109–10, 118n16
co-creation of Shakespeare, W., 170
Coleridge, Samuel Taylor
   ghost of Shakespeare, W., and, 23–25, 28n38
   sentimental drama and, 23–25
Colmer, Francis, 82
The Comedy of Errors, 102
comic device, ghost of Shakespeare, W., as, 13–14, 19–21
conception, of Shakespeare, S., 40, 94–95, 98, 100–101, 105n6
conjecture, as response to 11 September 2001, 113–15
conspiracy
   authorship and, 115–16, 150, 159
   Emmerich and, 116
   Marlowe, in interpretations of, 115–16
   as response to 11 September 2001, 115–16, 120n50
containment, 169
Cooper, Susan, 132–33

courtship/marriage, Shakespeare, W.
  Ackroyd on, 99–100
  Bate and, 102–3
  Burgess on, 106n11
  business acumen of Shakespeare, W., and, 99–100, 103
  The Comedy of Errors and, 102
  conception, of Shakespeare, S., and, 40, 94–95, 98, 100–101, 105n6
  Duncan-Jones on, 97–98, 103, 105n6
  Edmondson on, 104
  Greenblatt on, 98–99, 103
  Greer on, 98, 104, 106n8
  Hamlet and, 101
  Holderness on, 105n5
  Honan on, 95–96
  marriage licence in, 94, 104n1
  The Merchant of Venice and, 103
  Potter and, 106n9, 106n12
  as reciprocal, 96
  religion of Shakespeare, W., and, 40, 99
  Rio on, 40
  Sonnet 143 and, 102
  The Taming of the Shrew and, 102–3
  Twelfth Night and, 102
  Upstart Crow and, 162–63
  Venus and Adonis and, 102
  Weis on, 100–102
cross-dressing
  Blackwood and, 128
  Cue for Treason and, 126
  novels for young readers and, 126, 128–29, 133–34
  Twelfth Night and, 133–34
  Two Gentlemen of Verona and, 133–34
  Will Shakespeare and the Pirate's Fire and, 128–29
Cue for Treason (Trease), 134, 137n22
  cross-dressing and, 126
  disguise in, 128–29
  escape in, 127

D

Danson, Lawrence, 53
Dávidházi, Peter, 74
The Da Vinci Code (Brown), 169
Deane, Anthony C., 70, 76
death
  of Hathaway, R., 96–97
  of Marlowe, 7, 108, 113
  of Shakespeare, H., 164
  of Shakespeare, W., 4
Dederer, Claire, 153
democracy
  patriot, Shakespeare, W., as, and, 87
  Tercentenary, 1916, and, 86–88
Denmark, ghost of Shakespeare, W., and, 21
Dennis, John, 15
De Profundis (Wilde), 58
  as comedy, 60–63
  Douglas, addressed to, 49
Derrida, Jacques, 111
DiPietro, Cary, 65n7
disguise
  Cue for Treason and, 128–29
  novels for young readers and, 126, 128–29
  Will Shakespeare and the Pirate's Fire and, 128–29
Dobell, S. T., 78–79
Dobson, Michael
  authority of Shakespeare, W., and, 10–11
  ghost of Shakespeare, W., and, 10–11, 18, 26n2
Douglas, Alfred
  autobiography and, 55–57
  De Profundis addressed to, 49
  Hallam and, 66n28
  'The Portrait of W. H.' and, 55–56
  'Two Loves,' 54, 57
  Wilde and, 6, 48–49, 54–57, 63, 65n11
Drunk History, 171
Drunk Shakespeare, 153

Dryden, John
    Betterton and, 11
    ghost of Shakespeare, W., and,
        11–12, 15
    Troilus and Cressida and, 11–12
Ducis, Jean-François, 16
Duncan-Jones, Katherine
    courtship/marriage, Shakespeare,
        W., and, 97–98, 103, 105n6
    Hathaway, R., and, 97
    Marlowe and, 108, 110–11
Dusinberre, Juliet, 108
Dustagheer, Sarah, 155, 161–62
Duval, Alexandre, 139

E

Edmondson, Paul, 104
11 September 2001
    Blair and, 111–12
    Bush and, 111–13
    conjecture as response to, 113–15
    conspiracy as response to,
        115–16, 120n50
    credibility as response to, 112–13
    crisis as response to, 111–12
    Derrida on, 111
    Kaplan on, 119n28
    Marlowe, impact on interpretation of, 4, 107, 111–17,
        119n28
    Žižek on, 111
Elizabeth I (Queen), 132–33
Elton, Ben, 154. *See also Upstart Crow*
Elze, Karl, 46n26
    character of Shakespeare, W.,
        and, 34–35
    religion of Shakespeare, W.,
        and, 39, 41
Emmerich, Roland, 116
empathic speculation, 5–6
escape
    Blackwood and, 127
    Cue for Treason and, 127
    Loving Will Shakespeare and,
        128–29
    novels for young readers and,
        127–28
    The Playmaker and, 127–28
    Will Shakespeare and the Pirate's Fire and, 127
Everett, Barbara, 105n3

F

Fagan, J. B., 19
fan fiction (fanfic), 150–51
Fazel, Valerie, 150–51
First Folio, 1623
    bardolatry and, 124
    Jonson and, 107
Fischer, Susan, 146
Fitton, Mary, *Sonnets* and, 59–60,
    67n37
Fletcher, John, 144, 146
Fordy, Tom, 164
Foucault, Michel, 110
France
    ghost of Shakespeare, W., and,
        14–15, 17–18
    Tercentenary, 1916, and, 83–85
Friesen, Heinrich von, 38
Fulda, Ludwig, 33, 44n6

G

Gabor, Tompa, 21–22
Garrick, David
    ghost of Shakespeare, W., and,
        14–15
    Stratford Jubilee, 1769, and, 70
Geddes, Louise, 150–51
gender
    cross-dressing and, 126, 128–29,
        133–34
    Hateley on, 136n10, 137nn22–23,
        138nn49–50
    novels for young readers and,
        126, 128–29, 133–34,
        136n10, 137n23, 137n25,
        138n50
    Shakespeare Tercentenary Observance in the Schools and Other Institutions and, 77–81

Genée, Rudolph, 44n3, 46n15
  nationalism and, 32, 37
George, David, 118n18
Germany
  bardolatry and, 32
  Brandl and, 74–75
  character of Shakespeare, W.,
    and, 34–35
  Fulda and, 33
  Gervinus and, 32–33, 37–38
  ghost of Shakespeare, W., and,
    15–17
  Handel and, 83
  Kulturkampf in, 40–42
  morality of Shakespeare, W.,
    and, 36–43
  naturalization of Shakespeare,
    W., and, 31–33, 74–75, 88
  nostrification and, 74–75, 83, 88
  religion of Shakespeare, W.,
    and, 36–43
  Richter and, 41
  Tercentenary, 1916, and, 73–76,
    82–86, 88, 91n26
Gervinus, Georg Gottfried,
    44nn1–2, 45n8, 46nn16–17
  Germany and, 32–33, 37–38
  religion of Shakespeare, W.,
    and, 37–38
ghost of Shakespeare, W., 26n5, 139
  authority of Shakespeare, W.,
    and, 7, 9–25
  authorship and, 26n2
  bardolatry and, 21–22
  Betterton and, 10–11, 13
  Coleridge and, 23–25, 28n38
  as comic device, 13–14, 19–21
  Denmark and, 21
  Dennis and, 15
  Dobson on, 10–11, 18, 26n2
  Dryden and, 11–12, 15
  Fagan and, 19
  France and, 14–15, 17–18
  Gabor and, 21–22
  Garrick and, 14–15
  Germany and, 15–17
  Granville and, 12
  Greenblatt and, 9
  Hamlet and, 10, 21–22
  Hawkes on, 20
  Holland and, 17
  intellectual property and, 22
  Knapp on, 26n2
  Lenz and, 15
  mockery of, 13–14
  Munk and, 21
  nationalism and, 14–18
  Rich and, 12–14
  Romania and, 21–22
  Rosenthal on, 22, 26n2
  Rowe and, 10–11
  Rylance and, 21
  Sand and, 17–18
  Schiller and, 16–17, 23–25
  Schink and, 16
  Schröder and, 15–16
  science fiction and, 28n34
  sentimental drama and, 23–25
  theatrical disputes and, 12–14
ghost of Wilde, 63–64
Gifford, W., 38
Goethe, Johann Wolfgang von, 36,
    45nn12–13
Gollancz, Israel
  patriot, Shakespeare, W., as,
    and, 77
  Tercentenary, 1916, and, 71–73,
    75, 77
Graham, Cyril
  'The Portrait of W. H.' and, 50–52
  Sonnet 20 and, 51
Granville, George, 12
Greenblatt, Stephen
  containment and, 169
  courtship/marriage, Shake-
    speare, W., and, 98–99, 103
  ghost of Shakespeare, W., and, 9
  Hamlet and, 5–6
  Marlowe and, 114–15
Greene, Robert, 110
  Halliday on, 118n11
  Nashe on, 109

Greer, Germaine, 98, 104, 106n8
Gurr, Andrew, 108

H

Habicht, Werner, 27n23, 74, 76
Hall, Linda, 133
Hallam, Henry, 66n28
Halliday, F. E., 118n11
Halsey, Katie, 169
Hamlet
    courtship/marriage, Shakespeare, W., and, 101
    Ducis and, 16
    ghost of Shakespeare, W., and, 10, 21–22
    Greenblatt on, 5–6
    Something Rotten and, 167–68
    Tercentenary, 1916, and, 68–69
    Upstart Crow and, 161, 163
'Hamlet' (Somoza), 140
    Hathaway, A., in, 142
    writing process depicted in, 141–44, 147
Handel, George Frideric, 32, 83, 92n54
Harris, Frank
    autobiography and, 59
    'The Portrait of W. H.' and, 52
    Wilde and, 6, 48–50, 56, 58–63
Harris, Robert, 127–29
Hateley, Erica
    Blackwood and, 126
    gender and, 136n10, 137nn22–23, 138nn49–50
    novels for young readers and, 126, 136n10, 137nn22–23, 138nn49–50
Hathaway, Anne, 4, 94
    age of, 96
    'Hamlet' and, 142
    novels for young readers and, 129–30, 132–33
    Upstart Crow and, 154, 159, 162–64
    Whateley and, 94–95, 101–2, 104n1
Hathaway, Richard
    death of, 96–97
    Duncan-Jones and, 97
    Honan and, 96
Hauptmann, Gerhart, 33, 44n5
Hawkes, Terence, 107, 116–17
    ghost of Shakespeare, W., and, 20
Henry IV Part Two, 154
Henry V
    imperialism and, 87–88
    novels for young readers and, 126
    Tercentenary, 1916 and, 84–88
    Upstart Crow and, 164
Hero and Leander (Marlowe), 108
hero worship, Carlyle on, 84
Heywood, Thomas, 147
Höfele, Andreas, 153
Holderness, Graham, 3
    courtship/marriage, Shakespeare, W., and, 105n5
    death of Shakespeare and, 4
    empathic speculation and, 5–6
Holl, Jennifer, 153
Holland, ghost of Shakespeare, W., and, 17
homosexuality
    Butler and, 56, 58
    Chettle on, 118n16
    Marlowe and, 118n16
    Shakespeare, W., and, 50–59, 64, 66n28
    Sonnets and, 50–59, 64, 66n28
Honan, Park, 106n10
    courtship/marriage, Shakespeare, W., and, 95–96
    Hathaway, R., and, 96
humanism, religion of Shakespeare, W., and, 38–40

I

iconoclasm, 169
identity
    personal, 131–32
    public, 132–33

imperialism
  Dobell and, 78–79
  Henry V and, 87–88
  Tercentenary, 1916, and, 78–79, 87
improvisation
  Blackwood and, 130–31
  Loving Will Shakespeare and, 130–31
  novels for young readers and, 130–31, 138n51
intellectual property, 22

J
Jones, Henry Arthur, 75
Jong, Erica, 105n5
Jonson, Ben, 147, 164
  First Folio, 1623, and, 107
  novels for young readers and, 134

K
Kafka, Franz, 141
Kaplan, E. Ann
  11 September 2001 and, 119n28
  trauma and, 112
Kenny, Thomas, 35
King John, 163
King of Shadows (Cooper)
  personal identity in, 132
  public identity in, 133
Kirkpatrick, Karey, 164–65. *See also Something Rotten*
Kirkpatrick, Wayne, 164–65. *See also Something Rotten*
Knapp, Mary E., 26n2
Kristeva, Julia, 119n36
Kulturkampf (War of Cultures), 40–42
Kuriyama, Constance
  credibility and, 112–13
  Marlowe and, 112–13, 119n38

L
Lanier, Douglas, 105n5
  Anonymous and, 116

Lee, Sidney
  Schoenbaum on, 136n7
  Tercentenary, 1916, and, 72, 90n15
Lenz, Jakob Michael Reinhold, 15
The Life and Genius of Shakespeare (Kenny), 35
Logan, Robert, 108
London, Tercentenary, 1916, in, 70–73
Lord Strange's Men, 108, 136n13
  Manley on, 117n5
Love's Labours' Lost, 154
Loving Will Shakespeare (Meyer)
  escape in, 128–29
  improvisation in, 130–31
  personal identity in, 132
  public identity and, 132–33
Luhrman, T. M., 119n37

M
Manley, Lawrence, 117n5
Marche, Stephen, 116
Marías, Fernando, 141
Marlowe, Christopher
  As You Like It and, 108
  authorship and, 6–7, 115–16
  Baines Note and, 110, 118n20
  Bolt on, 6–7, 115–16
  Chettle on, 109–10, 118n16
  conjecture in interpretations of, 113–15
  conspiracy in interpretations of, 115–16
  credibility in interpretations of, 112–13
  crisis in interpretations of, 111–12
  death of, 7, 108, 113
  Duncan-Jones on, 108, 110–11
  Dusinberre on, 108
  11 September 2001 impact on interpretation of, 4, 107, 111–17, 119n28
  Greenblatt on, 114–15
  Hero and Leander, 108

homosexuality and, 118n16
Kuriyama on, 112–13, 119n38
Logan on, 108
Rylance on, 115
Upstart Crow and, 157
marriage licence, Shakespeare, W., 94, 104n1
McKay, Percy, 92n51
Measure for Measure, 106n10
The Merchant of Venice, 91n33
courtship/marriage, Shakespeare, W., and, 103
Upstart Crow and, 160
Meyer, Carolyn, 128–33
A Midsummer Night's Dream
novels for young readers and, 132–33, 138n43
Upstart Crow and, 158
Miguel Will (Somoza), 140, 147
Cardenio in, 144–46
Cervantes in, 144–45
Fletcher in, 144, 146
misogyny, *Upstart Crow* and, 158, 160–61
mockery, of ghost of Shakespeare, W., 13–14
morality of Shakespeare, W., 36–43
Morgan, Jude, 162
Munk, Kaj, 21
musicals, *Something Rotten* and, 166–67

N

Nashe, Thomas, 118n14
Greene and, 109
nationalism, 31, 33
Genée on, 32, 37
ghost of Shakespeare, W., and, 14–18
novels for young readers and, 137n19
patriot, Shakespeare, W., as, and, 77–83
religion of Shakespeare, W., and, 40–42
Tercentenary, 1916, and, 73–84

naturalization of Shakespeare, W.
Germany and, 31–33, 74–75, 88
nostrification and, 74–75, 83, 88
Neill, Michael, 76
Norrenberg, Peter, 42
nostrification, Germany and, 75, 88
Dávidházi on, 74
Habicht on, 74
Handel and, 83
Pfister on, 74
novels for young readers, 5, 123–24, 136n4
bardolatry and, 134–35
by Blackwood, 125–27, 129–31, 138n49, 138n51
boy-actors in, 125–26, 130, 132, 134, 137n33, 138n40, 138nn37–38
cross-dressing and, 126, 128–29, 133–34
Cue for Treason, 126–29, 134, 137n22
disguise in, 126, 128–29
Elizabeth I in, 132–33
escape in, 127–28
gender and, 126, 128–29, 133–34, 136n10, 137n23, 137n25, 138n50
Hall on, 133
Hateley on, 126, 136n10, 137nn22–23, 138nn49–50
Hathaway, A., in, 129–30, 132–33
Henry V and, 126
improvisation in, 130–31, 138n51
Jonson in, 134
King of Shadows, 132–33
Loving Will Shakespeare, 128–33
A Midsummer Night's Dream in, 132–33, 138n43
nationalism and, 137n19
performance and, 125–35
personal identity in, 131–32
The Playmaker, 127–28, 131
public identity in, 132–33
Romeo and Juliet in, 126, 134
Shakespeare, S., in, 124, 129

spying in, 129–30
The Tempest in, 128
time-slips in, 132–33
Twelfth Night in, 133–34
Two Gentlemen of Verona in, 133–34
Will Shakespeare and the Pirate's Fire, 127–29
The Winter's Tale in, 131

O
O'Farrell, John, 165. *See also Something Rotten*
O'Sullivan, Maurice J., 143–44
Othello, 154

P
patriot, Shakespeare, W., as
   democracy and, 87
   Gollancz and, 77
   Shakespeare Day, 1916, and, 77, 79
   Shakespeare Tercentenary Observance in the Schools and Other Institutions and, 77–83
   Tercentenary, 1916, and, 77–83
Pérez Galdós, Benito, 71, 90nn8–12
performance
   As You Like It and, 125, 131, 135
   novels for young readers and, 125–35
   personal identity and, 131–32
   public identity and, 132–33
personal identity
   King of Shadows and, 132
   Loving Will Shakespeare and, 132
   novels for young readers and, 131–32
   performance and, 131–32
   The Playmaker and, 131
personal tragedy of Shakespeare, W., in *Upstart Crow*, 162–64
Pfister, Manfred, 74
physical appearance of Shakespeare, W., 171n15
   Upstart Crow and, 155–57
   Will and, 156–57
The Picture of Dorian Gray (Wilde), 48, 50, 52–53
Pius IX (Pope), 40–41
The Playmaker (Cheaney)
   escape in, 127–28
   personal identity and, 131
'The Portrait of W. H.' (Wilde), 6, 66n15
   Douglas and, 55–56
   Graham and, 50–52
   Harris, F., on, 52
   Ricketts and, 65n1
   at trial of Wilde, 53–54
Potter, Lois, 114
   courtship/marriage, Shakespeare, W., and, 106n9, 106n12
Protestantism, 36–43
public identity
   King of Shadows and, 133
   Loving Will Shakespeare and, 132–33
   novels for young readers and, 132–33
   performance and, 132–33

Q
quiet trauma, 112, 119n37

R
racism, *Upstart Crow* and, 157–58
Rafter, Denis, 144–45
Raich, J. M., 42
Reichensperger, August, 42
religion of Shakespeare, W.
   Baumgartner on, 42–43
   Birch on, 38
   Carlyle on, 39
   Chateaubriand on, 39
   courtship/marriage, Shakespeare, W., and, 40, 99
   Elze on, 39, 41
   Friesen on, 38
   Germany and, 36–43
   Gervinus on, 37–38

Gifford on, 38
Goethe on, 36
humanism and, 38–40
morality and, 36–43
nationalism and, 40–42
Richter on, 41
Rio on, 40
Shakespeare, S., and, 40
Simpson on, 40
Tercentenary, 1916, and, 81–83
Upstart Crow and, 157
Rich, John, 12–14
Richard II, 79–80
Richter, Thomas, 41
Ricketts, Charles, 65n1
Rio, A. F., 40
Rodin, Auguste, 85
Romania, ghost of Shakespeare, W., and, 21–22
Romeo and Juliet
novels for young readers and, 126, 134
Something Rotten and, 166
Upstart Crow and, 154, 160–61
Rosenthal, Laura J., 22, 26n2
Rowe, Nicholas, 10–11
Rylance, Mark
ghost of Shakespeare, W., and, 21
Marlowe and, 115

S

Salmon, Edward, 86–87
Sand, George, 17–18
Scheil, Katherine West, 152, 162
Schiller, Friedrich, 16–17, 23–25
Schink, Johann Friedrich, 16
Schoenbaum, S., 6, 118n16
Lee and, 136n7
Schröder, Friedrich, 15–16
science fiction, ghost of Shakespeare, W., and, 28n34
The Secret Life of William Shakespeare (Morgan), 162
sentimental drama, ghost of Shakespeare, W., and, 23–25
sex symbol, Shakespeare, W., as, 152

Shakespeare, Hamnet
death of, 164
Upstart Crow and, 162–64
Shakespeare, Susanna
conception of, 40, 94–95, 98, 100–101, 105n6
name, choice of, 106n13
novels for young readers and, 124, 129
religion of Shakespeare, W., and, 40
Upstart Crow and, 154, 161, 163
Shakespeare, William. *See specific topics*
Shakespeare amoureux (Duval), 139
Shakespeare Day, 1916, 77, 79
Shakespeare in Love, 151, 155
Shakespeare in Time of War (Colmer), 82
Shakespeare Tercentenary Observance in the Schools and Other Institutions
gender and, 77–81
Shakespeare Day and, 77, 79
Tercentenary, 1916, and, 77–83, 91n42
Shapiro, James, 109
authorship and, 116
Shaw, George Bernard, 48–50, 59–63
Shawcross, J. P., 79–82, 91n42
Shit-faced Shakespeare, 153
Simpson, Richard, 40
Smith, Emma, 169
Snyder, Susan, 154
Something Rotten
authorship in, 167–68
Bard-baiting in, 164–70
bardolatry and, 168
Hamlet in, 167–68
musicals in, 166–67
Romeo and Juliet in, 166
Somoza, José Carlos, 5, 149n9
Fischer on, 146
'Hamlet,' 140–44, 147
Marías on, 141
Miguel Will, 140, 144–47

Sonnet 20, 51
Sonnet 143, 102
Sonnets, 65n7
  Fitton and, 59–60, 67n37
  Graham and, 50–52
  homosexuality and, 50–59, 64, 66n28. *See also* 'The Portrait of W. H.'
Spain, Tercentenary, 1916, in, 68
spying, in novels for young readers, 129–30
Storm and Stress. *See Sturm und Drang*
Stratford Jubilee, 1769, 70
Stratford-on-Avon, Tercentenary, 1916, in, 70–73
Sturm und Drang (Storm and Stress), 31
sympathy, 110

T
The Taming of the Shrew
  courtship/marriage, Shakespeare, W., and, 102–3
  Upstart Crow and, 157, 160–61
Taylor, Gary, 151
The Tempest, 128
Tercentenary, 1864, 70–71
Tercentenary, 1916, 4
  Adam and, 83, 87, 92nn58–59
  Askew and, 82
  authorship and, 73
  Brandl and, 74–76
  cet idéal pour lequel on combat, Shakespeare, W., as, and, 83–88
  Colmer and, 82
  Deane and, 70, 76
  democracy and, 86–88
  France and, 83–85
  Germany and, 73–76, 82–86, 88, 91n26
  Gollancz and, 71–73, 75, 77
  Hamlet and, 68–69
  Henry V and, 84–88
  imperialism and, 78–79, 87

  Lee and, 72, 90n15
  London and, 70–73
  McKay and, 92n51
  nationalism and, 73–84
  Neill on, 76
  patriot, Shakespeare, W., as, and, 77–83
  religion of Shakespeare, W., and, 81–83
  Richard II and, 79–80
  Salmon and, 86–87
  Shakespeare Day in, 77, 79
  Shakespeare Tercentenary Observance in the Schools and Other Institutions and, 77–83, 91n42
  Shawcross and, 79–82, 91n42
  Spain and, 68
  Stratford-on-Avon and, 70–73
theatrical disputes, ghost of Shakespeare, W., and, 12–14
time-slips, in novels for young readers, 132–33
trauma
  Kaplan on, 112
  Kristeva on, 119n36
  Luhrman on, 119n37
  quiet, 112, 119n37
Trease, Geoffrey, 126–29, 134, 137n22
trials, of Wilde, 48–49, 52
  'The Portrait of W. H.' at, 53–54
Troilus and Cressida, Dryden and, 11–12
Twelfth Night
  courtship/marriage, Shakespeare, W., and, 102
  cross-dressing in, 133–34
  novels for young readers and, 133–34
  Upstart Crow and, 161
Two Gentlemen of Verona
  cross-dressing in, 133–34
  novels for young readers and, 133–34
  Upstart Crow and, 158

'Two Loves' (Douglas), 54, 57

U

Ulrici, Hermann, 33–34, 36
Upstart Crow
   authorship in, 159
   Bard-baiting in, 151–52, 154–64
   bardolatry in, 164
   courtship/marriage, Shakespeare, W., in, 162–63
   Dustagheer on, 155, 161–62
   Hamlet in, 161, 163
   Hathaway, A., in, 154, 159, 162–64
   Henry V in, 164
   King John in, 163
   Love's Labours' Lost in, 154
   Marlowe in, 157
   The Merchant of Venice in, 160
   A Midsummer Night's Dream in, 158
   misogyny in, 158, 160–61
   personal tragedy of Shakespeare, W., in, 162–64
   physical appearance of Shakespeare, W., in, 155–57
   racism in, 157–58
   religion of Shakespeare, W., in, 157
   Romeo and Juliet in, 154, 160–61
   Shakespeare, H., in, 162–64
   Shakespeare, S., in, 154, 161, 163
   The Taming of the Shrew in, 157, 160–61
   Twelfth Night in, 161
   Two Gentlemen of Verona in, 158

V

Vega, Ventura de la, 140
Vehse, Eduard, 37, 45n14
Venus and Adonis, 102
Vickers, Brian, 115
Vine, Angus, 169
Vischer, Friedrich Theodor, 32–33, 44n4

W

Wardle, Janice, 151–52, 165
War of Cultures. *See Kulturkampf*
Weis, René, 100–102
Wells, Stanley, 108
Whateley, Anna, 94–95, 101–2, 104n1
Wilde, Oscar
   autobiography and, 6, 49–50
   Butler and, 56, 58
   Danson on, 53
   De Profundis, 49, 58, 60–62
   Douglas and, 6, 48–49, 54–57, 63, 65n11
   ghosts of, 63–64
   Harris, F., and, 6, 48–50, 56, 58–63
   The Picture of Dorian Gray, 48, 50, 52–53
   'The Portrait of W. H.,' 6, 50–56, 66n15
   Shaw and, 48–50, 59–63
   trials of, 48–49, 52–54
Will, 160
   Bard-baiting and, 151
   physical appearance of Shakespeare, W., in, 156–57
   sex symbol, Shakespeare, W., as, in, 152
Will Shakespeare and the Pirate's Fire (Harris, R.)
   cross-dressing and, 128–29
   disguise in, 128–29
   escape in, 127
The Winter's Tale, 131
Wolf, Paul, 33, 44n7
World War I, 4, 33
   Blackadder Goes Forth and, 164
   Les Bourgeois de Calais and, 85
   See also Tercentenary, 1916
World War II, 119n28

Z

Žižek, Slavoj, 111

www.ingramcontent.com/pod-product-compliance
Lightning Source LLC
Chambersburg PA
CBHW072154100526
44589CB00015B/2223